Rank and Style

Russians in State Service, Life, and Literature

❧ ❧ ❧

Ars Rossika

Series Editor: David BETHEA
(University of Wisconsin — Madison and Oxford University)

ACADEMIC
STUDIES
PRESS

Rank and Style

Russians in State Service, Life, and Literature

Selected Essays
by IRINA REYFMAN

BOSTON / 2012

Library of Congress Cataloging-in-Publication Data:
A catalog record for this book as available from the Library of Congress.

ISBN - 978-1-936235-51-3

Book design by Ivan Grave

Published by Academic Studies Press in 2012
28 Montfern Avenue
Brighton, MA 02135, USA
press@academicstudiespress.com
www.academicstudiespress.com

To my sisters,
Tatiana and Elena

TABLE OF CONTENTS

Part One
RANK, STATE SERVICE, AND LITERATURE

Part Two
PUSHKIN AS THE OTHER

LIST OF ILLUSTRATIONS

FOREWORD

This volume presents a collection of articles written in the last fifteen years, between the early 1990s and the present. Twelve of these articles have been published before, and three are appearing for the first time in this collection. I have revised most of the previously published articles, adjusting them somewhat to fit the present volume, correcting mistakes, updating footnotes, and unifying the documentation style. I have also translated the articles that were first published in Russian.

The collection is divided into four parts. The first comprises the articles that reflect my new interest in the Russian imperial rank system and its impact on writers who belonged to the noble estate (*dvoriane*). The second part is about Pushkin as seen by other writers (Gogol, Zoshchenko), by his contemporaries, and (somewhat ironically) by himself. The third part is devoted to Tolstoy, mostly to his struggle with the questions of death and dying, but also to his early views of sex and marriage. The final part doesn't have a unifying theme or method: two articles are grounded in close readings of eighteenth-century poetry, while the third, although also based on a close reading of Leskov's story, places it in a broader cultural context and, particularly, in a dialogue with Dostoevsky.

The articles' provenance differs. Some are related to my previous book projects (on Trediakovsky and on dueling), while others look forward to my next book, provisionally titled *Ranks and Writing*. Yet others may be called "occasional" articles, written in response to invitations to participate in particular projects.

Finally, the Tolstoy section reflects my ongoing fascination with Tolstoy, mostly fed by my teaching his shorter works to under-graduates.

It is impossible to acknowledge every person who provided feedback and help with different articles at different stages of their existence. Whenever an article began as a conference talk, I thank everyone who asked pointed questions and offered suggestions. Whenever an article was first solicited for a particular publication, I thank the editors for their help and encouragement. I would like, however, to offer my special thanks to Andrew Kahn, whose faith in my work, generosity, and friendship are responsible for several articles in this collection; Marcus Levitt, a fellow eighteenth-century scholar, whose ideas continue to inspire my own thinking; Deborah Martinsen, a friend and colleague who is always ready to provide advice and help with all aspects of my work but especially with finding a good title; Elena Dushechkina, my sister and colleague in the field of Russian literature, whose opinion and advice I value beyond words; Georgy Levinton and the late Lora Stepanova for helping me to interpret the nickname of Leskov's character, Pitulina.

Special heartfelt thanks go to Nancy Workman, my long-suf-fering editor. A patient and expert article surgeon, she extracts or inserts where necessary. A perceptive reader, she always finds the most skillful way to express my meaning. Infelicities of content are mine; felicities of style are hers. I am also grateful to Kirsten Painter for her invaluable help with manuscript preparation. The volume owes its neat appearance and splendid index to Kirsten's keen un-derstanding of my work and her attention to detail. In conclusion, I would like to thank my anonymous ASP editor for his or her care-ful reading of the manuscript and suggestions for further improve-ments and corrections. All mistakes and deficiencies are, of course, mine.

I am happy to acknowledge the generosity of the Harriman Institute Publication Committee whose liberal support made this publication possible.

Finally, my thanks go to the following publishers for their permission to republish my work. "Writing, Ranks and the

Eighteenth-Century Russian Gentry Experience," in *Representing Private Lives of the Enlightenment*, ed. Andrew Kahn, SVEC 11 (Oxford: Voltaire Foundation, 2010): 149–66, is reprinted by permission of the Voltaire Foundation, University of Oxford. I also thank SEEJ and AATSEEL for permission to reprint "Poetic Justice and Injustice: Autobiographical Echoes in Pushkin's *The Captain's Daughter*," *Slavic and East European Journal* 38, no. 3 (1994), 463–78; Berkeley Slavic Specialties for "Turgenev's 'Death' and Tolstoy's 'Three Deaths,'" in *Word, Music, History: A Festschrift for Caryl Emerson*, ed. Lazar Fleishman et al., *Stanford Slavic Studies* 29 (Stanford, CA: Stanford University, Dept. of Slavic Languages and Literatures, 2005), 1:312–26; *Ulbandus* for "Aleksey Rzhevsky, Russian Mannerist," in *Ulbandus, the Slavic Review of Columbia University* 9 (2005/2006): 3–17; and "Dishonor by Flogging and Restoration by Dancing: Leskov's Response to Dostoevsky," in *Ulbandus, the Slavic Review of Columbia University* 13 (2010), 109–25. I also thank publishers who do not require special permission for republishing or assign copyright to authors. I acknowledge them in the list of all first publications at the end of this volume.

Note on Transliteration

I am using a dual system of transliteration, following the guidelines in J. Thomas Shaw's *Transliteration of Modern Russian for English-Language Publications*:

In the text and in all discursive parts of the endnotes, Shaw's "System I" is used, which anglicizes Russian proper names: the "y"-ending is used instead of "ii"; "yu"/"ya" is used instead of "iu"/"ia"; "ay"/"ey" is used instead of "ai"/"ei"; "x" replaces "ks," etc. Well-known spellings are used for famous people (e.g., Peter the Great). However, soft signs are only omitted when they are at the end of the name, or if the name is well-known (Tulub'ev vs. Gogol).

When citing Russian sources in the bibliography and notes, I use the Library of Congress system without diacritics (Shaw's "System II").

Part One

RANK, STATE SERVICE, AND LITERATURE

Preface

This part presents some of the articles I have written in preparation for my next book project, *Ranks and Writing*. The main goal of the project is to consider how obligatory or (after 1762) strongly expected participation in service hierarchy affected Russian writers of noble origin, both their identity as noblemen and their self-images as writers. I am particularly interested in finding out how the service and rank system affected their status as writers and, conversely, how their being writers complicated their position in the service hierarchy. I am also curious how this situation is reflected in their literary production.

The first article examines the way three eighteenth-century writers, Alexander Sumarokov, Andrey Bolotov, and Ippolit Bogdanovich, coped with this situation. Sumarokov insisted on remaining in the military service long after he had stopped fulfilling his service duties. He claimed that writing constituted service and should therefore be rewarded by advancement in ranks. Even though Sumarokov's effort to move up the rank ladder using his literary endeavors didn't work, his strategy to present writing as service to the state helped develop the image of the writer as an important and valuable member of society. In contrast, Bolotov retired from service as soon as he could and used writing to shape his existence as a member of the gentry living on his estate. He viewed his lifelong literary pursuits as strictly private, published little, and largely failed to make his experiment known. In his turn, Bogdanovich successfully created an image of himself as a dilettante poet writing for his own amusement—an image that had nothing in common with reality. The image of Bogdanovich as a carefree dilettante was developed by Nikolay Karamzin and thus entered the public domain. Sumarokov's and Bogdanovich's behavioral models proved useful for nineteenth-century writers who succeeded them.

The next article offers a reading of Gogol's "Notes of a Madman" as a story of Poprishchin's failure to groom himself into a proper gentleman by means of writing. Similar to the eighteenth-century Russian gentlemen writers discussed in the previous article, Poprishchin believes that writing is a prerogative of nobility. Since he writes (both as part of his service duties as a bureaucrat and privately, in his diary), he has no doubt that he is a true gentleman and is crushed when his (supposedly) low rank shows him his proper place in service hierarchy—the place that makes him unsuitable as Sophie's bridegroom.

The other two articles in this part deal with Pushkin: one with his prose fiction and another with his social reputation in the 1830s. In the first article, I investigate how Pushkin's own rank and status anxieties are reflected in his prose, from *The Blackamoor of Peter the Great* to *The Egyptian Nights*. The second article attempts to reconstruct contemporary reaction to Pushkin's court title of kammerjunker. While Pushkin himself viewed his new title with great displeasure, not only feeling that it was inappropriate for a person of his age and renown but also citing his dislike of court, many of his contemporaries, including some of his friends, were apparently amused by the situation. Moreover, some believed that Pushkin wanted a court title and that he wouldn't have been upset at all had he been granted the higher title of kammerherr. Without necessarily accepting all aspects of this view, we may nonetheless adjust somewhat the established image of Pushkin as entirely hostile to court.

Two more articles could have been included in this part. One of them, "Pushkin the Titular Councilor," will appear in the collection of articles *Taboo Pushkin: Topics, Texts, Interpretations* to be published by the University of Wisconsin Press. It traces Pushkin's short and not very successful civil service career and was first presented at the conference "Alexander Pushkin and Russian National Identity: Taboo Texts, Topics, Interpretations" that took place at the University of Notre Dame in January of 2009. I have chosen to include the second one, "Kammerjunker in 'Notes of a Madman,'" in the next part of this collection, because it is Gogol's view of Pushkin, not Pushkin's court title as such, that is the primary object of its inquiry.

1. Writing, Ranks,
and the Eighteenth-Century Russian Gentry Experience

For European elites, challenged by changes in the idea of what makes an aristocrat, writing became a new technology of self-fashioning through which they shaped their public and private identities. Jonathan Dewald has observed that one purpose of writing for the seventeenth-century French nobility was to separate

> themselves from their surroundings, establishing themselves as individuals and freeing themselves from a variety of con- straints. At the same time, with writing they entered a new kind of relationship with the society around them . . . The circulation of writing, like that of money, challenged the principles of a hierarchical society.[1]

Unlike their contemporaries in the West, nobles in pre-Petrine Russia as a rule did not practice any types of writing—indeed, many were illiterate.[2] Writing, for both literary and administrative purposes, was mainly the preserve of the clergy and, later, the state bureaucrats. A substantial aim of the Petrine reforms was to educate nobles.[3] As a result, in the eighteenth century, newly literate Russian elites turned to writing in search of modern modes of existence.

---

[1]   Jonathan Dewald, *Aristocratic Experience and the Origins of Modern Culture: France, 1570–1715* (Berkeley: Univ. of California Press, 1993), 174–75.

[2]   For estimates of literacy rates in seventeenth-century Muscovy, see Gary Marker, "Literacy and Literacy Texts in Muscovy: a Reconsideration," *Slavic Review* 49 (1990): 74–89. Marker concludes that the most optimistic estimates suggest that "rudimentary literacy rates . . . were well below 10 percent for the entire population," with the number of those who could write at about 3 percent. Less optimistic estimates give 3 to 5 and 1 to 2 percent, respectively (89).

[3]   See Marc Raeff, *Origins of the Russian Intelligentsia: The Eighteenth-Century Nobility* (New York: Harcourt Brace & World, 1966), esp. chap. "Home and School"; Brenda Meehan-Waters, *Autocracy and Aristocracy: The Russian Service Elite of 1730* (New Brunswick, NJ: Rutgers Univ. Press, 1982), 39–47.

They also became active producers of literature and, by the second half of the eighteenth century, began to dominate the literary sphere.

The swiftness with which the nobility created a literary field is the more remarkable in that it happened under the patronage system dominant in Russia in the eighteenth century.[4] Writers of noble status employed different strategies in dealing with it: some resisted it, unhappy about its inherent inequality; others ignored it; yet others participated in it fully, using it to their advantage—especially if the patron happened to be the monarch. The nascent market system was another factor that complicated the situation for noblemen reluctant to participate directly in the sale of the fruits of their literary labors. Both factors made eighteenth-century writers of noble rank ambivalent about their literary pursuits; therefore they often preferred to publish anonymously if at all.[5]

Although this ambivalence about professional writing and publishing persisted among Russian nobles well into the nineteenth century, it did not hinder their partaking in the production of literature. In contrast, in arts other than literature (painting, sculpture, music, and theater), nobles did not participate professionally in any significant numbers until the second half of the nineteenth century. Thus, literature was the only art nobles did not consider beneath their dignity to acknowledge publicly as their professional occupation.[6] Moreover, as Gareth Jones points out, beginning with

---

[4]   See William Mills Todd III, *Fiction and Society in the Age of Pushkin: Ideology, Institutions, and Narrative* (Cambridge, MA: Harvard Univ. Press, 1986), 51–52.

[5]   See, for example, V. A. Zapadov, "Problema literaturnogo servilizma i dilentantizma i poeticheskaia pozitsiia G. R. Derzhavina," in *XVIII vek* (Leningrad: Nauka, 1989), 16:56–75, esp. 69–70; Joachim Klein, "Poet-samokhval: 'Pamiatnik' Derzhavina i status poeta v russkoi kul'ture XVIII veka," in his *Puti kul'turnogo importa: Trudy po russkoi literature XVIII veka* (Moscow: Iazyki slavianskikh kul'tur, 2005), 498–520.

[6]   See Viktor Zhivov, "Pervye russkie literaturnye biografii kak sotsial'noe iavlenie: Trediakovskii, Lomonosov, Sumarokov," *Novoe literaturnoe obozrenie* 25 (1997): 55. Zhivov quotes statistical data on the participation of the nobility in literature provided in Vladimir Nahirny, *The Russian Intelligentsia: From Torment to Silence* (New Brunswick, NJ: Rutgers Univ. Press, 1983), 28.

the second half of the eighteenth century, "literary accomplish-
ments were considered to be one of the clearest indications of
nobility."[7]

At the same time, in post-Petrine Russia writing was not the
only—or even the main—tool of self-fashioning for nobles: service
to the state and the monarch offered a surer means of establishing
and maintaining one's noble status. The Table of Ranks, a list of
positions in the military, civil, and court services introduced by Peter
the Great in 1722, was a powerful means of forging a new noble
class that was to replace the Muscovite elites. It defined the nobility
as a service class, obliging every noble to serve, offering tangible
evidence of career progress, and, at the same time, providing a way
for gifted commoners to enter the noble estate. It also introduced
a new hierarchy—that of rank—within the noble class. Furthermore,
military service was given preference over the other two (hereditary
nobility, for example, was granted to commoners in the military
beginning with the fourteenth rank, while in the civil service it
began with the eighth rank).[8] The Table of Ranks thus determined
a post-Petrine Russian nobleman's status vis-à-vis his counterparts.

This chapter explores how the circumstances I have described
affected writers of noble status, particularly their authorial self-
image. I will pay special attention to the way participation in the
service and rank system (which was compulsory until 1762, and
after that remained customary and, for many, highly desirable)
complicated their view of writing as simultaneously a private
and a public activity. The aim is to determine what strategies of
authorial behavior they worked out as they dealt with the complex
and often contradictory hierarchies in which they were forced to
participate. I will also briefly consider the relevance of these models
for subsequent generations of Russian writers.

---

[7]   W. Gareth Jones, "The Russian Language as a Definer of Nobility," in
       *A Window on Russia: Papers from the V International Conference of the Study
       Group on Eighteenth-Century Russia, Gargnano, 1994*, ed. Maria Di Salvo and
       Lindsey Hughes (Rome: La Fenice Edizioni, 1996), 297.

[8]   See Table of Ranks, paragraphs 11 and 15, in *Zakonodatel'stvo Petra I*
       (Moscow: Iuridicheskaia literatura, 1997), 398 and 400.

Three comparable, though distinctive, figures serve as case studies. The first, Alexander Sumarokov, remained in the service as long as he could, despite significant pressure to retire. At the same time, he continued to write and publish and worked hard to establish a view of writing as service to the state and to be acknowledged as a servitor in good standing based on his status as a writer. The second, Andrey Bolotov, left service as soon as he could and used writing, which was his everyday occupation throughout his life, to forge his private identity as a nobleman. Writing—in every genre imaginable—shaped Bolotov's daily existence but was not a status-building activity for him. The third, Ippolit Bogdanovich, was the first Russian writer to construct a public persona of himself as a dilettante writing for pleasure in the privacy of his home, a servant to the Muses, not a servitor to the state. At the same time, paradoxically, he built on the success of his best-received narrative poem, *Dushen'ka* (*Psyche*, 1783), not only to earn the patronage of Catherine the Great but also to repair and advance his service career.[9]

Alexander Petrovich Sumarokov (1717–1777), the well-educated scion of a respectable family of servitors that became prominent in seventeenth-century Muscovy, was in many ways representative of the new post-Petrine nobility. His father, a supporter of Peter the Great's reforms, had a long and successful service career, retiring in 1762 in the rank of actual privy councilor (second class). In 1740, Sumarokov graduated from the newly established Noble Infantry Cadet Corps, the first educational institution for children of

---

[9]   I have chosen to put aside the case of Gavrila Derzhavin, as the most idiosyncratic of all and thus requiring a separate treatment. On some aspects of this topic, see Anna Lisa Crone, *The Daring of Deržavin: The Moral and Aesthetic Independence of the Poet in Russia* (Bloomington: Indiana Univ. Press, 2001), esp. chap. 9. Another idiosyncratic case that needs a special examination is M. N. Murav'ev, whose literary and service careers both began early and evolved in parallel. He was a highly visible and high-ranking official and an actively publishing writer, but at the same time, he consciously worked to present himself as a dilettante and his writing as a private affair. For a short presentation of his case, see E. N. Marasinova, *Vlast' i lichnost': Ocherki russkoi istorii XVIII veka* (Moscow: Nauka, 2008), 375.

the nobility, and began his service as a member of the staffs of several important statesmen, including Alexey Razumovsky (1709–1771), Empress Elizabeth's favorite and the head of the Leib Company, the guards regiment that helped Elizabeth ascend the throne in 1741. In his capacity as Razumovsky's aide-de-camp, Sumarokov ran the regiment's affairs. In 1755, he was promoted to the rank of brigadier (fifth class).

Parallel to fulfilling his military duties, Sumarokov built up a formidable literary career, actively producing in all genres and vying for the place of Russia's foremost author with two other prominent writers of the time, Vasily Trediakovsky and Mikhailo Lomonosov. Despite his success as a writer, the idea of leaving the service never occurred to Sumarokov. Moreover, when, in 1756, he was appointed director (manager) of the first Russian public theater (which officially became a court theater in 1759), he retained his military rank as brigadier.

Sumarokov is often regarded as the first professional writer in Russian literary history, and, whether one agrees with this view or not (Sumarokov never sold his literary works directly to publishers and felt uneasy about the very idea), he undoubtedly saw his literary activities as the center of his life.[10] It is surprising, in this context, to observe how much importance Sumarokov gave to his place in the service hierarchy. When his service career came to a halt following his appointment as theater director, he complained bitterly and repeatedly that he was being "passed over" for promotion (*menia obkhodiat*). In a letter of November 15, 1759, to Ivan Shuvalov (Elizabeth's favorite and the overseer of several Russian cultural institutions, including theater), Sumarokov writes: "I never took part in a war and perhaps never will, but I labor as much in time of peace as I would have in time of war, but they pass me over." The labor he has in mind is managing the theater and writing plays and poems. Furthermore, Sumarokov believes that this labor qualifies

---

[10]   For a discussion of the view of Sumarokov as the first professional writer, see Marcus Levitt, "The Illegal Staging of Sumarokov's *Sinav i Truvor* in 1770 and the Problem of Authorial Status in Eighteenth-Century Russia," *Slavic and East European Journal* 43 (1999): 299–300.

him for a military rank. Asking in the same letter to be appointed to the Academy of Sciences, he insists that as a member of the Academy he would have the right to remain in the military service: "I don't want a civil rank, since I am a senior brigadier, and I am not inclined to take off voluntarily the military uniform I have worn for twenty-eight years; and nothing prevents me from being in both the Academy Chancellery and the Conference."[11]

Sumarokov was "relieved of his duties" (*uvolen*) as theater director by Elizabeth's decree of June 13, 1761. In anticipation of this event, he vigorously campaigned for promotion ("My memory tells me that upon retirement everyone gets promoted, even if he has been in his current rank for only a year. And I have been senior brigadier and a most unhappy man for six years," 91) or, at least, for keeping his military rank. In his letter to Shuvalov of April 24, 1761, he writes, obviously not quite sincerely:

> Have mercy on me . . . and dismiss me. I just do not want a ci-
> vil rank, since, having worn a military uniform and boots all
> my life, it will not be easy for me to learn to wear shoes. After
> all, I am retiring, not going into the civil service, and I would
> rather be a captain [ninth class] than receive a higher civil
> rank. (92)

When, in September 1762, the newly enthroned Catherine conferred on Sumarokov the civil rank of actual state councilor (fourth class), following his request for promotion and as a sign of her benevolence, Sumarokov was not satisfied in the least: he felt that he had not gained anything, arguing that a military rank was in fact equivalent not to the civil rank with which it shared a line on the

---

[11]   G. P. Makogonenko, ed., *Pis'ma russkikh pisatelei* (Leningrad: Nauka, 1980), 86 and 87. All subsequent references to this edition will be given in the text. The Chancellery was the general assembly of all academicians and adjuncts, and the Conference was the assembly of all Academy members with collegiate ranks; see V. P. Stepanov's commentary to Sumarokov's letters, in *Pis'ma*, 193n10. Obviously, Sumarokov implies that his superior rank as a brigadier gives him the right to join the Academy without leaving the military service for the civil one. Here and throughout the chapter the translations are my own, unless indicated otherwise.

Table of Ranks but to the civil rank one slot above it. Having been promoted from the military rank of fifth class to the civil rank of fourth class meant, effectively, that he had not risen in the hierarchy of ranks. Sumarokov summarizes his grievances in his letter to the empress of May 3, 1764:

> After the general promotion that took place before the [1756–63 Seven Years] War, I was second or third brigadier, and not only have all brigadiers [fifth class], colonels [sixth class], and lieutenant-colonels [seventh class] overtaken me, but many of those below the seventh class; and now even those who in the time of Your Majesty's reign were promoted from lieutenant-colonels are my seniors in military rank, and I was never in civilian service. (96)[12]

Rejecting the rank conferred on him by the empress, Sumarokov concludes his letter with a plea: "I ask only to learn what I am: am I in service and in which one? Otherwise, retire me properly, as all good people are retired, with a proper rank" (97). He is asking for what, in his view, is his due: to be promoted to the next rank upon retirement, as a servitor in good standing. His requests were never satisfied: he died in 1777 in the rank of actual state councilor.

It can be argued that service was Sumarokov's main source of income, the way he supported himself and his family. True, his requests for promotion were often accompanied by requests for money, usually back pay. These requests were satisfied for the most part, even if not always immediately. Furthermore, after Sumarokov's retirement from the position of theater director, an arrangement was made to continue to pay him his allowances both as brigadier and as theater director.[13] Once she was in power, Catherine in her turn forgave his considerable debts to the Academy press and granted him the "lifetime privilege of having all his

---

[12] It is not quite clear what Sumarokov meant by "second or third brigadier": there were no classes within the rank. It is possible that Sumarokov means the order of promotion to the rank of brigadier, that is, that only one or two people were promoted to this rank earlier than he.

[13] For Elizabeth's decree, see *F. G. Volkov i russkii teatr ego vremeni: sbornik materialov* (Moscow: Izdatel'stvo Akademii Nauk SSSR, 1953), 144–45.

works printed at her cost."[14] Even in the 1770s, when Catherine's benevolence faded (and Sumarokov's financial situation drastically worsened after 1767, owing to a family quarrel that deprived him of much of his inheritance), the empress occasionally granted the writer monetary support. All this suggests that, for Sumarokov, anxiety over rank was a separate issue from anxiety over his financial situation.

Furthermore, the option of publishing for money was available to Sumarokov, and he considered taking it, if half-heartedly, as is evident from his letter to Catherine of January 13, 1773:

> Perhaps, having worked for fame, I should undertake the writing of novels, which could bring me a good income, because Moscow likes this kind of writing. Now, is it really becoming for me to write novels, especially in the reign of the wise Catherine, who, I am sure, doesn't have a single novel in her entire library? When Augustus rules, then Virgils and Ovids write, and Aeneids are held in respect, not Bovas the king's sons.[15] I, however, wouldn't dishonor myself even if I wrote a Bova, although I wouldn't gain much honor either. (163)

What is remarkable in this passage is the mixture of contradictory views of the writer: as a client writing to laud a powerful patron (Virgil lauds Augustus, and Sumarokov, Catherine), as a producer of saleable goods (an identity that Sumarokov tries on hesitantly and reluctantly), and as a nobleman serving the state (evident in Sumarokov's use of the vocabulary of honor).[16]

---

[14]   Marcus Levitt, "Aleksandr Petrovich Sumarokov," in *Early Modern Russian Writers: Late Seventeenth and Eighteenth Centuries*, ed. Marcus Levitt, vol. 150 of *Dictionary of Literary Biography* (Detroit, MI: Gale Research / Bruccoli Clark Layman, 1995), 376–77.

[15]   *Bova the King's Son* is one of the chivalric romances adapted in Muscovite Russia and extremely popular among lowbrow eighteenth-century readers. These romances were despised by Russian classicists, Sumarokov in particular.

[16]   See Levitt, "Illegal Staging," 317, for his analysis of the place the notion of honor played in Sumarokov's view of authorship.

It was Sumarokov's position as servitor to the state that helped him resist the patronage system.[17] Even though at times he accepted the role of a client of powerful patrons—such as Shuvalov and, later, Catherine's favorites Grigory Orlov and Grigory Potemkin as well as Catherine herself—at other times, he attempted to reject it.[18] He writes in a letter to Shuvalov of June 10, 1758:

> In all truth, I haven't asked for a present, which I have never done and will never do, but requested from your cabinet a loan for the theater, and it was not any kind of political game on my part. I would sooner become a beggar and be exposed to various misfortunes than be among those who seek patrons in order to profit from them. (79)

His view of his writing as a fulfillment of service duties helped him justify his protestations.

Sumarokov consistently presents his writing as the fulfillment of service duties. In October 1758, he complains to Elizabeth that he has not been paid for nine months and lists his managing the theater and his writing as service: "I . . . must live on what I have thanks to my rank and my labors, laboring as hard as I can in versification and theater" (83). He goes on to compare his literary efforts to his service as Razumovsky's aide-de-camp. Arguing that he deserves promotion (in his letter to Shuvalov of November 15, 1759), Sumarokov again insists that his writing is comparable in importance to other types of service:

> My [literary] exercises do not have the slightest similarity to either court or civil duties, and therefore I do not impede anyone's progress, but my labors are no smaller than anyone else's, and they are of some use, if literature is considered useful in this world. (86)

Continuing his fight for promotion in a letter to Shuvalov of April 24, 1761, Sumarokov directly labels his achievements in

---

[17]   See Zhivov, "Pervye russkie literaturnye biografii," 58.

[18]   On Sumarokov's participation in the patronage system, see Todd, *Fiction and Society*, 53–55.

literature as service to the state and the empress: "I have served exactly thirty years, and tomorrow it will be twenty years that I have served h[er] m[ajesty] [i.e., Elizabeth]" (92).

Sumarokov uses the same argument in his letters of complaint to Catherine. In August of 1762, he writes that he has been "passed over":

> And I am offended more than anyone, because, without any fault on my part, having labored both in fulfillment of my duties as well as beyond them in literature, I have been left behind everyone, not only behind my peers, but also behind those who were much junior to me in rank. (94)

According to Sumarokov's reasoning, writing was additional service on his part and should have particularly qualified him for promotion. Sumarokov ends up asserting the superiority of literary activity over other types of service. In his letter to Catherine of March 4, 1770, he declares: "Sophocle, le prince des poètes tragiques qui était en même temps le général des Athéniens et camarade de Periclès, est encore plus connu sous le nom de poète qu'en qualité de général" (139). Thus, gradually, Sumarokov comes to see his literary activities as not just comparable to, but superior to the types of services legitimized by Peter in the Table of Ranks. What astonishes in his position is the trouble he has assigning value to himself as a writer outside the rank system. He needs a rank to confirm the significance of his writing activities, both in the eyes of the public and his own eyes. This explains Sumarokov's reluctance to retire and his insistence on his right to be promoted.[19]

While interpreting his writing as service to the state, Sumarokov sometimes mentions the Muses. Curiously, however, these references are consistently placed in the context of service. At least once Sumarokov directly calls his relations with the Muses "service" (91). On another occasion, he reports to Catherine about a rare period of harmony in his life as a playwright: "The Muses, the local governor-general, the chief of the police, the impresarios, and

---

[19]   On Sumarokov's insistence in his correspondence that writing equals service, see Marasinova, *Vlast' i lichnost'*, 374–75.

the actors are in total agreement with me" (125). Characteristically, Sumarokov never complains that his service to the state interferes with his service to the Muses, but does explain his failure to succeed in his service career by his devotion to them: "The main reason for all of this is my love for poetry, because, having relied on it and literature, I cared not so much for rank and possessions as for my Muse" (174).

Crucially, the idea of literature as a private pursuit is absent from Sumarokov's view of himself as a writer. Only once does Sumarokov seem to express a desire for a "Parnassian refuge" (*parnasskoe ubezhishche*, 118), but even then he justifies his wish for a retreat by his eagerness to be useful to the state. He writes to Catherine in February of 1769:

> In my letter to the count [G. A. Orlov], I also asked for a small humble estate. I need only to have a Parnassian refuge there, and it would bring more profit in the form of verses and other compositions than it gives grain to the state treasury. (118; cf. 116)

Once he received the desired "Parnassian refuge," it did not figure in his representations of his authorial pursuits at all. Clearly, Sumarokov viewed writing as a public activity, as a fulfillment of his service duty to the state and the monarch, its success to be reflected by his place in the system of ranks.

Certain expressions in Sumarokov's letters suggest that for him rank not only indicated his place in the service hierarchy but defined who he was as a human being. This is clearly evident in his question to Catherine in his letter of May 3, 1764: "What am I?" (*chto ia?*). The expression also crops up earlier in the same letter, with a similar anguished overtone:

> I, by the way, don't have a place or position. I am not in the military, not in the civil service, not at court, not in the Academy, and not retired. I dare to submit my request to Your Imperial Majesty, so that something might be done with me in order for me to know what I am. (96)[20]

---

[20]   Thomas Newlin detects "existential panic" in these formulations; see his *The Voice in the Garden: Andrei Bolotov and the Anxieties of Russian Pastoral,*

Sumarokov obviously had trouble conceiving himself outside the service hierarchy, and his writing (which, as Lomonosov caustically claimed in his letter to Ivan Shuvalov of January 19, 1761, Sumarokov put "above all human knowledge") was not quite enough for him to define his identity.[21] It is noteworthy that when Sumarokov wants to claim his status as poet, he does so by adding a third component to the formula, "an officer and a gentleman." He uses it in this form twice in his correspondence, in Russian ("Dvorianin i ofitser, i stikhotvorets sverkh togo," that is, "I am . . . a gentleman and an officer, and a poet to boot," 73) and in French ("poète, gentilhomme, et officier," 78).

In contrast, Andrey Bolotov (1738–1833), arguably the most prolific Russian writer ever, viewed writing as primarily an activity of private self-fashioning. As a teenager, he amused and educated himself by copying his favorite books, both translations of European fiction and traditional Russian literature, such as saints' lives. As a young officer stationed in Königsberg during the Seven Years War, he discovered "the pleasures of letter writing," initiating a correspondence with the navy officer N. E. Tulub'ev.[22] In 1789, when Bolotov began his formidable writing enterprise, the memoir *The Life and Adventures of Andrey Bolotov, Depicted by Himself for His Descendants*, he adopted an epistolary form, addressing entries to an imaginary intimate "Dear friend." In addition to the *Life and Adventures* (on which he worked until the late 1820s, eventually penning thirty-seven manuscript volumes that covered his life from the year he was born to the early nineteenth century), Bolotov also kept several diaries and various kinds of journals, minutely documenting his life and circumstances. He also wrote prolifically in other genres, including poetry, drama, literary criticism, books for children, and treatises on economy, agriculture, philosophy, and religion. Bolotov continued writing well into his eighties, eventu-

---

1738–1833 (Evanston, IL: Northwestern Univ. Press, 2001), 223n13.

21   Mikhail Lomonosov, *Polnoe sobranie sochinenii* (Moscow: Izdatel'stvo Akademii Nauk SSSR, 1957), 10:545.

22   Thomas Newlin, "Andrei Timofeevich Bolotov," in *Early Modern Russian Writers*, ed. Levitt, 38.

ally producing, in Thomas Newlin's estimation, "the equivalent of some 350 volumes of written material."[23] As Newlin suggests, the purpose of Bolotov's lifelong writing activity was, in significant part, to create a model of Russian private gentry experience that lacked precedents in the life of the eighteenth-century service-bound nobility.[24]

Like every eighteenth-century Russian nobleman before 1762, Bolotov was obliged to serve: at the age of ten he was enlisted in the regiment of which his father was commander. Even though his service was nominal, and his time mostly occupied with schooling and partly spent away from the regiment, he was promoted twice—first to corporal and then to sergeant. Bolotov began actual service at the age of seventeen, still in the rank of sergeant, and was made a commissioned officer in 1757.

Bolotov's career shaped up reasonably well, but he disliked service, viewing it as a hindrance to his private pursuits (which, like Sumarokov, he often calls "exercises"). His resentment of his service duties is often mentioned in his memoir. In "letter" 61, for example, he complains that his clerical duties as an officer stationed in Königsberg were difficult and boring and describes how he rejoiced when, having cleared up a backlog of paperwork, he was able to free himself for more interesting occupations:

> Now, continuing my story, I will tell you that as this life was for me at the beginning somewhat difficult and boring, so afterwards it became pleasant and merry . . . When I finished up this difficult work, there was much less writing left for me to do, and finally there was so little that I had hardly one page a day to write. Therefore I could finish this small work in half an hour, and I not only did not have to go to the office in the afternoon, but sometimes even in the morning I did not have any work and could, with the permission of my little old man, absent myself and sometimes even spend the entire day at home. This circumstance, which allowed me more leisure and free time . . . , pleased me, because I could devote a longer time to my exercises and live as I wished, without

---

23   Ibid., 37.

24   Newlin, *Voice in the Garden*, 8–10, and esp. chap. 2.

any concern that I would be sent to perform some company duties or appointed to guard detail.[25]

Later, when Bolotov's knowledge of German landed him a job in the governor's chancellery as a translator and interpreter, he again became upset by the large volume of boring paperwork. Even the governor's benevolence did not quite console him:

> But when, on the other hand, I recalled the difficult and tedious translations that bored me silly in a single day, when I pictured how I would be obliged to go to the chancellery every day and to spend the entire day toiling incessantly over them and be deprived completely of all the freedom so pleasant to me, these thoughts diminished my delight [at being accepted in the governor's house] and concerned me indescribably. Most of all I grieved that I would be tied down [by my duties] and would not have a minute, so to speak, of free time for myself, time that I could use for my own interesting exercises.[26]

Only in retrospect does Bolotov acknowledge that his busyness kept him out of trouble, crediting his new duties and his association with colleagues in the chancellery as good for his education.[27]

In describing his subsequent service in St. Petersburg, Bolotov continues to complain that it is a tedious hindrance to his private occupations. He therefore chose to retire as soon as he could, right after Peter III granted the Russian nobility freedom from obligatory service with his decree of 1762. Bolotov writes in his memoir how ecstatic he felt on the day his retirement became official:

> Finally, said date of June 14, the most memorable day in my life, arrived, and I received my so passionately desired

---

[25]   Andrei Bolotov, *Zhizn' i prikliucheniia Andreia Bolotova, opisannye samim im dlia svoikh potomkov* (Moscow: Terra, 1993), 1:399–400. Bolotov calls his commander "the little old man" (*starichok*).

[26]   Bolotov, *Zhizn' i prikliucheniia*, letter 63, accessed January 10, 2011, http://az.lib.ru/b/bolotow_a_t/text_0080.shtml.

[27]   Ibid., letter 64, accessed January 10, 2011, http://az.lib.ru/b/bolotow_a_t/text_0080.shtml.

dismissal . . . In such a way on that day my fourteen-year military service came to an end, and, having received my dismissal, I became a free and independent man forever.[28]

Having retired at the age of twenty-three with the rank of army captain (ninth class), Bolotov returned to civil service between 1774 and 1797 and eventually retired with the rank of collegiate assessor (sixth class). He took great care, however, not to let his service interfere with his private pursuits.

Bolotov arrived on his estate in September of 1762. When the autumn weather put a stop to the urgently necessary improvements (which happened to be planting his first garden), he turned to reading and writing in order to fill his lonely leisure.[29] Soon he realized that it was precisely these occupations that made his life in the country meaningful and pleasurable:

> In a word, the effect my learned exercises produced was that, instead of boredom, I was beginning even then to perceive all the pleasure of country life, free and independent, unconstrained and tranquil; and I was not burdened in the least either by [free] time, or by my solitude.[30]

Intellectual pursuits were so important for Bolotov that, in looking for a bride, he sought a partner with similar interests. Unfortunately, soon after the wedding, he realized that he had not succeeded: "I did not find and could not notice in her even the slightest inclination toward reading books or to anything concerning learning."[31] He hoped that with time his young wife would develop these interests so central to his own existence,

---

28   Bolotov, *Zhizn' i prikliucheniia*, 2:157.

29   Newlin comments on the correspondence between gardening and writing for Bolotov—his two favorite occupations while in the country. See Newlin, *Voice in the Garden*, 115 and 231n38. On Bolotov's gardening projects, see Andreas Schönle, *The Ruler in the Garden: Politics and Landscape Design in Imperial Russia* (New York: Peter Lang, 2007), chap. 2. Schönle also comments on the analogy between Bolotov's gardening activities and his writing (124).

30   Bolotov, *Zhizn' i prikliucheniia*, 2:214.

31   Ibid., 2:303.

but, to his disappointment, this never happened. He was lucky enough, however, to find a kindred soul in his mother-in-law. His ideal of private gentry existence was thus complete: he had his independence, plenty of time to read and write, and a person with whom to share his intellectual interests. Later, his son Pavel became his "best friend and dear comrade and interlocutor."[32]

Bolotov's literary pursuits were largely private: he published almost exclusively in non-literary and non-autobiographical genres, such as pedagogy, philosophy, science, gardening, and economics, the one exception being his drama *The Unfortunate Orphans*. Neither his poetry nor his memoirs and diaries went to print in his lifetime. It was not for the public that he wrote in these genres but to give shape to his pastoral existence in the privacy of his estate. In this, he followed a literary tradition that imagined life in the country as necessarily including intellectual activities, such as reading and writing.[33] Based on Horace's Second Epode, this pastoral ideal was first formulated for Russians by Antiokh Kantemir in his satire "On True Happiness" (1738) and survived at least until 1834, when Pushkin sketched his unfinished poem "It's Time, My Friend, It's Time." It is crucial, however, that Bolotov not only wrote prolifically about a life in the country that was independent and full of intellectual pursuits, but also succeeded in implementing this literary topos in real life.

My third case, Ippolit Bogdanovich (1743–1802), worked on his narrative poem *Dushen'ka* during a time in his service career that was filled with uncertainty as well as activity. Firstly, his civil service career faltered: in March of 1779, he was transferred from the Foreign College, where he served as a translator in the rank of collegiate assessor (eighth class), to the Office of Heraldry, but the new appointment was without pay. Bogdanovich could not afford to serve without compensation and had to resign. He was able to return to service (to the newly established State Archive) only in October of 1780. Bogdanovich also experienced difficulties in his parallel career as editor of several state-sponsored periodicals

---

[32]   Ibid., 3:470.

[33]   Newlin, *Voice in the Garden*, 29–32.

published by the Academy of Sciences, including the official newspaper *St. Petersburg News*. In July of 1782, the Academy Conference, its secretariat, accused him of printing articles in *St. Petersburg News* that were "poorly chosen and often childish."[34] In August, more accusations followed. As a result, in December of 1782, Bogdanovich was forced to resign from his position as editor, and Catherine was informed of his alleged blunders. No doubt, in the late 1770s and the early 1780s, Bogdanovich must have been both overwhelmed by the volume of his duties and distressed by his bad luck in his service career.

Curiously, Bogdanovich's service woes did not affect the persona that he developed as a writer. *Dushen'ka*, which was composed during roughly the same years (canto 1 appeared in print in 1778 and the entire poem in 1783), fostered in the minds of both Bogdanovich's contemporaries and posterity a very different image of its author: not that of a busy, impecunious servitor whose career was being threatened, but that of "a carefree Bohemian" writing in his (seemingly abundant) spare time. As Thomas Barran states in his biography of Bogdanovich, "This persona does not agree with the biographical facts. Bogdanovich adopted an authorial pose in the preface to *Dushen'ka* that may have provided the impetus for the rewriting of his biography."[35] Indeed, the first sentence in Bogdanovich's introduction to the 1783 edition reads: "To entertain myself in hours of idleness was my only motivation when I began writing *Dushen'ka*." He goes on to claim that he did not even plan to publish it until the praise of his friends compelled him to do so. Bogdanovich concludes his introduction with an assertion of his dilettante status as a writer: "I am . . . not from among the established writers."[36]

---

34   Quoted in N. D. Kochetkova, "Ippolit Fedorovich Bogdanovich," in *Slovar' russkikh pisatelei XVIII veka*, ed. N. D. Kochetkova et al. (Leningrad: Nauka, 1988), 1:106.

35   Thomas Barran, "Ippolit Fedorovich Bogdanovich," in *Early Modern Russian Writers*, ed. Levitt, 33.

36   I. F. Bogdanovich, *Stikhotvoreniia i poemy* (Leningrad: Sovetskii pisatel', 1957), 45.

Dushen'ka was hugely successful. Most importantly, it gained Bogdanovich Catherine's patronage: in March of 1783, the entire print run of the poem was acquired by the Academy of Sciences, and in November of 1783, the poet was elected to the Russian Academy (created the same year to emulate the Académie française). The Empress herself encouraged Bogdanovich in his literary pursuits, and he produced several plays for the Hermitage Theater, beginning with the 1786 adaptation of *Dushen'ka* for the stage. His labors as a court playwright were rewarded with substantial sums of money and a diamond ring. More importantly, the poem also allowed Bogdanovich to relaunch his service career. In March of 1784, he was promoted to the rank of court councilor (seventh class); in 1788, he received the rank of collegiate councilor (sixth class) and became the head of the State Archive. His literary activities gradually came to an end after this appointment. He retired in 1795.[37]

The image of Bogdanovich as an idle and carefree poet creating his poem in the privacy of his home to amuse himself in his spare time was amplified and consolidated by Nikolay Karamzin in his 1803 article, "On Bogdanovich and His Works." Claiming that the image of the author can be discerned from the poem itself, Karamzin writes:

> He lived at the time on Vasilevsky Island, in a quiet, isolated little home, devoting his time to music and verse in happy insouciance and freedom; . . . he loved to go out on occasion, but he loved even more to return to where the Muse awaited him with new ideas and colors.[38]

The legend of Bogdanovich as the carefree creator of the charming *Dushen'ka* not only ignored the realities of his early struggles as a poorly paid bureaucrat but also completely disregarded his destitute and unhappy post-retirement life. It also

---

[37]   See Kochetkova, "Ippolit Fedorovich Bogdanovich," 106–8; Joachim Klein, "Bogdanovich i ego 'Dushen'ka,'" in *Puti kul'turnogo importa*, 476–77.

[38]   Nikolai Karamzin, "O Bogdanoviche i ego sochineniiakh," in his *Izbrannye stat'i i pis'ma* (Moscow: Sovremennik, 1982), 118. I quote Barran's translation, "Ippolit Fedorovich Bogdanovich," 33.

overlooked his desperate and unsuccessful attempts to return both to service and to the literary scene in the early 1800s. In June of 1801, Bogdanovich petitioned the Russian Academy for help in publishing his ode on the coronation of Alexander I and his collected works, but his petition was rejected. On several occasions in 1802, he sent his works to the Academy for publication, but they were rejected as well. In his accompanying letters, Bogdanovich wrote of his utter poverty, which had forced him to sell his library. It is noteworthy that in his letters this self-proclaimed dilettante also begged for an opportunity to return to service or at least to be rewarded "either with a rank, or with a cross, or with any other state decoration, but not with . . . a small one-time monetary allowance, which humiliates the spirit and extinguishes zeal in a nobleman."[39] These requests were also ignored, and Bogdanovich died soon thereafter.

Nineteenth-century Russian writers inherited from eighteenth-century literati of noble status several models of authorial behavior that negotiated between the public and private spheres. One type is exemplified by Sumarokov, who strove to cast away the patronage system and placed his literary activities in the context of state service. He believed that rank, a public criterion of his standing within the service hierarchy, was needed to give value to his writing. Thus, writing was not a private activity for him: in his formulation, "service to the Muses" suspiciously resembles service to the state. At the same time, Sumarokov rejected publishing for money as an activity that would dishonor him as author and nobleman. Sumarokov's view of writing as state service was aimed at elevating the status of literature in the eyes of his contemporaries. Even though Sumarokov's attempts were not quite successful during his lifetime, they proved essential for the eventual construction of the image of the Russian writer as an influential public figure.[40]

A second model is exemplified by Bolotov. Engrossed in his lifelong writing activity, Bolotov did not regard it as service,

[39]   Quoted in Kochetkova, "Ippolit Fedorovich Bogdanovich," 108–9.

[40]   See Zhivov, "Pervye russkie literaturnye biografii," 54–55.

was not interested in service ranks, and did not look for patrons. Furthermore, as Newlin puts it, "throughout his life Bolotov remained oddly ambivalent about the whole business of being published."[41] Perhaps not so oddly: unlike Sumarokov, who insisted that his writing was valuable service to the state, Bolotov saw his writing as a private activity that defined personal, even intimate, space for him—the space he perceived as suitable for gentry existence. Bolotov's experiment in creating an authorial identity entirely independent of the idea of service and the Table of Ranks remained without consequence in his own time, at least in part because his authorial reticence kept his literary pursuits private. It is safe to assume that it did not affect the public view of writers in any significant way. Furthermore, it is not even clear whether Russians—who, during the late-eighteenth and nineteenth centuries, grew to expect a writer to be a public figure—would ever have approved of this kind of love of privacy in a writer. Even after the publication of Bolotov's *Life and Adventures* in the 1870s, Russians, while acknowledging his importance as a memoirist, did not warm to the description of writerly existence that he offered. Perhaps it was not public enough and thus not heroic enough for the Russian taste. Early in the twentieth century, Alexander Blok, the pre-eminent Symbolist poet, devoted his undergraduate thesis to comparing Bolotov and the writer and publisher Nikolay Novikov, and confirmed the durability of this attitude: Blok hails Novikov, a highly visible public figure, and presents Bolotov, with his subdued authorial aspirations and love of privacy, as a philistine, a man without "citizenry interests" (*obshchestv[ennykh] interesov*).[42]

Unlike Sumarokov and Bolotov, Bogdanovich eagerly participated both in the service hierarchy and in the patronage system. At the same time, in his introduction to *Dushen'ka*, he

---

[41] Newlin, "Andrei Timofeevich Bolotov," 40.

[42] I. Vladimirova [Irina Reyfman], M. Grigor'ev [Mark Altshuller], and K. Kumpan, "A. A. Blok i russkaia kul'tura XVIII veka," *Blokovskii sbornik,* ed. D. E. Maksimov et al. (Tartu: Tartuskii gosudarstvennyi universitet, 1980), 4:84.

attempted to present writing as a private activity, that of a dilettante who indulges in it in his free time and for his own pleasure. Unlike Bolotov, Bogdanovich's authorial self-image had no basis in reality. Nevertheless, it took root and, once developed further by Karamzin, fully supplanted his true biography as a writer. Bogdanovich's (quite public) image as the carefree and independent author of the charming *Dushen'ka* was used by Karamzin to forge the idea of writing as a private occupation separate from service to the state. Later in the nineteenth century, Bogdanovich's self-constructed persona of a dilettante writing in the privacy of his home and publishing only when pressed by his friends proved useful for other Russian writers, including Pushkin, in working out the idea of writing as both a private and a public activity.

Largely illiterate until the eighteenth century, Russian nobles took to writing with a vengeance in the post-Petrine era. Like their European counterparts, some used writing to define their private sphere of existence or to formulate an authorial position that made them, at least nominally, independent of the state and its hierarchies. At the same time, obligatory or, later in the century, expected service to the state made any non-service activity suspect, forcing Russian noblemen to justify their right to write. Moreover, because they had trouble imagining themselves outside the service hierarchy institutionalized in the Tables of Ranks, they attempted to elevate writing to the status of state service. Paradoxically, their strategy helped establish writing, and writing literature in particular, as a highly regarded public activity in Russia.

2. What Makes a Gentleman?
Revisiting Gogol's "Notes of a Madman"

In pre-modern Europe, nobles were physical creatures, and their social status depended on their bodily strength and physical skills. The noble class—whose main occupations were war, hunting, and participating in tournaments—defined itself in terms of bravery, prowess, and strength. Intellectual pursuits, in contrast, were largely irrelevant to a noble's standing within his class.

The situation began to change with the advent of modernity, when the notion of aristocracy underwent a gradual transformation, resulting in cardinally new ideas of what an aristocrat was. First, land ownership and wealth became the definers of the aristocrat's status vis-à-vis his peers. Wealth provided leisure, which then gave rise to genteel behavior, with its preoccupation with such non-heroic qualities as manners and decorum. In the formulation Domna Stanton offers in her book *The Aristocrat as Art*, these new qualities allowed an aristocrat to demonstrate his "capacity for idleness." To quote Stanton again, the only labor "deemed worthy of an aristocrat" was now the kind that shaped his own self.[1]

A good portion of this labor was directed at external features: grooming, fashionable clothing, and good manners. The product was the aristocrat as aesthetic object: an *honnête homme*, a *petit-maître*, a fop. Eventually, the idea of good breeding began to include internal characteristics as well: wit, education, and, especially, an ability to write well. For the English aristocracy, education becomes necessary around the mid-sixteenth century.[2] For the French nobility, this change came about one and a half to two

---

[1]   Domna C. Stanton, *The Aristocrat as Art: A Study of the* Honnête Homme *and the* Dandy *in Seventeenth- and Nineteenth-Century* French Literature (New York: Columbia University Press, 1980), 2 and 3.

[2]   Lawrence Stone and Jeanne C. F. Stone, *An Open Elite? England 1540–1880* (Oxford, UK: Clarendon Press, 1984), 262–66.

centuries later. Stanton points out that for the French nobility, "the seventeenth century was bent on intellectualizing or civilizing the noble."[3] She stresses the role of salons in this civilizing effort. But in his book *Aristocratic Experience and the Origins of Modern Culture*, Jonathan Dewald looks beyond the salons and finds aristocrats drawn to intellectual pursuits everywhere. He also emphasizes the particular importance of writing for the seventeenth-century French nobility:

> Nobles turned to writing in a variety of surprising circumstances, as a part of both public and intimate life. They wrote political reflections and love letters; many began assessing their lives in written form, producing memoirs for their own amusement or the instruction of their families. They closely followed contemporary poetry, and they participated intently in contemporary discussions of linguistic purity. Most striking, in the course of the seventeenth century good writing came to be closely associated with nobility itself.[4]

In Russia, elites didn't turn to writing until the eighteenth century. Only in post-Petrine Russia did being able to write—and to write well—become, as Gareth Jones argues in his article "The Russian Language as a Definer of Nobility," "one of the most important definers of the true Russian nobleman."[5] Autobiographical narratives especially attracted the newly literate Russian nobles: characteristically, tables 1 and 2 in Andrey Tartakovsky's *Russian Memoirs in the Eighteenth and the First Half of the Nineteenth Centuries* show that noblemen predominated among eighteenth-century memoir and diary writers.[6]

---

3   Stanton, *Aristocrat as Art*, 48.

4   Jonathan Dewald, *Aristocratic Experience and the Origins of Modern Culture: France, 1570–1715* (Berkeley: Univ. of California Press, 1993), 174.

5   W. Gareth Jones, "The Russian Language as a Definer of Nobility," in *A Window on Russia. Papers from the V International Conference of the Study Group on Eighteenth-Century Russia, Gargnano, 1994.* Maria Di Salvo and Lindsey Hughes, editors (Rome: La Fenice Edizioni, 1996), 293.

6   A. G. Tartakovskii, *Russkaia memuaristika XVIII—pervoi poloviny XIX v.* (Moscow: Nauka, 1991), 244–70.

For the Russian eighteenth-century nobility, the self-fashioning process (for which writing served as one of the most important means) was replete with particular anxieties because, close to the end of the *ancien régime* as it was, the noble class in Russia was not simply adapting to the challenges of modernity but creating itself anew. For all practical purposes, the post-Petrine *shliakhetstvo* (or *dvorianstvo*, as it became to be called later in the eighteenth century) was a newly formed aristocratic class. *Dvorianstvo* incorporated former boyars, former servitors (*dvoriane*), and commoners who were able to enter the noble class either thanks to the Table of Ranks or to *sluchái*, or imperial favor. The conspicuous lack of homogeneity in the newly formed noble class became a source of tension. Those members of the noble class who considered themselves the heirs of the pre-Petrine aristocracy resented the newcomers, whom they perceived as interlopers. Imperial favorites, of course, integrated faster and more easily than those working their way up the ladder of ranks, but the perception of both groups as intruders lingered well into the nineteenth century.

Many issues divided the newly emerging Russian noble class. One of the most important was its members' attitude toward service, which, unlike in the West, was obligatory—absolutely obligatory until 1762 and essentially so thereafter. The established nobility considered service a duty, though oftentimes an unwelcome one. Civil service in particular, especially its entry-level positions, was a chore beneath the dignity of the established nobility, to be avoided if at all possible.

Consider, for example, Alexander Sumarokov's reluctance to abandon the military service even after he was appointed, in 1756, director of the first Russian public theater and stopped fulfilling military duties in any meaningful way. Yet he continued to insist, passionately, that he had the right to remain in the military and be promoted to the next military rank.[7] In contrast, for commoners, the civil service provided a chance to enter the noble class by climbing the ladder of rank.

---

[7] See my article "Writing, Ranks, and the Eighteenth-Century Russian Gentry Experience" in this collection.

Another divide was cultural: the established members of the
noble class considered former commoners to be lacking in education
and polish. The irony, from the perspective of my topic, was that
the allegedly illiterate upstarts were predominantly bureaucrats,
whose primary occupation was writing and who, historically, were
the oldest secularly educated group in Russia. It was the so-called
prikaznaia shkola (that is, seventeenth-century bureaucrats) that
produced the first examples of Russian secular poetry. They also
were the first translators of secular books, particularly fiction, into
Russian. Furthermore, as a rule, commoners who received their
noble status through the Table of Ranks came from the historically
literate estates, most often from the clergy.[8] Nonetheless, the
new producers of culture, the eighteenth-century nobility, often
dismissed their contributions and portrayed them as illiterate,
unkempt, and ill-mannered. For Sumarokov, clerks (*pod"iachie*)
are the epitome of illiteracy. He concludes his essay addressed to
typesetters, instructing them in correct spelling and usage:

> You know that not only many translators but also some
> authors are less literate than clerks . . . And don't think that
> clerks are more skillful than you . . . just because they are
> richer than you; every day you note that illiterate people are
> always richer than literate ones. And they are called scribes
> [*pistsami*] ironically, because they don't know how to write,
> and this is not their [true] occupation: their occupation is to
> fleece [*obirat'*].[9]

Skepticism toward the education and breeding of *raznochintsy*
continued well into the nineteenth century and can be clearly
seen, for example, in Pushkin's treatment of Nikolay Nadezhdin.
In one of his *Table-talk* sketches, he writes: "I met Nadezhdin at
Pogodin's. He seemed to me very low-class [*prostonarodnyi*], *vulgar*

---

8   See Marc Raeff, *Origins of the Russian Intelligentsia: The Eighteenth-Century
     Nobility* (New York: Harcourt Brace & World, 1966), 52.

9   Aleksandr Sumarokov, "K tipografskim naborshchikam," in his *Polnoe
     sobranie vsekh sochinenii*, 2nd ed. (Moscow: v universitetskoi tipografii u
     N. Novikova, 1787), 4: 315.

[Pushkin uses the English word here], dull, arrogant, and without any manners."[10] Nikolay Nekrasov's lampoon of Dostoevsky as an ill-mannered upstart, *How Great I Am!* (*Kak ia velik!*), written in the 1850s, is another, even more striking, example.

Against this background of class warfare within the Russian noble estate, the story of Aksenty Poprishchin— a hereditary civil servant and, most probably, a newly-minted nobleman—in Gogol's "Notes of a Madman" is instructive. Students of Gogol have extensively discussed the fact that Poprishchin composes government documents for a living (his less able double, Akaky Akakievich Bashmachkin of "The Overcoat," only copies them). More significantly, Poprishchin also keeps a private diary. In the chapter on "Notes of a Madman" (entitled therein "Diary of a Madman") in his book *Exploring Gogol*, Robert Maguire analyzes the autobiographical impulses behind Gogol's desire to make Poprishchin a writer. He also points out that by keeping a diary Poprishchin creates "a record of private self," constructing for himself a private space different from the one that his official position accords him.[11] This, as Dewald argues, is one of the important purposes writing served for seventeenth-century French nobles: it helped them separate "themselves from their surroundings, to establish themselves as individuals."[12]

What kind of an individual is Poprishchin trying to become by writing in a diary?[13] I propose that he uses writing (as we know, unsuccessfully) to construct his identity as a nobleman. More specifically, he tries to lay claim to the identity of a cultured and refined nobleman, an *honnête homme*, and fails—and not only because of his personal inadequacies. For one, his attempt at self-

10   Aleksandr Pushkin, *Polnoe sobranie sochinenii v 16-ti tomakh* (Moscow: Izdatel'stvo Akademii Nauk SSSR, 1937–59), 12:159.

11   Robert A. Maguire, *Exploring Gogol* (Stanford, CA: Stanford Univ. Press, 1994), 52.

12   Dewald, *Aristocratic Experience*, 174.

13   For an analysis of Gogol's own efforts at self-fashioning, see Richard Gregg, "À la recherche du nez perdu: An Inquiry into the Genealogical and Onomastic Origins of 'The Nose,'" *Russian Review* 40, no. 4 (1981): 365–77.

fashioning comes too late, after the Russian noble class had essentially closed its ranks to ambitious newcomers: not only was the service rank that granted noble status continually being raised, but integration into the society of nobles was becoming increasingly more difficult. At the same time, the era of the *raznochintsy*—the time when education, not heredity, began to mark the cultural elite—had not yet arrived. Furthermore, the Table of Ranks itself, Peter's utopian system for shaping a new noble class based on government service rather than birth, sets Poprishchin up for failure because it didn't anticipate hostility toward newcomers and imagined a homogeneous noble estate. Finally, the genre Poprishchin chooses to construct his identity as a nobleman, the diary, also trips him up: while an effective tool for creating personal spaces, the diaristic genre—intrinsically introversive and even claustrophobic—is not conducive to enhancing others' opinions about its author or changing his place in the world.

While Poprishchin's status as a nobleman may seem ambiguous from the outside, he himself does not perceive it this way. He repeatedly declares that he is a nobleman. In the first entry, describing his setting out for the department on a rainy morning, he remarks: "As for members of the noble class [*iz blagorodnykh*], only my comrade a civil servant dragged himself along [*nash brat chinovnik plelsia*]."[14] He makes similar remarks in entries for October 4, November 12, and December 3. In his article "The Suffering Usurper: Gogol's *Diary of a Madman*," Richard Gustafson calls Poprishchin's claims to nobility aggressive.[15]

Moreover, Poprishchin insists that his nobility is inherited. Fuming in his diary over the rude treatment he receives from a lackey, he exclaims, rhetorically: "Do you know, stupid flunky, that I am a civil servant, that I am of noble origin?" (*ia blagorodnogo*

---

14   Nikolai Gogol', "Zapiski sumasshedshego," in his *Peterburgskie povesti*, ed. O. G. Dilaktorskaia (St. Petersburg: Nauka, 1995), 111. All subsequent references to this edition are given in the text.

15   Richard F. Gustafson, "The Suffering Usurper: Gogol's *Diary of a Madman*," *SEEJ* 9, no. 3 (1965): 268–69.

proiskhozhdeniia; 113). In the November 6 entry, he directly asserts that he has been born into the noble class: "Am I a descendant of some commoner, a tailor, or a noncommissioned officer? [*Razve ia iz kakikh-nibud' raznochintsev, iz portnykh, ili iz unter-ofitserskikh detei?*]. I am a gentleman" (113).

Whether this is true can be contested. Poprishchin's service rank, titular councilor, is the one that granted commoners in civil service a so-called *lichnoe* (personal, or lifetime) nobility but not hereditary nobility, for which promotion to the next (eighth) rank of collegiate assessor was needed. Gogol may have used the rank of titular councilor to signal Poprishchin's precarious status as a nobleman, as Maguire argues. However, many hereditary nobles did not make it to the higher ranks either. Pushkin, for one, never advanced beyond the very same rank of titular councilor. Gogol's text doesn't give us any reason to doubt Poprishchin's assertions that he is indeed a hereditary nobleman.

It is quite safe to suppose, nonetheless, that if Poprishchin was born a nobleman, his nobility was of very recent origin. His first name and surname point to this: unlike his counterpart—or foil— Evgeny of Pushkin's *The Bronze Horseman*, whose name marks him as a pedigreed aristocrat (even though he has fallen on hard times), both Aksenty and Poprishchin mark Gogol's character as a recent member of the noble class. Aksenty, which is a corrupted Avksenty, derives from the Greek for "to increase, grow," and Poprishchin refers to *poprishche*, or career. He is an upstart, he owes his nobility to service (most probably his father's), and his ensuing anxiety about his status as a nobleman is evident in his repeated claims to be a nobleman.

Even if Poprishchin is aware of the inferiority of his position as a civil servant and a recent nobleman, he does not admit it. On the contrary, as we remember, he believes that civil servants and military officers are on an equal footing: "What kind of artful dodgers [*bestiia*] our civil servants [*nash brat chinovnik*] are! By God, they wouldn't yield to any military officer" (111). Furthermore, Poprishchin shares the hereditary nobility's disdain for newly minted nobles. He praises a vaudeville that satirizes upstarts:

> They also put up some sort of a vaudeville with amusing
> rhymes about lawyers, especially about some collegiate
> registrar . . . , and about merchants, they say openly that they
> are swindling everyone and that their sons lead a dissolute
> life and use every means to become noblemen [*lezut v
> dvoriane*]. (114)

It is, of course, telling that Poprishchin remarks caustically on the
collegiate registrar (fourteenth class). This rank is the lowest that
afforded its bearer lifelong nobility (up until 1845), whereas the
titular councilor was the highest.

Not only does Poprishchin share the aristocratic disdain for
social upstarts, but he also fills his life with aristocratic pursuits —
very similar to the ones enumerated by Dewald and Stanton. He
reads poetry and prose, he regularly attends the theater (and criticizes
his colleagues who do not), and he has a gallant (or, in Gustafson's
formulation, courtly) love affair: he admires his beloved Sophie
from afar, he walks under her windows at night, he daydreams of
her beauty and stops just when his dreams are about to become
improper, and he attempts to wait on her — risking his life — when
she drops her handkerchief. Granted, his genteel behavior is always
inadequate: the poetry he admires is old-fashioned (he reads
a late-eighteenth-century poem by Nikolay Nikolev and believes it
to be "Pushkin's composition" [*Pushkina sochinenie*], 113); the prose
that he likes is penned by Faddey Bulgarin, whose reputation as
a mediocre writer, fair or not, had been well established by the
1830s; in theater, he prefers vulgar vaudevilles, and his courting is
clumsy and ineffectual. Even the danger he put himself in to serve
his beloved is comically vulgar:

> She looked at me, then at the book, and dropped her handker-
> chief. I darted out, but slipped on the damned parquet floor
> and nearly got my nose smashed [*chut'-chut' ne raskleil nosa*];
> I kept my balance, however, and got the handkerchief. (112)

Still, in Poprishchin's own view, he behaves like a true gentleman.

Poprishchin's notorious neglect of his service duties can also
be interpreted as a feature of aristocratic behavior. Many young
noblemen who entered the civil service served nominally, showing

up late and staying only for a couple of hours. The *arkhivnye iunoshi* ("archival dandies," in James Falen's translation), mentioned by Pushkin in chapter 7 of *Eugene Onegin*, are one well-known example. Pushkin himself—in the years of his service in Petersburg, Kishinev, and Odesssa—is arguably another.[16] These young aristocrats served because it was customary and because service gave them status within the noble estate (without a service rank, their official title would be that of "minor," *nedorosl'*), but they did not take their duties seriously and were not much concerned with career advancement.[17] Likewise, early on in his diary, in earnest or not, Poprishchin declares that he serves for status: "Yes, I'll admit, if not for the nobility of my service, I would have left the department long ago" (110). And unlike his presumed double, Akaky Akakievich, who is diligent and even passionate about his service, Poprishchin shirks his duties long before his not showing up in the office can be explained by the deterioration of his mental condition.

Most importantly for his self-image as a gentleman, Po-prishchin writes. It is crucial that, in his view, writing is not something incidental and easily accessible to everyone. Writing marks him as a true gentleman: "Only a gentleman can write properly," he declares in the very first entry (111). He dismisses any writing by non-nobles as inadequate: "Sure, some shopkeepers' clerks and even serfs scribble once in a while, but their writing is for the most part mechanical: it has no commas, no periods, no style" (111). He critiques Madgie's writing, approving of her spelling and grammar (116) but disapproving of her style (117) and choice of subject matter (118). He obviously believes himself to be an expert writer.

---

[16] For a discussion of Pushkin's attitude to service, see Irina Reyfman, "Pushkin the Titular Councilor," in *Taboo Pushkin: Topics, Texts, Interpretations*, ed. Alyssa Dinega Gillespie, in the "Publications of the Wisconsin Center for Pushkin Studies" Series, general editors David M. Bethea and Alexander A. Dolinin (Madison: University of Wisconsin Press, forthcoming spring 2012).

[17] For a rare example of a nobleman (Pushkin's contemporary and friend) who chose not to serve at all, even nominally, see Iu. M. Lotman, "Liudi i chiny," in his *Besedy o russkoi kul'ture: Byt i traditsii russkogo dvorianstva (XVIII–nachalo XIX veka)* (St. Petersburg: Iskusstvo—SPB, 1994), 28.

Poprishchin, it can be concluded, does everything he can
to shape himself into a proper nobleman. And he thinks he is
succeeding: he believes that he is only a step away from winning
the hand of the general's daughter. And then everything comes
crashing down: he loses Sophie to a kammerjunker, and his carefully
constructed self-image as a gentleman disintegrates. Why?

Poprishchin blames his failure on Teplov's superior rank. It is,
however, not at all clear that Teplov is in fact his superior in rank.
If in the original Table of Ranks kammerjunker was a court title of
the ninth class (that is, the same as titular councilor in civil service),
in 1809 it became an honorary title (*zvanie*), awarded for special
services of the individual or his family. Its bearer was required to
be in the military or civil service. Beginning in 1836—that is, two
years after Gogol's story was written—a correlation between the
title of kammerjunker and rank was established: no one with a rank
lower than titular councilor could be recommended for the title
of kammerjunker. This system was not in place when Gogol was
working on his story, and, according to Semyon Reiser, the group
of kammerjunkers that Pushkin joined in December 1833 included
servitors from the fourteenth class (one person) to the fifth class (two
people). This allows us to assume that Teplov's rank conceivably
could have been equal to Poprishchin's—or even lower. The latter
is particularly plausible, since Poprishchin is no Bashmachkin
and in fact is rather successful in his career: from the description
of his last visit to the department we learn that he is a desk chief,
stolonachal'nik, which means that he had about ten people reporting
to him.[18] In contrast, Teplov's service record is not mentioned at
all, and may easily be quite unimpressive. It is obvious that when
Poprishchin compares the title of kammerjunker with the rank of
general ("everything goes to kammerjunkers or generals," 119),
he is off the mark from the viewpoint of the Table of Ranks. He
perceives the inequality but misplaces its source.

The problem, of course, is that the Table of Ranks did not
work as Peter envisioned it would. Instead of creating a homoge-

18   See Dilaktorskaia's commentary to "Notes of a Madman," in Gogol',
      "Zapiski sumasshedshego," 293n22.

neous noble class based on merit, it not only oftentimes failed to reward achievement but also institutionalized inequality among the ranks and types of service. Most importantly, it did little to erase the difference between the pedigreed and service nobility. Even if his rank was insignificant, kammerjunker Teplov was still socially superior to titular councilor Poprishchin, despite the latter's considerable service success. Teplov's social superiority was based not on his service record, but on his established status as a nobleman, which is made evident by his title of kammerjunker, given to him (I quote from the 1809 decree) as "a sign of the Tsar's particular attention to the family or to the achievements of their ancestors."

As we remember, in desperation Poprishchin tries to take a "shortcut" to achieve high social status, bypassing the Table of Ranks and using yet another model offered by the eighteenth century: rapid promotion or, in his case, self-promotion to a high position. His examples are obvious. One was Alexander Menshikov, a person of unknown origin whom Peter elevated to the rank of the military officer of the first class (*general-fel'dmarshal*), also bestowing on him such titles as Most Radiant Prince (*Svetleishii Kniaz'*) of the Russian and Holy Roman Empires and Duke of Izhora. Another is likely to be Alexey Razumovsky, who was born a Cossack but became Elizabeth's lover and, as the tradition has it, her secret husband, whom she elevated to the rank of *general-fel'dmarshal* and made a count. The third model was Emelian Pugachev, a Cossack who, in 1772, declared himself to be Peter III, Catherine II's husband killed in the course of her 1762 coup d'état. All three were commoners, and Poprishchin refers to this fact himself: "See how many examples there are in history: some commoner, not even a gentleman but a tradesman [*meshchanin*] or even a peasant—and all of a sudden it turns out that he is some grandee [*vel'mozha*] or even a sovereign [*gosudar'*]" (119). As we know, Poprishchin chooses to follow in Pugachev's steps, and his attempt at self-promotion fails, landing him in an insane asylum.

Poprishchin's inadequacy as a nobleman created by the Table of Ranks is thus one reason for his inability to win Sophie. The other is the failure of his writing enterprise: not only is Poprishchin historically late with his self-fashioning effort, but he also chooses the wrong genre for it. As mentioned above, a diary works well to create a private space but does little to connect its writer with a larger community, as writings intended for publication, correspondences, or even memoirs do. A diary does nothing to change the writer's place in the existing social hierarchy or to transform the hierarchy itself.

Gogol seems to be drawing our attention to the limitations of the diaristic genre by contrasting it with the dogs' correspondence. Let us disregard the fact that Poprishchin himself creates the corresponding dogs, but let us note that he creates them unequal. The dogs' unequal relations are underscored at their first appearance in the story, when Fidèle reproaches Madgie for not writing to her, suspecting a slight. In the first letter we are allowed to read, Madgie pointedly reminds Fidèle about her inferior status by complaining about her "petit bourgeois" (*meshchanskoe*) name (116). Indeed, in her article "Through Gogol's Enchanted Spaces," Ksana Blank argues that Fidèle's owner is likely to be a servant, because Poprishchin retrieves Madgie's correspondence from the kitchen located in the sixth floor of Zverkov's house. As Blank points out, only the back of this house (which was very famous and well-known to Gogol, who lived there in the early 1830s), the portion served by the service staircase, had six floors; the more prestigious front section of the house, served by the main staircase, had only five. (It should be noted, however, that when Poprishchin initially follows the two ladies to Zverkov's house, he reports that they go up to the fifth floor; 112).[19] Questions of social hierarchy continue to be prominent in Madgie's letters. She discusses pedigrees and polite behavior (117). She tells Fidèle about her rejection of a socially inferior suitor in favor of the gallant (*kavaler*) Trésor (118). The dogs' writing to each other, however, mediates their inequality; they are able to remain friends, and Fidèle gains in status.

In contrast, Poprishchin's diary does not connect him to anyone. Nobody knows that he is keeping a diary. Nobody is aware of his self-image as a gentleman. His effort at self-fashioning

---

19   Ksana Blank, "Po zakoldovannym mestam Gogolia," *Novoe Literaturnoe Obozrenie* 11 (1996): 177–79.

is not validated by his peers. Furthermore, the private space that Poprishchin's diary creates for him is a trap, since it prevents him from apprehending how others see him and thus changing in response. In his examination of the diaristic genre, *A Book of One's Own: People and Their Diaries*, Thomas Mallon points out: "One can always have things as one wants them in a diary; it is easy to believe that one's own authorized version and the truth are the same thing."[20] And this is what Poprishchin evidently believes. Characteristically, he easily explains away his department head's attempt to wake him from his dreams of marrying Sophie as jealousy of Poprishchin's supposed success with the girl: "I know, I know why he is mad at me. He is jealous: he has seen, perhaps, the signs of benevolence that are shown predominantly to me [*predpochtitel'no mne okazyvaemye znaki blagoraspolozheniia*]" (113). Poprishchin also easily dismisses the comical portrayal of himself that he finds in Madgie's letter—which, if Poprishchin is the author of the letter, can be interpreted as his own momentary recognition of the way things really are. He, however, refuses to accept it: "You are lying, you wretched, nasty dog!" (118).

His inaccurate self-image ultimately becomes his ruin, leading to his madness and confinement in the asylum. Only in the last entry is Poprishchin able momentarily to escape the trap he has created for himself. To do so, he discards the entire social system within which he has been trying to establish himself, abandons the conventions of diary writing, and appeals for help directly to his (perhaps imaginary) mother—revealing by this universal gesture his purely human essence, unprotected by rank, title, or text.

---

[20]   Thomas Mallon, *A Book of One's Own: People and Their Diaries* (New York: Ticknor and Fields, 1984), 209.

3. *Writing and the Anxiety of Rank:*
Pushkin's Prose Fiction

Alexander Pushkin turned to prose fiction in 1827, when he began working on *The Blackamoor of Peter the Great*. The body of his prose fiction is not large: finished and unfinished works as well as outlines, sketches, and variants fit into a single volume of any standard popular edition of his writings. Of about thirty contemplated works, Pushkin completed only four: *The Tales of Belkin*, "The Queen of Spades," "Kirdzhali," and *The Captain's Daughter*. Of these, "Kirdzhali," a biography of a brigand subtitled "a tale," can hardly be called a work of fiction. It is a tale (*povest'*) only in the idiosyncratic sense that Pushkin sometimes gives the word to emphasize the narrative's supposedly factual nature. The rest of Pushkin's attempts at prose fiction remained in various states of incompletion, ranging from several relatively polished chapters (*The Blackamoor of Peter the Great*, *Dubrovsky*, and *The Egyptian Nights*) to fragments that begin in *medias res* and end as abruptly ("The Guests Were Arriving at the Dacha," "In the Corner of a Small Square," and "We Were Spending the Evening at the Dacha") to outlines of several lines or paragraphs.

Paul Debreczeny, in his *Other Pushkin*, explains the large number of abandoned projects by Pushkin's inexperience as a prose writer and his search for effective narrative voices.[1] In contrast, Monika Greenleaf argues that Pushkin's tendency to abandon his prose projects can be accounted for by his general bent toward fragmentariness.[2] She develops Yury Tynianov's idea that there are no firm boundaries between Pushkin's "sketched programs and his finished prose" and that sometimes his "rough drafts became in

---

[1]   Paul Debreczeny, *The Other Pushkin: A Study of Alexander Pushkin's Prose Fiction* (Stanford, CA: Stanford Univ. Press, 1976), 25–55.

[2]   Monika Greenleaf, *Pushkin and Romantic Fashion: Fragment, Elegy, Orient, Irony* (Stanford, CA: Stanford Univ. Press, 1994), 1–18.

themselves finished products." Tynianov points to "Kirdzhali" and "A Journey to Arzrum" as examples of published work in which "the boundary between a program and a [finished] work" is not fully established.[3] Svetlana Evdokimova, in her *Pushkin's Historical Imagination*, names *The Blackamoor of Peter the Great* as yet another example of a work that Pushkin never finished but parts of which he nonetheless published.[4]

Recent scholarship has begun to plumb the connection between Pushkin's "life text" and his literary texts.[5] Read together, they reveal the extent to which different forms of anxiety surface throughout Pushkin's life as a frequent theme in his poetry and prose. It can be suggested that Pushkin's anxieties could have played a role in his abandoning some of his prose pieces. For example, Catharine Nepomnyashchy argues that Pushkin's uneasiness about his mixed racial origin, intensified by his plans to marry, could have made it impossible for him to continue the story of his African protagonist in *The Blackamoor of Peter the Great*. Pushkin's disquiet about the increasing commercialization of literature and the corresponding rise of prose fiction could also be a strong factor in his not finishing *The Blackamoor* and, later, *The Egyptian Nights*. Both sets of anxieties were linked to Pushkin's uneasiness about selling things that should not be sold: people, love, or the fruits of artistic creation.[6] While it is always risky to divine the connection between a writer's creative psychology and biography, such speculation is worthwhile because

---

3   Iu. N. Tynianov, "Pushkin," in his *Pushkin i ego sovremenniki* (Moscow: Nauka, 1968), 162.

4   Svetlana Evdokimova, *Pushkin's Historical Imagination* (New Haven, CT: Yale Univ. Press, 1999), 255n2.

5   See, for example, A. A. Faustov, *Avtorskoe povedenie Pushkina* (Voronezh: Voronezhskii gosudarstvennyi universitet, 2000), 7–8, 164–242; A. L. Ospo-vat, "Imenovanie geroia 'Kapitanskoi dochki,'" *Lotmanovskii sbornik* 3 (2004): 262–64; and Irina Reyfman, "Poetic Justice and Injustice: Autobiographical Echoes in Pushkin's *The Captain's Daughter*," chap. 5 in this collection.

6   Catharine Theimer Nepomnyashchy, "The Telltale Black Baby, or Why Pushkin Began *The Blackamoor of Peter the Great* but Didn't Finish It," in *"Under the Sky of My Africa": Alexander Pushkin and Blackness*, ed. Catharine Theimer Nepomnyashchy, Ludmilla Trigos, and Nicole Svobodny (Evanston, IL: Northwestern Univ. Press, 2006), 150–71.

Pushkin himself raised the issue of his black descent, first fleetingly in a footnote to chapter 1 of *Eugene Onegin* and later when defending himself in his poem "My Genealogy" against racist slurs cast by his literary enemies in 1830.[7]

Nepomnyashchy's theoretical premises parallel A. A. Faustov's notion of authorial behavior (*avtorskoe povedenie*). Faustov propounds the idea of the "unity of the biographical author and the author creator" and the corresponding importance of reading the writer's "life text" and his or her literary texts together.[8] Faustov offers an illuminating analysis of yet another source of anxiety for Pushkin throughout his life and a frequent theme in his poetry and prose: the concept of fate and the need for correct behavior in the face of fateful events.[9] Both Faustov and Nepomnyashchy scrutinize the autobiographical impulses—in particular, personal concerns and anxieties—that spurred Pushkin's creativity and, simultaneously, gave him writer's block.

I propose to probe concerns about rank and social status that form a theme in Pushkin's prose fiction. Pushkin's uneasiness about his social status in general, and his service rank in particular, is well known, and the way it makes itself evident in his poetry has been thoroughly studied.[10] His prose fiction, however, has been largely neglected. Its close examination shows that the issue of rank and status is present in virtually every piece and that it frequently constitutes the core of the narrative. Furthermore, in a substantial number of works it has clear personal significance. Manifestations

---

7   Catherine Theimer Nepomnyashchy, "The Note on Curiosity in Pushkin's *The Blackamoor of Peter the Great," Pushkin Review* 4 (2001): 44–45.

8   Faustov, *Avtorskoe povedenie Pushkina*, 7–8. Cf. David M. Bethea, *Realizing Metaphors: Alexander Pushkin and the Life of the Poet* (Madison: Univ. of Wisconsin Press, 1998).

9   Faustov, *Avtorskoe povedenie Pushkina*, 164–242.

10   See, for example, Waclaw Lednicki, *Pushkin's "Bronze Horseman": The Story of a Masterpiece* (Berkeley: Univ. of California Press, 1955), 58–72; Sam Driver, *Puškin: Literature and Social Ideas* (New York: Columbia Univ. Press, 1989), 67–76; Catriona Kelly, "Pushkin's Vicarious Grand Tour: A Neo-Sociological Interpretation of 'K vel'mozhe' (1830)," *Slavonic and East European Review* 77 (1999): 1–29.

of personal meaning differ, depending on what aspect of his self-image Pushkin presents in a particular work. Pushkin's many identities, both in life and in literature, included those of a Negro, a Russian gentleman of old bloodline, a poet, and a member of high society, to name only the most important ones. Some identities brand him as an outsider, the Other, while others indicate his desire to be an accepted member of a group. Pushkin's sentiment about his Otherness was clearly ambivalent: he both highlighted and resented it. This ambivalence made him sensitive about his social standing and rank. The rest of this chapter will examine some of Pushkin's social anxieties as they manifest themselves in his prose fiction.

"An Ugly Descendant of Negroes": Gannibal's Integration into Russian Culture

The Blackamoor, which fictionally constructs the history of Pushkin's African great-grandfather, Abram (Ibrahim) Gannibal, consistently foregrounds the status of his ancestor as an outsider both racially and socially. In Pushkin's reconstruction, Ibrahim's status as an outsider both in France and in Russia allows him to play the role of a mediator between the European and the Russian, the new and the old.[11] To fulfill his role as mediator, however, Ibrahim must be integrated, at least to some degree, into the societies in which he lives. In France, this integration is possible due to his merits: in the public sphere, he is accepted thanks to his education, intelligence, and bravery; and in the private sphere, he succeeds by gaining the love of a high-society woman. In Russia, three integrative mechanisms are at work in the public sphere: the Emperor's personal favor, service, and family ties. Ibrahim's integration depends on all three, and he seems to be on the road to success. However, he underestimates the importance of the private sphere, and the existing text of the novel suggests that this sets him up for failure.

Pushkin frequently evokes Ibrahim's status as Peter's favorite. In the first paragraph of the novel, he calls Ibrahim Peter's godson

---

[11]   Evdokimova, Pushkin's Historical Imagination, 153–54, 169–71.

(*krestnik*) and his favorite (*liubimets*). In the same paragraph, Peter's special treatment of Ibrahim is highlighted: the tsar abandons his usual financial prudence for the sake of his godson and generously bestows on him both money and "fatherly advice."[12] Pushkin continues to remind the reader about Ibrahim's status as Peter's favorite throughout the novel. Ibrahim shares the status of an outsider made prominent by Peter's favor with two other characters in the novel: the tsar's wife, Catherine, and Peter's childhood friend, Alexander Menshikov.

Ibrahim's status is also defined by his service rank. In France, he attains a considerable military rank—captain, earned in a military school and in the theater of war. After Ibrahim returns to Russia, his designated rank of lieutenant captain is only superficially a demotion and, in fact, an advance, because he now serves in a regiment captained by the tsar himself. As a tangible sign of Peter's favor, the new rank represents a powerful tool for Ibrahim's integration into Russian society. Unsurprisingly, all Russian dignitaries immediately seek his friendship: "The courtiers surrounded Ibrahim, each trying in his own way to show esteem for [*oblaskat'*] the new favorite" (20).

Ibrahim's rank is supposed to make him a living symbol of a new kind of social hierarchy introduced by Peter: one based on merit rather than blood. Although Ibrahim rises due to Peter's favor rather than actual governmental service, Peter bestows both his love and the service rank on Ibrahim as a reflection of his merit. This is not necessarily at odds with Peter's social policy. The character of Menshikov reminds the reader of the fact that there could be worthy favorites (Catherine and Ibrahim) and unworthy ones.

The Table of Ranks and personal favor provided opportunities for social mobility in eighteenth-century Russia; stability, on the other hand, came from family connections. The Rzhevsky household exemplifies the traditional social hierarchy of kinship (as instituted in the protocols of precedence, or *mestnichestvo*), demonstrated by

---

12   Alexander Pushkin, *Complete Prose Fiction*, trans. Paul Debreczeny (Stanford, CA: Stanford Univ. Press, 1983), 11. All subsequent references to this edition are given in the text.

the order in which guests sit down for dinner. True to the custom of the day, Pushkin purposefully notes that "the other guests sat according to the rank of their families, thereby evoking the happy old days of the order of precedence" (27). It is significant that the prominence of Ibrahim's family in his native land mitigates the problem of his race for Rzhevsky: "'He is not of common birth,' said Gavrila Afanasevich, 'he is the son of a black sultan'" (32). Ibrahim further strengthens his position with Rzhevsky by showing respect for the traditional clan hierarchy. Peter argues that Ibrahim's full integration into Russian society requires a union with the old Russian aristocracy through marriage, and Ibrahim accepts Peter's argument: "Marriage with the young Rzhevskaya will affiliate me with the proud Russian gentry, and I will no longer be a newcomer in my adopted fatherland" (34).

According to Pushkin's plans for the novel, Ibrahim's marriage to Natalya Rzhevskaya was to be unhappy: Natalya was to be unfaithful and would bear him a white child. Ironically, the father of her illegitimate child was to be Valerian, a figure who—as orphan, ward, and son of an executed state criminal—is a total social outsider and thus, in Rzhevsky's view, an unacceptable candidate for Natalya's hand. And yet he was to win Natalya's heart and ruin Ibrahim's marriage. Ibrahim's full integration into Russian society was thus set to fail, and the failure was to be caused by his lack of success in the personal sphere.

It is well known that the life stories of the fictional Ibrahim and his historical self differ. Abram Gannibal's and his descendants' integration into Russian culture, while ultimately successful, was even messier than Pushkin's fictitious account of it. Peter did not bless Abram's first marriage because he was long dead by the time his godson married. Abram's first wife was not a woman from the Russian gentry, but a beauty of Greek descent who was repeatedly unfaithful to him and bore him a white daughter. Even before his scandalous divorce was granted, Gannibal cohabited with and then married a German woman, who spoke no better than broken Russian, but was faithful to her black consort and gave birth to several children, Pushkin's grandfather Osip among them. Osip did marry into a Russian gentry family, that of the Pushkins: his wife

was a distant cousin of the poet's father. This first union between
the exotic newcomers and the Russian gentry was not very happy:
it included infidelities, jealousy, and bigamy. It did, nonetheless,
produce Nadezhda Gannibal, who once again married a Pushkin
and gave birth to the poet—completing, it seems, the Gannibals'
integration into the Russian social and cultural milieu. Colorful
as they were, the lives of the historical Gannibals could hardly
have served Pushkin's purposes in *The Blackamoor*. Their marital
misfortunes cast doubt on the very success of their integration and
thus on Pushkin's own place in Russian society, which could have
been yet another powerful reason for Pushkin not to finish this
novel, begun when he was in search of a bride.

"I Am a Russian Gentleman, Pushkin": The Old Gentry and the New Aristocracy

While the Gannibal connection highlighted Pushkin's status as an
outsider, his Pushkinian lineage should have placed him comfortably
within the Russian privileged noble class. The Pushkins, however,
were not a particularly prominent family: they did not belong to
the powerful and wealthy group contemporaries dubbed "the new
aristocracy," which had risen to prominence in the previous century,
in many cases thanks to their personal ties to monarchs. Pushkin
attributed his family's marginality to their allegedly independent
behavior at several historical turning points in the seventeenth
and eighteenth centuries, when the gentry had to take sides in
the struggle for the throne. To compensate for his family's lack of
present prominence, Pushkin laid claim to an old and respectable
bloodline and asserted his ancestors' historical significance.[13]

Pushkin's own service rank was also remarkably insignificant,
and his service career was utterly unimpressive. Upon graduation

---

[13]   See Aleksandr Pushkin, "Oproverzhenie na kritiki," in his *Polnoe sobranie
sochinenii v 16-ti tomakh* (Moscow: Izdatel'stvo Akademii Nauk SSSR, 1937–
59), 11:160–62; "Nachalo avtobiografii" (ibid., 12:311–13). Mark Altshuller
shows the fictional character of Pushkin's accounts about his ancestors'
historical prominence and their political disobedience; see his *Mezhdu
dvukh tsarei* (St. Petersburg: Akademicheskii proekt, 2003), 186–98.

from the Lyceum, he was appointed to the College of Foreign Affairs with the rank of collegiate secretary (tenth class). In 1824, at the same time when Pushkin was ordered to live on his father's estate in Mikhailovskoe, he was dismissed from service without the usual promotion to the next rank—a sign of imperial disapproval. On November 14, 1831, at his own request, the poet was reinstated as a collegiate secretary at the College of Foreign Affairs. On December 6, 1831, he was promoted to the rank of titular councilor (ninth class). Pushkin's new service position brought him a yearly income of five thousand rubles and access to the Imperial archives. On December 31, 1833, Pushkin was granted a court title of kammerjunker. The thirty-four-year-old Pushkin was deeply insulted by this undistinguished title, which, in his view, was unbecoming to a paterfamilias and renowned poet. He never advanced any further.[14]

Pushkin's awareness of the service rank system is evident in one of *The Tales of Belkin*, "The Stationmaster." The entire story, of course, is about differences in social status: its main character, the humble stationmaster Samson Vyrin, loses his beautiful daughter Dunya to Minsky, a dashing young aristocrat and cavalry captain (seventh class). Convinced that Minsky will abandon his socially inferior lover, Vyrin travels to St. Petersburg to save her, but is thrown out both from Minsky's quarters and from the apartment he keeps for Dunya. Years later, Dunya shows up in her native village dressed as a grand dame and with three children in tow, only to learn that her father has drunk himself to death.

---

[14]   For a detailed analysis of Pushkin's service record, see Irina Reyfman, "Pushkin the Titular Councilor," in *Taboo Pushkin: Topics, Texts, Interpretations*, ed. Alyssa Dinega Gillespie, in the "Publications of the Wisconsin Center for Pushkin Studies" Series, general editors David M. Bethea and Alexander A. Dolinin (Madison University of Wisconsin Press, forthcoming spring 2012). For an overview of Pushkin's complaints about his title of kammerjunker, see N. A. Gastfreid, *Pushkin: Dokumenty gosudarstvennogo i S.-Peterburgskogo glavnogo arkhivov ministerstva inostran-nykh del, otnosiashchiesia k sluzhbe ego 1831–1837 gg.* (St. Petersburg: A. Benke, 1900), 38–40 and Irina Reyfman, "Pushkin the Kammerherr: On Pushkin's Social Reputation in the 1830s," chap. 4 in this collection.

This inverted version of the standard fallen woman story begins with a lengthy discussion of the system of ranks in Russia. The first paragraph portrays the sorry lot of stationmasters, whose rank of fiscal clerk-of-registration (*kollezhskii registrator*, fourteenth class) barely protects them from physical abuse at the hands of irate travelers demanding horses. It also outlines the complicated rank system that governs the dispensation of horses at post stations.

The third paragraph of the story describes the narrator's past youthful resentment of the rank system, which governs not only the dispensation of horses at post stations but also the distribution of food at governors' dinner tables. By the time he tells the story, however, the narrator's rank has risen (the fictitious editor A. P. informs us that Belkin heard "The Stationmaster" from titular councilor A.G.N.), and his resentment has apparently dissipated: "Nowadays both the one and the other seem to me to be in the order of things." He now seems to find wisdom in the rank system—or does he? He concludes wryly: "Indeed what would happen to us if the rule convenient to all, 'Let rank yield to rank,' were to be replaced by some other, such as 'Let mind yield to mind'? What arguments would arise! And whom would the butler serve first?" (94). Such a "defense" of the rank system actually mocks it as an absurdity that was bound to create awkward situations not only for the young A.G.N., but also, by extension, for the low-ranking Pushkin.

Another of *The Tales of Belkin*, "The Shot," reveals Pushkin's discomfort with his social standing more directly. In this story, Silvio's opponent, Count B***, is portrayed as a representative of the "new aristocracy." Silvio calls him "a young man from a rich and distinguished family [*znatnoi familii*]" and "a brilliant child of fortune [*blistatel'nyi schastlivets*]." He then again stresses the count's social prominence and wealth: "Picture . . . an exalted [*gromkoe*] name, and money, more that he could count, in an inexhaustible supply" (69–70). The young man's title suggests the recent origin of both his exalted name and wealth (the first Russian count was Boris Sheremetev, who received the title in 1706, as a reward for putting down a revolt in Astrakhan).

We cannot tell whether Silvio is a middling nobleman or a foreigner (Silvio, the narrator informs us, is not his real name), but we have reason to believe that his conflict with Count B*** is as much over a difference in social standing as it is over a difference of dispositions. This supposition is supported by Silvio's behavior as a duelist: it mimics that of many middling Russian noblemen who resorted to unconventional dueling behavior (*breterstvo* or *bretteur* behavior, as it was known) to force socially superior opponents to acknowledge their equal status.[15] Silvio resents Count B***'s nonchalant conduct at the dueling site, rightly seeing it as dismissive and insulting. He wants the count to take him seriously, and to achieve this he violates the rules of proper dueling by interrupting the duel.

It seems, however, that Pushkin was not completely certain whose side to take, Silvio's or the count's, which signals his ambivalence regarding his own position vis-à-vis the two groups of nobility. It is telling that he distributes features of his own behavior between Silvio and Count B***. He makes Silvio join Alexander Ypsilanti's uprising against the Turks (in which, the narrator reports, Silvio is killed)—an action Pushkin himself contemplated in the early 1820s.[16] At the same time, the count's behavior in "The Shot" (eating cherries under the barrel of a gun) repeats Pushkin's nonchalance during his 1822 duel with the officer Zubov. Unlike Count B***, however, Pushkin withstood Zubov's shot and subsequently refused either to return fire or to reconcile—a harsher insult than the one inflicted on Silvio by Count B***, who shoots at Silvio and agrees to await the return shot indefinitely. Pushkin initially ended the story at that point (the manuscript of the first version states: "The ending has been lost"). In this version, Silvio, like Zubov, would have been left without recourse. Two days later, Pushkin added chapter 2, which reports on Silvio's retaliation.

---

[15]   See Irina Reyfman, *Ritualized Violence Russian-Style: The Duel in Russian Culture and Literature* (Stanford, CA: Stanford Univ. Press, 1999), 80–84.

[16]   Iu. M. Lotman, *Aleksandr Sergeevich Pushkin: Biografiia pisatelia* (Leningrad: Prosveshchenie, 1981), 78.

"The Shot" was written in September of 1830 in Boldino, where Pushkin went to take possession of the nearby village of Kistenevka, allotted to him by his father on the occasion of his impending marriage. His situation thus resembled that of Count B*** as depicted in chapter 2. The fact that Pushkin was quarantined in Boldino because of a cholera epidemic and was in danger of dying emphasizes the similarity. Identifying with the newly married Count B***, who was facing death because of his youthful imprudence, Pushkin may have been rethinking his own former dueling behavior. The story reworks the denouement of the Zubov episode, thereby correcting Pushkin's mistreatment of the officer.

Pushkin's insulting conduct with Zubov was typical for the Kishinev period of his life. His years in Kishinev (a location that was clearly on his mind when he wrote "The Shot") were particularly difficult for him socially. Lotman writes:

> A collegiate secretary and a versifier [*stikhotvorets*] in a world where everything was defined by rank, a person without means amidst people well provided for and spending money freely, a twenty-year-old youth amidst seasoned military officers or grand Moldavian boyars, Pushkin was a person whose dignity was constantly assaulted.[17]

One line of defense was Pushkin's perpetual readiness to duel. It is well known that his mentor in dueling affairs in Kishinev was Lieutenant Colonel I. P. Liprandy, a famous *bretteur* and Pushkin's acknowledged original both for the character of Silvio and for the story's narrator, Lieutenant Colonel I.L.P.

Not only does Liprandy split into two characters in "The Shot," but one of those characters, the narrator, also undergoes a strange metamorphosis in the course of the story: while he is independent and dignified in his interactions with Silvio in chapter 1, he inexplicably assumes an obsequious tone with Count B*** in chapter 2. The narrator himself explains it with reference to current poverty: "Having grown unaccustomed to luxury in my poor corner . . . I now felt timid" (72). While this might explain a mo-

---

17   Lotman, *Aleksandr Sergeevich Pushkin*, 86–87.

mentary awkwardness, it cannot justify the narrator's servile tone throughout his brief conversation with the count, where he addresses him by title (Your Excellency, or *Vashe siiatel'stvo*) nine times. Moreover, he twice uses the title not as an address, but as a substitute for the pronoun "you" ("I bet Your Excellency could not hit..."; 73). Such usage powerfully signals the speaker's implied lower status.

The narrator's behavior is particularly conspicuous because there is no reason for him to feel inferior. Granted, at the time of his visit to Count B***'s estate, Lieutenant Colonel I.L.P. is retired and living in his ancestral "poor little village" (71). Nonetheless, his status as a gentleman, his respectable military rank (seventh class), and his education (Silvio, as we remember, liked to talk to him "about different subjects"; 68) make him the count's equal in everything but wealth. Furthermore, the narrator seems to be the only true exponent of the honor code in the story: it is against his reaction that the behavior of the two duelists is measured. This gives him an enormous moral advantage over the count, who twice shoots at Silvio and does not endure a single shot himself.

Every first person narrator is simultaneously the author's creation and, inevitably, his alter ego; and I.L.P.'s behavior echoes Pushkin's own insecurities, both those of the Kishinev period and especially those of the time he wrote the story. About to be married and facing a cholera epidemic, he would have identified with Count B***, as I have argued. At the same time, living in Boldino, near his ancestral "poor little village" of Kistenevka, Pushkin could not have failed to perceive the vast distance between them: unlike the count, he had no title, no respectable service rank, no luxurious estate, no rich bride, and only a paltry independent income. The letters he wrote to friends when leaving for Boldino convey his concern that his royalties would not cover the cost of his wedding and impending household expenses. Pushkin symbolically purges himself of these worries by making his look-alike narrator in "The Shot" fawn before the count. The exorcism worked: as is well known, Pushkin's involuntary sojourn in Boldino made the autumn of 1830 one of the most productive, and thus lucrative, periods of his life.

In the unfinished novel *Dubrovsky*, once again events are set in motion by a conflict between a wealthy and powerful upstart (Troekurov) and a middling nobleman (Andrey Dubrovsky). Pushkin begins by establishing the two characters' essential equality as noblemen: "Of the same age, born of the same social class, and educated the same way, they were to some extent similar in character and disposition" (146). This is how middling nobility and Pushkin himself would have wanted to see relations within the noble class. However, just as this way of thinking did not work in real life, it does not work in the novel: Troekurov accepts Dubrovsky as his equal only up to a certain point. As soon as he feels Dubrovsky has slighted him, he forgets their old friendship and begins to behave like an all-powerful and ruthless new aristocrat: he takes away Dubrovsky's village, Kistenevka (which, tellingly, is named after the village allotted to Pushkin himself in 1830).

Although Troekurov is introduced as a person "of distinguished birth" (145), Pushkin indicates that his prominence is of recent origin. As we learn from the ruling read during the court procedure that deprives Dubrovsky of his estate, Troekurov's father was of humble station: he began his career in the rank of provincial secretary (thirteenth class at the time) and eventually rose to the rank of collegiate assessor (eighth class).[18] Not only were provincial officials at the bottom of the state service hierarchy, but we cannot even be sure that Troekurov's father was a hereditary nobleman, for while the court ruling refers to the "noble birth" of every noble person mentioned, it says no such thing about the elder Troekurov. True, he did rise to the rank that would have secured him a place in the hereditary noble class, and his son rose even higher, to the rank of general *en chef*—that is, full general (second class). Yet, for all his service success, Troekurov behaves like an upstart. He is boorish and enjoys flattery. Most conspicuously, he lacks the sense of honor expected from a gentleman: he agrees to take his friend's estate by means of chicanery.

---

[18]   Pushkin inserted into the text of the chapter a copy of a real court ruling on a similar case, changing only the dates and names. See commentary to Pushkin, *Dubrovskii*, in *Polnoe sobranie sochinenii v 16-ti tomakh*, vol. 8, bk. 2, p. 1054.

In contrast, Dubrovsky is portrayed as a man of honor. A retired lieutenant of the guards (ninth class, but one should remember that the guards were the most respectable of all military services), he is independent and dignified despite his modest financial situation. He knows how to respond to an offense to his honor. In his reply to Troekurov's insulting demands, he writes: "I do not intend to tolerate jests from your serfs, nor will I tolerate them from you, for I am not a buffoon but a nobleman of ancient lineage [*starinnyi dvorianin*]." In fact, the last clause of his retort echoes the response of the nineteen-year-old Pushkin to a certain Major Denisevich, who declined Pushkin's challenge to a duel because of the challenger's youth and low service rank. To this, Pushkin responded: "I am a Russian nobleman [*Ia russkii dvorianin*]." Denisevich was forced to apologize.[19] The connection is made stronger by Dubrovsky's concluding his letter with a formula that may indicate his readiness to duel: "I remain at your disposal [*Za sim ostaius' pokornym ko uslugam*]."[20] Pushkin thus "lends" Andrey Dubrovsky not only the name of his estate but also his own behavior as a gentleman.

Pushkin does not have much in common with the younger Dubrovsky, the true hero of the novel and a quintessential Romantic outcast. Could this be one of the reasons Pushkin did not finish *Dubrovsky* and moved on to *The Captain's Daughter*, a novel full of personal significance? Among other things, the main character in *The Captain's Daughter*, Petr Grinev, is a poet, and one of Pushkin's goals in this novel is to examine a poet's behavior amid social unrest.[21] In his other prose work of the 1830s, he is concerned with the poet's status in a society that did not provide a comfortable position for a writer of noble origin attempting to make a living by his trade.

---

19   I. I. Lazhechnikov, "Moe znakomstvo s Pushkinym," in *A. S. Pushkin v vospominaniiakh sovremennikov v dvukh tomakh* (Moscow: Khudozhestvennaia literatura, 1985), 2:174.

20   Pushkin, *Dubrovskii*, in his *Polnoe sobranie sochinenii v 16-ti tomakh*, vol. 8, bk. 1, p. 164. Debreczeny's translation, "I remain your humble servant" (148), does not convey this meaning.

21   See Reyfman, "Poetic Justice and Injustice." On the importance of rank and name in *The Captain's Daughter*, see Ospovat, "Imenovanie geroia 'Kapitanskoi dochki,'" 262–64.

"This Rubbish": The Poet as Aristocrat and Sellout

Pushkin confronts this question most directly in *The Egyptian Nights*. One of the two main characters in the story, Charsky, is a society man and a poet who conceals his gift, calling inspiration rubbish (*drian'*), and who hides from everyone when it overcomes him. He does this because, as an aristocrat, he does not fit the two prevailing institutions of literature in Russia: the system of patronage (inherited from the eighteenth century) and professional writing (taking shape in Pushkin's lifetime). As William Mills Todd III puts it, Charsky cannot resolve the "conflict between social position, literary commerce, and inspiration."[22]

This conflict certainly had personal significance for Pushkin, who, particularly in his younger years, fashioned himself as a society man and dandy, and was constantly on the alert for any attempts to treat him as a client looking for patronage. He wrote to Vyazemsky on June 7, 1824: "None of us would want *the magnanimous patronage of an enlightened grandee. This fell into decay [obvetshalo] together with Lomonosov. Our present-day literature is and has to be nobly independent.*"[23] In the 1830s, without abandoning the dandy persona altogether, Pushkin came to respect the professionalism of his eighteenth-century predecessors. In his "Journey from Moscow to Petersburg," he puts Lomonosov's alleged flattery of his superiors in historical perspective and admires his occasional voicing of independence. He paraphrases Lomonosov's proud words to his patron, Ivan Shuvalov: "I do not want to be a fool either at the tables of high-born gentry or for other earthy rulers or even for the Lord God."[24] Remarkably, Lomonosov's words are echoed in Dubrovsky's retort to Troekurov quoted above. Moreover, Pushkin would

---

[22]   William Mills Todd III, *Fiction and Society in the Age of Pushkin: Ideology, Institutions, and Narrative* (Cambridge, MA: Harvard University Press, 1986), 108.

[23]   Pushkin, *Polnoe sobranie sochinenii v 16-ti tomakh*, 13:96. The emphasis is Pushkin's.

[24]   Pushkin, "Journey from Moscow to Petersburg," in *Polnoe sobranie sochinenii v 16-ti tomakh*, 11:254.

rephrase these words again, in his diary of 1834, in connection with his ill-fated title of kammerjunker: "I can be a subject, even a slave, but a flunky and a jester I will not be even for the heavenly ruler."[25] Pushkin clearly grew to perceive Lomonosov as a fellow writer and a worthy model.

Even more importantly, Pushkin came to respect professionalism. The eighteenth-century poet and literary theorist Vasily Trediakovsky, the butt of Pushkin's jokes in the 1820s, receives high praise as a professional in the "Journey" as well as in Pushkin's other writings in the 1830s.[26] Pushkin's new thinking shapes his concept of the professional writer in *The Egyptian Nights*. Charsky's stated dilettantism no longer suits Pushkin, whereas Charsky's foil in the story—an Italian *improvisatore*, for all his repulsiveness— embodies Pushkin's idea of a true poet. To be sure, the *improvisatore* seems to represent not only the worst case of clientage but also the commercialization of literature in its crudest form: he sells the fruits of his inspiration directly to consumers, as if from a market stall. And yet it is to him that Pushkin planned to lend his own poetry: the two poems the Italian creates on demand. In contrast, we are not shown any of Charsky's poems. His refusal to acknowledge the importance of the reading public makes his writings irrelevant. It is entirely plausible to suppose that Pushkin's own similarity to the *improvisatore* unsettled the author and interfered with his finishing the piece. But in the fragment that has been written, it is the *improvisatore* who is Pushkin's alter ego.

A Writer of Prose as an Insignificant Person

As we recall, the first paragraph of "The Stationmaster" discusses the sad lot of stationmasters, harassed because of their low service rank. The paragraph ends rather unexpectedly, with a statement on

---

[25]   Pushkin, *Polnoe sobranie sochinenii v 16-ti tomakh*, 12:329 (entry of May 10, 1834).

[26]   On Pushkin's treatment of Trediakovsky, see Irina Reyfman, *Vasilii Trediakovsky: The Fool of the "New" Russian Literature* (Stanford, CA: Stanford Univ. Press, 1990), 196–225.

the low-ranking stationmasters' narrative talents. They are declared better narrators than high-ranking officials: "For my part, I must confess that I would rather listen to them than to some official of the sixth class travelling on government business" (94).[27] In the third paragraph, as we recall, the narrator—seriously or not—hails the rank system that governs the distribution of horses at post stations and food at official dinners. He then abruptly returns to his story ("But let me return to my story"; 94), leaving the reader to wonder how his apparent approval of the rank hierarchy reflects on his own ability as a narrator and, most importantly, on his previous statement that the hierarchy of narrative talent runs contrary to the hierarchy of rank.

As a matter of fact, in Pushkin's prose of the 1830s, none of the first-person narrators are socially prominent. The narrator of "The Shot" is seized with a sudden social inferiority complex. The narrator of "The Stationmaster," for all his apparent social success, remains a modest titular councilor. The rank of the alleged narrator of *The Tales of Belkin* is not identified, but it is unlikely that this dull-minded fellow could have made a decent career in his seven years in an undistinguished infantry regiment. The narrator of the unfinished "A History of the Village of Goriukhino," Belkin's double (initially, Pushkin planned to make the history Belkin's other creation), began his service as a cadet and, it seems, was able to rise only to the first commissioned officer's rank, that of ensign (fourteenth class). Even Petr Andreevich Grinev, the narrator of Pushkin's last work of prose fiction, *The Captain's Daughter*—who, like Pushkin, is of a "good old family"—is unable to rise above the very same rank of ensign. In *Pushkin and Romantic Fashion*, Greenleaf suggests: "The poet in prose was one step away from the mad clerk, the next figure into which modern society would project its own sense of disorientation and self-pity."[28] This means that Pushkin's narrators of prose fiction are one step away from Gogol's pathetic heroes Aksenty Poprishchin

---

27   I have slightly altered Debreczeny's translation to emphasize that the narrator of "The Stationmaster" listens more than he talks.

28   Greenleaf, *Pushkin and Romantic Fashion*, 315.

and Akaky Bashmachkin, titular councilors scribbling away in mad inspiration.

As, of course, is the Titular Councilor Alexander Pushkin. In a fit of self-mockery, he gets the narrator of "A History of the Village of Goriukhino" in trouble with higher-ranking officers for his love of writing and writers. Still a cadet, he spends a week in St. Petersburg on official duty and, sitting in a café, spots "B., the author" (123). He chases after him to pay his respects, but, to his utter chagrin, he bumps into one higher-ranking officer after another, and every one of them stops him and demands that he stand at attention. B. disappears, and the poor cadet catches up with some solicitor instead. Chasing after B.—that is, Faddey Bulgarin, a financially successful prose writer and Pushkin's bitter enemy— and being stopped at every step by one's superiors could serve as a comic representation of Pushkin's own struggle for both respectable social status and financial success as a writer.

4. Pushkin the Kammerherr: On Pushkin's Social Reputation in the 1830s

As is well known, in late December of 1833, Pushkin was granted the court title of kammerjunker (junior chamberlain or junior kammerherr). Russian cultural memory has preserved a view of this event according to which the poet was extremely unhappy with this title, considering it beneath his status and age, and suspecting that the title was granted to him so that his beautiful wife could be invited to court balls. This view, based on Pushkin's diaries and letters as well as contemporary memoirs, is generally correct, but does it reflect the entire picture?

I will not address the question of whether Nicholas's alleged improper interest in Natalya Nikolaevna Pushkina was the impulse behind his granting Pushkin the title. True or not, contemporary speculations on this matter undoubtedly upset Pushkin; no wonder he referred to them repeatedly in his correspondence and his diary. In a recent article, "Pushkin's Year of Frustration, or How *The*

Golden Cockerel is Made," Boris Gasparov convincingly argues that Pushkin's 1834 fairy tale *The Golden Cockerel* was written partly in response to the sexual undertones of the entire episode, including speculations about Natalya Nikolaevna and the tsar.[1]

My focus, however, is on the rumors concerning Pushkin himself: I will attempt to reconstruct what contemporaries thought about Pushkin receiving the court title. How did they see the incident and his reaction to it? Was it viewed the same way that it is seen now by the majority of scholars and educated Russians— that is, that the title was unexpected, unwanted, insulting, and was accepted only because it was impossible to decline a favor from the tsar? Or was their view perhaps different? Did Pushkin's contemporaries sympathize with his situation? If his enemies didn't, did his friends? I realize that such a reconstruction can be only speculative, but nonetheless I would like to attempt it, to make the currently accepted image of Pushkin's stoically suffering the insult he couldn't avenge a little bit more complicated. I hope my reconstruction will offer a picture somewhat closer to the actual situation.

Many contemporaries registered Pushkin's discomfort, perhaps indignation and even wrath, in reaction to receiving the title, and this, as I said, is what the existing cultural memory has preserved. What is not often recalled is that for many around Pushkin, including those who liked and even loved him, this situation was comical, and Pushkin knew it. Sophia Karamzina, the historian's daughter, writing to the poet Ivan Dmitriev on January 20, 1834 (that is, less than a month after the title was officially conferred), described Pushkin's feelings rather flippantly: "Pushkin was deeply afraid [*krepko boialsia*] of bad jokes on account of his unexpected kammerjunker status, but now he has calmed down, attends balls, and enjoys the solemn beauty of his wife." (Karamzina goes on to joke about Natalya Nikolaevna's jealousy of Pushkin's attentions to other women.)[2] However, it is likely that Pushkin calmed down (if

---

1   Boris Gasparov, "Pushkin's Year of Frustration, or How *The Golden Cockerel* is Made," *Ulbandus Review* 12 (2009/2010): 41–62.

2   "Prilozheniia k pis'mam N. M. Karamzina: 1. Izvlecheniia iz perepiski rodnykh Karamzina v pervoe vremia posle ego smerti," in Nikolai

he actually did) not because there were no jokes, but because he could do little to prevent them. Petr Vyazemsky's son Pavel, who knew Pushkin quite well, writes in his memoirs:

> Friends did not spare Pushkin's pride [*samoliubie*] on account of his belated kammerjunker title. I remember Sobolevsky's poem:
>
> > Пушкин камер-юнкер,
> > Раззолоченный как клюнкер.
>
> (Pushkin the kammerjunker, /gilded like a golden coin.)

Pavel Vyazemsky continues: "It was Sobolevsky who invented the name *kliunker* for a golden coin, using it as proof that there is a word that rhymes with kammerjunker."[3] The joker, Sergey Sobolevsky, one of the poet's closest friends, is referring here to the kammerjunker uniform, which featured rich golden decorations. As we see, he bends over backwards to ridicule his friend, inventing a new meaning for a word of German derivation, which, according to Dahl's dictionary, actually meant a train of carts carrying gold.

Petr Vyazemsky (whom we also have to consider among Pushkin's closest friends, even though—especially toward the end of Pushkin's life—one may question the sincerity of his friendship) made similar jokes. On May 28, 1834, he wrote to Pushkin, forwarding to him Ivan Myatlev's invitation for dinner:

> Come without fail. It will be really fun. You have to be there at 4 o'clock, that is, today. In addition, Myatlev is
>
> > Любезный родственник, поэт и камер-гер.
> > А ты ему родня, поэт и камер-юнкер:
> > Мы выпьем у него шампанского на клункер,
> > И будут нам стихи, на м<ате>рный манер.[4]

Karamzin, *Pis'ma k I. I. Dmitrievu* (St. Petersburg: Imperatorskaia Akademiia Nauk, 1866), 439.

[3]   Pavel Viazemskii, "Aleksandr Sergeevich Pushkin, 1826–1837," in *A. S. Pushkin v vospominaniiakh sovremennikov v dvukh tomakh* (Moscow: Khudozhestvennaia literatura, 1985), 2:192.

[4]   Aleksandr Pushkin, *Polnoe sobranie sochinenii v 16-ti tomakh* (Moscow: Izdatel'stvo Akademii Nauk SSSR, 1937–59), 15:152.

(Myatlev is a dear relative, a poet and kammerherr. / And you are his relative, a poet and kammerjunker. / At his place we will drink champagne worth a *klunker* / And [Myatlev — known for his burlesque poetry] will read his obscene poetry to us.)

Vyazemsky is, of course, quoting Vasily Pushkin's 1812 poem "To P. N. Priklonsky," which begins with the line "Dear relative, poet and kammerherr" — a line that entered the parlance of the Pushkin circle and was used by Pushkin in his own poem addressed to Vyazemsky on the occasion of his receiving the title of kammerherr on August 5, 1831, which begins "Dear Vyazemsky, poet and kammerherr."[5] In his invitation, Vyazemsky jokingly presents himself, Myatlev, and Pushkin as members of the same family by pointing out that all three of them have court titles. Given the fact that both Vyazemsky and Myatlev were kammerherrs, whereas Pushkin was only a kammerjunker, it is doubtful that Pushkin was entirely amused by Vyazemsky's joke.

In his article on *The Golden Cockerel*, Gasparov rightly reminds us that the additional insult of this joke comes from the sexual associations of the word *kammerherr* itself. Not only does the German *herr* sound like a vulgar Russian synonym for penis, but a detail of the kammerherr's uniform, a golden key that was worn on the lower back, invited homosexual connotations. As Gasparov points out, "In the Arzamasian parlance [it] was interpreted as 'the key to one's bottom' (*kliuch k zadu*), implying the way the distinction was allegedly often earned." The title of kammerjunker, or junior kammerherr, by definition must have been even less respectable.[6]

In this context, the allegations that Pushkin actively sought out the title of kammerjunker had to be even more upsetting for him than the needling but friendly jokes. Such allegations seem to have been rather widespread. Yakov Polonsky, a poet and good

---

5   See Irina Paperno, "O rekonstruktsii ustnoi rechi iz pis'mennykh istoch-nikov (Kruzhkovaia semantika i domashniaia literatura v Pushkinskuiu epokhu)," in *Semantika nominatsii i semiotika ustnoi rechi* (Tartu: Tartu Riiklik Ülikool, 1978), 1:125–26.

6   Gasparov, "Pushkin's Year of Frustration," 53–54.

acquaintance of Pushkin's younger brother, Lev, wrote down his own reminiscences about the episode: "Some of his enemies spread rumors and even published that Pushkin attained this title by using intrigues and flattery" (he then goes on to quote Lev's refutation of these rumors).[7] Pushkin's good friend N. M. Smirnov (husband of A. O. Smirnova-Rosset) records similar allegations in his 1842 memoir:

> Moreover, in relation to this case a vile lampoon appeared, in which they talked about the change in Pushkin's feelings, alleged that he had become a fawner, a petty person [*malodushnyi*], and he, who valued his fame, was afraid that this opinion would be accepted by the public and would deprive him of his popularity [*narodnosti*].[8]

Likewise, Pavel Nashchokin, perhaps Pushkin's closest friend in his later years, reported to Petr Bartenev (who, as we know, interviewed many of Pushkin's contemporaries to collect information about the poet): "Many accused [Pushkin] of seeking out the kammerjunker title."[9] In his memoirs, V. I. Safonovich, a casual acquaintance of Pushkin who met him at Natalya Zagrazhskaya's, gives us a taste of what people outside Pushkin's inner circle thought and said:

> Pushkin was a kind of enigmatic, two-faced [*dvulichnoe*] creature. He was eager to be accepted among the aristocracy [*kidalsia v znat'*]—but [at the same time] wanted to be popular; he would appear in a salon—but would behave grossly [*griazno*]; [he] would seek the good graces of people with influence and of upper circles—but had nothing genial [*gratsioznogo*] in his manner and behaved haughtily. He was both a conservative and a revolutionary. He accepted the title

---

7   "Rasskazy L. S. Pushkina v zapisi Ia. P. Polonskogo," in *A. S. Pushkin v vospominaniiakh sovremennikov*, 1:57.

8   N. M. Smirnov, "Iz pamiatnykh zapisok," in *A. S. Pushkin v vospominaniiakh sovremennikov*, 2:281.

9   P. V. Nashchokin and V. A. Nashchokina, "Rasskazy o Pushkine, zapisannye P. I. Bartenevym," in *A. S. Pushkin v vospominaniiakh sovremennikov*, 2:231.

of kammerjunker with pleasure, but would mill [*vertelsia*] around people who didn't particularly like the court.[10]

To add insult to injury, many among Pushkin's contemporaries believed that he was upset not because he had been granted an unwanted court title, but because, in his view, this title was not high enough: they believed that, had he received the title of kammerherr, he would have accepted it gladly. In his earlier (1834) description of Pushkin's reaction to receiving the title, Smirnov explains his displeasure precisely in this way:

> He claimed that it would be strange if he put on the court uniform—he, the former critic of the court; *mais le fin mot de la chose*, [was] that he was annoyed that he had not been made a kammerherr. The Emperor didn't figure this out [*ne dogadalsia*], and he was given the golden uniform [of kammerjunker], so that he, and especially his beautiful wife, could be invited to court.[11]

Likewise, Petr Vyazemsky wrote to Grand Duke Michael soon after the poet's death, on February 14, 1837:

> I have to admit: Pushkin didn't like his kammerjunker uniform. What he didn't like in it was not the court service, but the uniform of kammerjunker. Despite my friendship with him, I will not hide that he was conceited and vain. The kammerherr's key was a distinction that he would have appreciated; but it seemed to him improper that at his age, at the height of his career he was made kammerjunker in the manner of youths and society debutants. This is the entire truth about his prejudice against the uniform. It came not out of opposition, not out of liberalism, but out of vainglory and personal touchiness.[12]

---

10   V. I. Safonovich, "Vospominaniia," *Russkii arkhiv* 4 (1903): 492.

11   K. P. Bogaevskaia, "Iz zapisok N. M. Smirnova," *Vremennik Pushkinskoi kommissii, 1967–1968* (Leningrad: Nauka, 1970), 8.

12   Kn[iaz'] P. A. Viazemskii to Vel[ikii] kn[iaz] Mikhail Pavlovich, February 14, 1837, *Russkii arkhiv* 1 (1879): 390.

Accurate or not (and regardless of what one thinks about Vyazemsky's true feelings toward Pushkin), this is strong testimony, especially from a person who had witnessed his friend's death two weeks before.

Fig. 1: Pushkin with
a kammerherr's key
(Reproduced in *Literaturnoe
nasledstvo* 16–18 [1934]: 983)

The rumors about Pushkin's alleged desire for a higher title were apparently quite prevalent. Pushkinist Leonid Grossman writes in his 1934 article: "Such opinions spread widely in Petersburg 'high society,' giving rise to ironic remarks, epigrams, lampoons [*paskvili*], and caricatures."[13] Smirnov, as we remember, mentions a "vile lampoon" (*merzkii paskvil'*) in his 1842 memoir. Grossman does not give any concrete references to epigrams and lampoons in his article but analyzes in detail a caricatured portrait of Pushkin that depicts him holding the kammerherr's key in his hand and pressing it to his lips (see figure 1). The meaning of the caricature is clear: Pushkin's kissing the key represents his alleged passionate desire to become a kammerherr. It also implies the sexual overtones

---

13   Leonid Grossman, "Neizvestnoe izobrazhenie Pushkina," *Literaturnoe
nasledstvo* 16–18 (1934): 983.

of this desire, which suggests that the kammerherr jokes spread well beyond Pushkin's immediate circle. Grossman does not discuss the possible provenance of the caricature, but dates this amateur drawing to somewhere between 1834 and 1836, with 1834 being the most probable date.

We have no evidence that Pushkin was aware of the gossip that he desired the kammerherr's key, but he certainly knew the rumor that he actively sought out the title of kammerjunker. According to Nashchokin (as recorded by Bartenev), Pushkin repudiated this rumor in the following way:

> When [Pushkin] told Nashchokin about this [rumor], he argued that he could not have sought it out, because three years earlier Benkendorf himself had offered him the title of kammerherr, but he rejected it, noting, "You want me to be reproached like Voltaire" [who, as we know, was reproached for accepting a position at the court of Frederick the Great].[14]

It is hard to tell what exactly Pushkin had in mind when he mentioned Benkendorf's offer. Here I can suggest only speculations by way of an explanation.

One possible basis for Pushkin's assertion can, perhaps, be found in his correspondence with Elizaveta Khitrovo, Mikhail Kutuzov's daughter and a high-society lady with considerable influence, who happened to have tender feelings for Pushkin. In her letter to the poet, written in May 1830 shortly before his marriage to Natalya Goncharova, Khitrovo first forgives him his impending marriage and then proposes to help him relaunch his career, citing the tsar's benevolent attitude toward him and promising, in order to help, to "tear herself into forty-six thousand pieces for him."[15] Responding to her, Pushkin says, "Thank you, but no thank you," expressing an aversion to civil service and court titles:

---

14   Nashchokin and Nashchokina, "Rasskazy o Pushkine," in *A. S. Pushkin v vospominaniiakh sovremennikov*, 2:231.

15   Pushkin, *Polnoe sobranie sochinenii v 16-ti tomakh*, 14:92; original in French.

It is very kind on your part, madam, to take an interest in my situation in relation to the master [that is, Nicholas]. But what sort of a position, in your opinion, can I take at his side? I don't see a single proper one. I abhor paperwork . . . To be a kammerjunker doesn't befit my age; besides, what would I do at court? Neither my income nor my occupation allows me this.[16]

It is interesting to consider the French term for the court title that Pushkin rejects in this letter: *gentilhomme de la chambre*. The French system of the Officers of the Crown was of course quite different from the Russian Table of Ranks, and the Russian usage of the French term not only did not correspond to it but also appeared to have been used rather loosely: it could be applied both to kammerherrs and kammerjunkers. For example, A. B. Kurakin (who became a kammerjunker in 1771) is called "Gentilhomme de la Chambre de sa majesté imperial de toutes les Russies" in the title of his letter published in 1775 by François Henri Turpin as an introduction to Turpin's tragedy *Cyrus*. We may assume that this is how Kurakin the kammerjunker signed his letter. S. G. Domashnev, who received the title of kammerjunker in 1773 and that of kammerherr in 1778, signed his *Discours sur l'importance de l'histoire*, delivered in 1776 at the Academy of Sciences in Petersburg (of which he was appointed director in 1775) and published in 1778, "M. de Domaschneff, gentilhomme de la Chambre de l'imperatrice," making it difficult to decide which title is actually meant. Finally, in the rough draft of a French letter written in March of 1794 from Petersburg to an unknown person (perhaps to S. R. Vorontsov), F. V. Rostopchin, updating his correspondent on rumors about upcoming diplomatic appointments, informs him that baron Gustav Ernest (Gustav Ottonovich) Stackelberg is said to be slated for an appointment to Copenhagen and had been made a *gentilhomme de la chambre*.[17] Since G. E. Stackelberg was made kammerjunker in 1789

---

[16]   Ibid., 93; original in French.

[17]   F. V. Rostopchin, "Pis'mo grafa F. V. Rostopchina o sostoianii Rossii v kontse ekaterininskogo tsarstvovaniia," *Russkii arkhiv* 1, no. 3 (1878): 294. The translation provided on p. 297 gives Stackelberg's title as kammerjunker.

and kammerherr in 1794, it is more than likely that Rostopchin has in mind the latter appointment and thus uses *gentilhomme de la chambre* for kammerherr.[18] Russians thus used *gentilhomme de la chambre* to indicate both kammerherr and kammerjunker, but Pushkin's assertion in his letter to Khitrovo that the title of *gentilhomme de la chambre* does not befit his age clearly signals that he was rejecting the idea of the title of kammerjunker, not kammerherr.

We cannot be sure whether Khitrovo followed up on her suggestion despite Pushkin's refusal to accept her offer or, if she did, whether any rumors were generated by her actions. It is equally impossible to determine whether the title of kammerherr was actually offered to Pushkin at that point. If it was, and Pushkin declined (which is doubtful, since, even coming from Benkendorf, it had to be authorized by Nicholas, and imperial appointments could not be refused), the added irony of his reference to Voltaire would have been the fact that the French *philosophe* carried both titles: *gentilhomme de la chambre du Roy* in France and kammerherr at Frederick's court.

It is also possible that Nashchokin's story echoes a different set of events, partly described in Filipp Vigel's letter written in the summer of 1831. In this letter, Vigel expresses his support for Pushkin's plans (in the wake of the demise of his *Literary Gazette*) to start a new "political-literary" journal that he intended to offer (I quote from Pushkin's program for the journal) "to the government, as an instrument of its influence on the general opinion."[19] Vigel, whom Pushkin had known since the time of "Arzamas," recommended that Pushkin reconnect with Sergey Uvarov, another fellow Arzamasian and, at the time, the president of the Academy of Sciences. In 1831, Uvarov was on the verge of becoming one of the most powerful statesmen in the Nicholaevan empire: in 1832, he

---

18   Rostopchin obviously had in mind the younger Stackelberg, not his father Otto Magnus Stackelberg, also a diplomat, who was made kammerherr in 1771, long before the time the letter was written.

19   Pushkin, "Materialy i zametki, sviazannye s izdaniem gazety 'Dnevnik,'" in his *Sobranie sochinenii v 10-ti tomakh*, ed. D. D. Blagoi (Moscow: Izd. Khudozhestvennoi literatury, 1962), 6:373.

would be appointed deputy minister, and in 1833, minister of public education. The same year he would come up with his famous (or infamous) triad—Orthodoxy, Autocracy, and Nationality—which would become the ideological basis of Nicholas's reign. Uvarov's support would thus have been a serious help both for Pushkin's plan and for his career.

In his letter to Pushkin, Vigel insists that Uvarov is ready to provide such help, that he has been informed of Pushkin's plan for the journal, "approves of it, is enthusiastic about it,"[20] and is ready to talk about it with Benkendorf (whose endorsement would be needed to start a new publication). Vigel spends considerable time describing Uvarov's enthusiasm about Pushkin's plan. For a thorough discussion of the reasons for Uvarov's alleged enthusiastic reaction, I refer the reader to Mariya Maiofis's book *A Proclamation to Europe*, in which she convincingly argues that, at the time "Arzamas" was active, Arzamasians saw themselves not as private persons getting together to dine on goose, have a good time, and poke fun at their literary opponents, but as high-minded patriots aspiring to advise the tsar on matters of internal and foreign affairs at a time when, they believed, radical changes in these areas were imminent. Maiofis also argues that this spirit was rekindled at the beginning of Nicholas's reign, and that the three former Arzamasians—Uvarov, Vigel, and Pushkin—could have been united by it.[21] Despite Uvarov's supposed enthusiasm, Pushkin's project failed. However, the poet's relatively good and collaborative relations with Uvarov continued, though gradually deteriorating, until December 1835, when Pushkin wrote a poem mocking Uvarov, "On the Recovery of Lucullus," after which, as is well known, their relations swiftly went downhill, ending in mutual vitriolic hatred.

What interests me in Vigel's letter of 1831 is his assertion that, in addition to supporting Pushkin's plans for the journal, Uvarov

---

[20]   Filipp Vigel' to Aleksandr Pushkin, 1831, in Pushkin, *Polnoe sobranie sochinenii v 16-ti tomakh*, 14:202; original in French.

[21]   Mariya Maiofis, *Vozzvanie k Evrope: Literaturnoe obshchestvo "Arzamas" i ros-siiskii modernizatsionnyi proekt 1815–1818 godov*, Historia Rossica Series ([Moscow]: Novoe Literaturnoe Obozrenie, 2008), 658–68.

was ready, even eager, to promote Pushkin's social standing in any way possible. Vigel asserts: "[Uvarov] cannot wait to see you an honorary member of his Academy of Sciences. The first vacant seat in Shishkov's Russian Academy has to be given to you, has to be set aside for you."[22] Moreover, Vigel suggests that Uvarov may help him obtain the title of kammerherr:

> As a poet, you don't have to serve, but why wouldn't you become a courtier? If a laurel wreath decorates the brow of a son of Apollo, why couldn't the kammerherr's key decorate the behind of a scion of an ancient noble family?[23]

Given the fact that both Vigel and Uvarov were known homosexuals, Vigel's proposition had to have sounded at least somewhat improper.

It is impossible to say what in Vigel's letter originates with Uvarov and what is included on his own initiative. We do know that in October of 1831, Uvarov translated (or rather transposed) into French Pushkin's "To the Slanderers of Russia" (he sent it to Pushkin on October 8).[24] In January of 1833, he facilitated Pushkin's election to the Russian Academy. We also know that Pushkin's appointment as kammerherr never took place, but whether Uvarov ever undertook any steps in this direction is impossible to determine. In any case, Pushkin's alleged assertion that he was offered and refused the title may have originated in this episode (as he asserted to Nashchokin in 1834, this offer was made "three years ago": the chronology thus matches). One thing is still certain: it could not have been an official appointment or even a real offer; if it were, as I have already pointed out, Pushkin would not have been in a position to refuse it.

---

22   Filipp Vigel' to Aleksandr Pushkin, 1831, in Pushkin, *Polnoe sobranie sochinenii v 16-ti tomakh*, 14:202.

23   Ibid. Vigel's information about the service requirement is not quite accurate: beginning in 1809, every holder of a court title had to be in the military or civil service; perhaps, he meant that for Pushkin such service would have been nominal—as indeed it was after Pushkin returned to service in the fall of 1831.

24   For Uvarov's letter with the translation, see Pushkin, *Polnoe sobranie sochinenii v 16-ti tomakh*, 14:232; for Pushkin's response, see ibid., 236.

Eventually, as we know, Pushkin petitioned to be reinstated at the College of Foreign Affairs, was allowed to return to service, and was promoted to the rank of titular councilor. He was made kammerjunker, not kammerherr—most likely because, according to Semyon Reiser's article analyzing the ranks and ages of Pushkin's fellow kammerjunkers, as a titular councilor, "according to the rules and traditions, Pushkin could not lay claim to the title of kammerherr."[25]

In conclusion, it is worth mentioning that some admirers of Pushkin in today's Russia have a hard time accepting this outcome, and Russian cultural memory has preserved a legend, popular among amateur historians, that toward the very end of his life—or even after his death—Pushkin was granted the title of kammerherr.[26] This legend is based mostly on wishful thinking but also on the fact that in the documents of the military court investigation held after Pushkin's fatal duel, he is consistently called "kammerherr."[27] All the investigators, as well as D'Anthès and Pushkin's second, Konstantin Danzas, use this title. The only person who calls Pushkin kammerjunker is Petr Vyazemsky.[28] Finally, an inquiry about Pushkin's title was made to the court chancellery; and after the response came back stating that it was kammerjunker, the correct title was used by all parties.[29] There is no factual basis to the legend, and the story of the postmortem promotion reflects not facts, but Pushkin's unshakably high status in Russian cultural memory.

---

[25]   S. A. Reiser, "Tri stroki dnevnika Pushkina," *Vremennik Pushkinskoi komissii, 1981* (Leningrad: Nauka, 1985), 152.

[26]   See G. I. Tiraspol'skii, "Opiska ili simvol?" *Voprosy literatury* 5 (2001): 331–35; Anatolii Korolev, "Kamerger dvora ego imperatorskogo velichestva," *Neva* 4 (2006), accessed December 4, 2010, http://magazines.russ.ru/neva/2006/4/ko17.html. Tiraspol'sky realizes that the opinion is erroneous but sees it as poetic justice. Korolev believes that Nicholas promoted Pushkin after his death.

[27]   *Duel' Pushkina s Dantesom-Gekkernom: Podlinnoe voenno-sudnoe delo 1837 g.* ([Moscow]: Rosslit, 1992), 15ff, up to 115.

[28]   For Vyazemsky's use of Pushkin's title, see ibid., 46.

[29]   Ibid., 115 and 116.

Part Two

PUSHKIN AS THE OTHER

Preface

The four articles in this part are united by their subject matter: Pushkin as he appears in his own work (*The Captain's Daughter*), in stories by Gogol and Zoshchenko ("Notes of a Madman" and "The Sixth Tale of Belkin," respectively), and in popular imagination, as a man dying a painful death. The first article contends that in *The Captain's Daughter*, among other things, Pushkin considers some personal questions, such as the behavior of a poet caught up in a bloody revolt. I argue that both Grinev and his adversary, Shvabrin, are endowed with "poetic" traits and are associated in Pushkin's mind with several poets, including Pushkin himself.

The next article interrogates a broader question of Gogol's opinion of Pushkin, using as an example Gogol's "Notes of a Madman." I concur with a view—not entirely new but recently supported by several excellent studies—that Gogol's attitude toward Pushkin was much more complex and far less positive than popular consensus has it.

The third article analyzes the documents (letters, diary entries, memoirs, and medical records) generated in the last few days of Pushkin's life, while he lay on his death bed. The article argues that the accounts of Pushkin's death were uncommonly detailed and graphic and made public the spectacle of the wounded poet's dying body. Such frankness ran against the traditional reticence about deaths in duels, however bloody and painful they may have been. Accounts of Pushkin's death undermined this tradition and thereafter allowed portrayals of wounded and dying duelists to appear both in documentary and literary accounts.

The last article looks at Zoshchenko's pseudo-imitation of Pushkin's *Tales of Belkin*, written at the time when preparations for Pushkin's centennial of 1937 were under way. It argues that multi-layered stylistic play, together with both obvious and hidden references not only to Pushkin but also to Tolstoy, Konstantin Leont'ev, and Zoshchenko himself, allow the writer to assert his artistic freedom at a time when this was hard to do openly.

5. Poetic Justice and Injustice:
Autobiographical Echoes
in Pushkin's The Captain's Daughter

Interpreting a literary work, a scholar generally is expected to respect the author's will regarding the final redaction of the text and confine him- or herself to this final version. In reality, this hardly ever happens, since different versions, rough drafts, early outlines, and other materials frequently exist that not only assist in understanding the final product but also allow a glimpse into the author's creative process itself. Sometimes it appears that the author desires that we watch him write, by offering parallel versions (such as the so-called omitted chapter in *The Captain's Daughter* or the chapter "At Tikhon's" in *Demons*—regardless of the reason that compelled Pushkin and Dostoevsky to exclude these chapters from the final versions of their works) or incorporating certain details into the main text, which otherwise would not make sense. These details might signal to the reader that the author has left out something significant that he or she, nonetheless, does not want to be completely lost. The reader can then follow the author's lead and can attempt to recover this hidden information. Thereby, the reader comes to be invited as a participant in the author's creative process. Pushkin—for whom creative play was an integral part of his work—is known for leaving such clues. The "ears" that "stick out" in *Boris Godunov* provide one famous example; the omitted stanzas in *Eugene Onegin*, represented only by numbers, mark another. In *The Captain's Daughter*, the name of Vasily Trediakovsky is one clue that invites the reader to the inner workings of Pushkin's creative process.

In *The Captain's Daughter*, Trediakovsky's name is mentioned only once, but at a very dramatic point in the story: in the scene leading to the duel between Grinev and Shvabrin. Shvabrin ridicules the love song that Grinev presents for his judgment by comparing it to Trediakovsky's poetry:

But to my great disappointment Shvabrin, who had generally been indulgent, this time unhesitatingly declared that my song was no good. "And why?" I asked, concealing my annoyance. "Because," he replied, "such verses are worthy of my teacher, Vasily Kirilych Trediakovsky, and strongly remind me of his amatory couplets."[1]

Pushkin's use of Trediakovsky's name in this passage was a short-hand reference to a culturally accepted stereotype: to Trediakovsky's reputation as the most wretched versifier ever, a ridiculous pedant, and the author of hideous poetry and prose that made people either laugh or fall asleep.[2] The stereotypical image of Trediakovsky was extremely useful in literary polemics. To condemn a literary opponent, one had simply to compare him to Trediakovsky or to claim that he was the opponent's teacher or ancestor. Pushkin was keenly aware of this tradition and used Trediakovsky's name as a polemical tool throughout his literary career. The image of Trediakovsky as an ancestor of all bad poets suited equally well the needs of the young Pushkin quarreling with the Archaists in the 1810s and the mature Pushkin entering angry polemics with Mikhail Kachenovsky's and Nikolay Nadezhdin's *Messenger of Europe* (*Vestnik Evropy*) in the late 1820s.

While Pushkin never ceased using the comical image of Trediakovsky for polemical purposes, his views of the poet changed over time. In the 1810s, Pushkin seemed to accept his reputation as a bad poet without reservations. In the 1820s, however, Pushkin's attitude shifted, partly because he revised the very principles upon

---

[1] Aleksandr Pushkin, *Polnoe sobranie sochinenii v 16-ti tomakh* (Moscow: Izdatel'stvo Akademii Nauk SSSR, 1937–59), 8:300; *Complete Prose Fiction*, trans. Paul Debreczeny (Stanford, CA: Stanford Univ. Press, 1983), 287. I have omitted the qualifier "former," which Debreczeny has inserted before the word "teacher" in his translation and which is absent in the original. All future references to both the original and the translation are given in the text: the first numbers indicate the volume and page of the original, while the second number indicates the page of the translation.

[2] On Trediakovsky's reputation, see Irina Reyfman, *Vasilii Trediakovsky: The Fool of the "New" Russian Literature* (Stanford, CA: Stanford Univ. Press, 1991); on Pushkin's manipulation of the stereotypic image of Trediakovsky, see ibid., chap. 5.

which the "Arzamas" members' mockery of Trediakovsky and the Archaists had been based. In the 1830s, the image of Trediakovsky as an ancestor of all bad poets lost much of its validity for Pushkin. Behind the stories about Trediakovsky the pedant—laughed at, despised, and beaten by everyone—Pushkin began to discern the features of Trediakovsky the professional, the bold experimenter, a man haunted by misfortunes and tragically unappreciated by his contemporaries and literary descendants.

Pushkin's treatment of Trediakovsky in the 1830s, however, was not univocal. He continued to exploit the humorous aspects of his reputation, an attitude plainly displayed in the passage from *The Captain's Daughter*. Shvabrin's comment reproduces common notions about Trediakovsky as the provider of bad models. Pushkin thus playfully imitates (or parodies) the contemporary tradition. This interpretation, however, does not explain why Trediakovsky appears in Shvabrin's comment not only as a bad model for Grinev's song, but also as the critic's own teacher. While Grinev is portrayed as the writer of a memoir and a poet, whose poetry later won Sumarokov's praise ("Alexander Petrovich Sumarokov was some years later to accord much praise to them," 8:300; 287), nowhere else in the novel Shvabrin is portrayed as having anything to do with literature.[3] Furthermore, Pushkin knew perfectly well that it was highly unusual to declare Trediakovsky one's own teacher. Russian writers in the late eighteenth and early nineteenth centuries tried to avoid any comparisons with Trediakovsky, to prevent any allusions to him as their predecessor, and to downplay anything that could suggest their artistic indebtedness to him.

A notable exception to this general rule was Gavrila Derzhavin. In his *Memoir*, written in 1812–13, he names Trediakovsky, together with Lomonosov and Sumarokov, among his models. He states that in the early 1760s, while trying his hand at poetry, he turned to "the book about poetry composed by Mr. Trediakovsky" to

---

3   For a discussion of Grinev as Sumarokov's disciple, see V. E. Vatsuro, "Iz istoriko-literaturnogo kommentariia k stikhotvoreniiam Pushkina," *Pushkin: issledovaniia i materialy*, Institut russkoi literatury (Pushkinskii dom) (Leningrad: Nauka, 1986), 12:319–23.

learn about versification.[4] Yakov Grot, the editor and commentator of Derzhavin's *Works*, quotes an even more explicit statement from "an 1805 notebook," where the poet declares: "I derived the rules of poetry from Trediakovsky's works."[5] The entry on Derzhavin in Metropolitan Evgeny's *Dictionary of Russian Secular Writers*—based on an autobiographical essay Evgeny had asked the poet to write for this purpose—cites a similar statement.[6] Derzhavin clearly intended to flout the prevailing trend and acknowledge Trediakovsky as his teacher.

Derzhavin's memoir was first published long after Pushkin's death. Pushkin was aware of the memoir's existence (in the commentary to chapter 5 of his *History of Pugachev* [*Istoriia Pugacheva*, 1834] he mentions that Derzhavin had left "a memoir, unfortunately, still unpublished") and asked Derzhavin's heirs for permission to examine the poet's papers concerning the Pugachev events, but access was denied.[7] It is thus unlikely that Pushkin knew the statement in Derzhavin's memoir. Nonetheless, Pushkin could have read Evgeny's *Dictionary* entry on Derzhavin. First published in 1806, in the magazine *Friend of Enlightenment* (*Drug prosveshcheniia*), Evgeny's essay includes the following statement:

> He [Derzhavin] kept busy reading various books and sometimes also writing little poems, getting instruction

---

4   Gavrila Derzhavin, *Sochineniia v 9-ti tomakh*, ed. Iakov Grot (St. Petersburg: v tipografii Imperatorskoi Akademii Nauk, 1864–83), 6:443. Derzhavin refers to Trediakovsky's *New and Brief Method for Composing Russian Verse* (1735), probably its second, revised version published in volume one of his *Compositions and Translations in Verse as Well as in Prose* (1752).

5   Ibid., 6:443n.

6   Evgenii [Bolkhovitinov], *Slovar' russkikh svetskikh pisatelei* (Moscow: v Universitetskoi tipografii, 1845), 1:168. About the entry on Derzhavin in Evgeny's *Dictionary* as an autobiography, see Iakov Grot, "Perepiska Evgeniia s Derzhavinym," *Sbornik obshchestva russkogo iazyka i slovesnosti* 5, no. 1 (1868): 66, 71.

7   Iakov Grot, *Materialy dlia biografii Derzhavina: 1773–1777, Deiatel'nost' i perepiska Derzhavina vo vremia pugachevskogo bunta* (St. Petersburg: v tipografii Imperatorskoi Akademii Nauk, 1861), 1; for Pushkin's remark, see his *Polnoe sobranie sochinenii v 16-ti tomakh*, 9:110.

from the poetic rules of foreign writers and even more of
Mr. Trediakovsky, in other respects attempting to imitate
Lomonosov's genius.[8]

Pushkin also could have known about Derzhavin's accepting attitude toward Trediakovsky from his *Discourse on Lyrics or on Ode in
General*, parts of which were published in *Readings in the Colloquium
of Lovers of the Russian Word* (*Chteniia v Besede liubitelei russkogo slova*)
in 1811–14. The poet opens his discussion of the ode with a reference to Trediakovsky's pioneering efforts in the field of lyrics.[9]

Finally, in the 1830s, Pushkin was likely to believe that
Derzhavin's attitude toward Trediakovsky was similar to his own
at that time and combined respect for the poet with the ability to
enjoy the potential for play offered by his reputation as an ancestor
of bad poets. In the early nineteenth century, a cycle of short poems
circulated among the educated public. Popular opinion either took
them for Trediakovsky's original poems or considered them parodies
of his poetry, often ascribing them to Derzhavin. Either way, these
utterly absurd poems proved for the reading public Trediakovsky's
alleged lack of talent. They contributed greatly to the formation of
Trediakovsky's negative reputation. The poems' origins varied. One
of them was Derzhavin's humorous epigram "Impromptu for Marfa
Ivanovna Arbenina," written around 1808.[10] Another was lifted from
Trediakovsky's 1755 essay "On Ancient, Middle, and New Russian
Poetry," where it is quoted as an example of a corrupt practice of
distorting words for the sake of rhyme.[11] Others were anonymous
parodies of Trediakovsky's poetry, which oral tradition attributed

---

[8]   Evgenii [Bolkhovitinov], "Derzhavin," *Drug prosveshcheniia* 1 (1806): 277.

[9]   Gavrila Derzhavin, "Rassuzhdenie o liricheskoi poezii," *Chteniia v Besede
        liubitelei russkogo slova* 2, no. 1 (1811): 3.

[10]   Derzhavin, "Eksprompt dlia Marfy Ivanovny Arbeninoi," in his *Sochineniia*,
        3:507. A contemporary recalls that the poem circulated in Moscow in 1808–9
        (ibid., 3:507n).

[11]   Vasilii Trediakovskii, "O drevnem, srednem i novom stikhotvorenii
        rossiiskom," in his *Izbrannye proizvedeniia* (Moscow: Sovetskii pisatel', 1963),
        431.

to Derzhavin.[12] According to A. O. Smirnova-Rosset, Pushkin knew one such poem and quoted it to her in the early 1830s:

> Pushkin said that his favorite poet was Trediakovsky, and after him Count Khvostov. To prove Trediakovsky's charm he quoted two lines:
>
> > O leto, leto, tem ty mne ne liubovno,
> > Chto akhti ne gribovno.
>
> (O summer, summer, you are not agreeable to me, / Since you are not rich in mushrooms.)[13]

Pushkin could have shared the popular belief about Derzhavin's authorship of the parodies, including this one. The fact that he did not mention it to Smirnova-Rosset doesn't mean much: it was not unusual for Pushkin to use Trediakovsky's comical image for literary play.

But what does the villain Shvabrin have to do with the great poet Derzhavin? There is at least one connection: the Pugachev rebellion. As a native of Kazan *guberniya*, Derzhavin volunteered for service in the secret military unit dispatched to the Volga region to carry out intelligence operations on Pugachev and his followers. In this capacity, Derzhavin took a very active part in suppressing the uprising. He saw the campaign as an opportunity to

---

12   Four such poems were published in Iurii Tynianov, *Mnimaia poeziia: Materialy po istorii poeticheskoi parodii XVIII i XIX vv.* (Moscow: Academia, 1931), 135. In his commentary (419), Tynianov gives references for only two of them, Derzhavin's "Impromptu" and the quotation from Trediakovsky's essay, but does not identify his sources for the other two and does not discuss the question of attribution. A. A. Morozov, in his introduction to *Russkaia stikhotvornaia parodiia (XVIII-nachalo XX v.)* (Leningrad: Sovetskii pisatel', 1960), quotes one of the unattributed poems but evades the question of authorship, introducing it simply as "a poem stuck in [the editor's?] memory" (*zastriavshie v pamiati stikhi*, 10).

13   A. O. Smirnova-Rosset, "Iz 'Avtobiograficheskikh zapisok,'" *A. S. Pushkin v vospominaniiakh sovremennikov* (Moscow: Khudozhestvennaia literatura, 1985), 2:171. The poem most likely dates to no earlier than the first quarter of the nineteenth century, since the word *gribovno* is not listed in *Slovar' russkogo iazyka XVIII veka* (Leningrad: Nauka, 1989), 5:234, with an extensive database of one hundred thousand words.

advance his stagnating career and did everything to demonstrate his zealousness and military skill. Among other commissions, he was entrusted with capturing Pugachev himself, even though he did not succeed. In turn, the rebels announced a ten-thousand-ruble reward for Derzhavin's head. Having acted energetically and capably throughout the campaign, Derzhavin won the respect of his superiors, from A. I. Bibikov to A. V. Suvorov, but in the end fell into disfavor with the last commander in chief, Count Petr Panin. Panin, who was suspicious of Derzhavin's actions during Pugachev's capture of Saratov, demanded explanations, and even threatened to hang Derzhavin along with Pugachev. Panin's allegations against Derzhavin implied not only cowardice and incompetence but treason. Derzhavin eventually cleared his name, but his military career was damaged, and in 1777, he left the military for the civil service.[14]

Pushkin's "Remarks on the Rebellion" ("Zamechaniia o bunte," his supplement to the *History of Pugachev*, written for the tsar) and the notes Pushkin took while doing research for the *History* show his considerable interest in Derzhavin's activities during the Pugachev revolt. In his brief preface to the *History*, Pushkin asserts that one of the important reasons for exploring the Pugachev rebellion was the fact that Derzhavin (along with other prominent figures of the time) figured in these events. Accordingly, Pushkin gives a detailed account of the poet's actions and movements during the time he was assigned to the Volga region, paying attention to his activities as an able and ambitious officer, to the events that led to his quarrel with his superiors, and to the early indications of his literary abilities.

---

[14]   For a detailed account of Derzhavin's activities during the Pugachev rebellion see Grot, *Materialy dlia biografii*; for Panin's inquiries and his threat, see 122 and 143. In his letter to Panin, published by Grot, Derzhavin defends his actions and points out that the allegations of treason do not stand up to logic (134). For a different take on Derzhavin's behavior in this incident and on Pushkin's view of it, see David M. Bethea, *Realizing Metaphors: Alexander Pushkin and the Life of the Poet* (Madison: Univ. of Wisconsin Press, 1998), 198, 206–17. Bethea agrees, however, with my general claim in this article about Derzhavin's "presence" in *The Captain's Daughter*.

One episode of Derzhavin's service in the Volga region especially attracted Pushkin's attention: Derzhavin's allegedly cruel actions against the rebels near the village Malykovka of Saratov *guberniya*, where he was assigned for almost the entire duration of the campaign. Pushkin discusses this episode three times: in the main text of the work, in the "Remarks on the Rebellion," and in the preparatory notes. In the notes, the story is attributed to D. O. Baranov (1773–1834):

> (I heard this from Senator Baranov.) Derzhavin, having approached a certain village near Malykovka with two Cossacks, learned that a large crowd had gathered and intended to go over to Pugachev. He went directly to the assembly building and demanded an explanation from the scribe Zlobin . . . on why the crowd had gathered and who had ordered this. The leaders stepped forward and declared that they were on the way to join His Majesty Petr Fyodorovich [that is, Pugachev] and even began to threaten Derzhavin. He ordered two of them hanged, and ordered the crowd to bring lashes and had the entire village flogged. The crowd scattered. Derzh[avin] convinced them that three regiments were following him.[15]

Pushkin incorporated a toned-down version of the same episode into the main text of his treatise.[16] In the preparatory notes, he added a commentary that he ascribed to his other informant, the poet Ivan Dmitriev: "Dmitriev claimed that Derzhavin hanged them out of poetic curiosity."[17] Pushkin found this information important enough to include it in the "Remarks on the Rebellion," a supplement to the *History* that contained material that he considered noteworthy but unsuitable for publication in the main text:

---

15   Pushkin, "Dmitriev. Predaniia," in his *Polnoe sobranie sochinenii v 16-ti tomakh*, 9:498.

16   Pushkin, *Istoriia Pugacheva*, in his *Polnoe sobranie sochinenii v 16-ti tomakh*, 9:44.

17   Pushkin, "Dmitriev. Predaniia," in his *Polnoe sobranie sochinenii v 16-ti tomakh*, 9:498.

"I. I. Dmitriev claimed that Derzhavin hanged these two peasants
more out of poetic curiosity than military necessity."[18]

Dmitriev was one of the eyewitnesses with whom Pushkin
consulted during his work on the *History*. A native of Simbirsk
guberniya, he had spent his adolescence in the region where the
rebellion was brewing, before his family fled to Moscow at the
beginning of the uprising. Later, as a fifteen-year-old student of
a military school, Dmitriev witnessed the execution of Pugachev
in January of 1775. Pushkin wrote down Dmitriev's account of
the Pugachev events under the title "Dmitriev. Legends." He was
also familiar with Dmitriev's memoir, *A View of My Life* (*Vzgliad na
moiu zhizn'*), still unpublished at the beginning of the 1830s, and he
quoted Dmitriev's description of the execution in the last chapter
of his *History of Pugachev*, as well as in the commentary to this
chapter.

Baranov's story and, especially, Dmitriev's interpretation
are of doubtful historical validity. True, both Derzhavin's memoir
and Grot's very detailed account of Derzhavin's service during
the Pugachev campaign mention Derzhavin's reckless behavior,
including references to non-existent regiments that allegedly were
on their way to reinforce Derzhavin's scanty company, but neither
source accords with Baranov's story. True, Derzhavin commanded
executions and floggings, including the one in Malykovka when,
in order to instill fear into the hearts of the inhabitants and thus
ensure their loyalty, he staged a very theatrical execution of the
murderers of a certain Tishin—who, together with his wife and
small children, had been mercilessly slaughtered. In all these
cases, however, Derzhavin either followed orders or his actions
were justified by military necessity and (as in the case with the
murder of the Tishins) the cruelty of the rebels' actions. Baranov's
story and Dmitriev's comment thus form a legend that reflects
historical facts but interprets and changes them so as to present
a certain image of Derzhavin—namely, the image of a person for
whom the need for "poetic" exploration outweighs humaneness

---

18   Pushkin, "Zamechaniia o bunte," in his *Polnoe sobranie sochinenii v 16-ti
        tomakh*, 9:373.

and practical considerations. Pushkin's title for Dmitriev's reports about the Pugachev events, "Dmitriev. Legends," suggests that he understood the legendary nature of this image. Nonetheless, Pushkin apparently attributed some value to the legend about Derzhavin and believed that the allegedly poetic impulse behind Derzhavin's actions reflected an important aspect of his personality.

Notably, Dmitriev apparently "lent" Derzhavin his own fascination with executions. Describing his reaction to the beheading of Pugachev in his memoir, Dmitriev acknowledged that, unlike his older brother who could not watch the execution and turned his face away "in order not to see the stroke of the ax," he himself only pretended to be unable to watch but in fact "secretly tried to catch every movement of the outlaw. What was the reason for this? Certainly, not my cruelty, but only my desire to see how a person behaves in such a decisive, terrible moment."[19] Pushkin had to know this passage, since it follows the description of Pugachev's beheading that Pushkin quoted twice in his treatise. It is unlikely that he failed to notice the similarity of the two poets' reactions to executions—"poetic curiosity."

Pushkin's interest in Derzhavin's confrontation with the rebels was likely to be heightened by its resemblance to Nicholas's actions during the 1831 cholera riots in military settlements near Novgorod. Pushkin referred to this episode three times: twice in his 1831 diary (July 26 and July 29) and once in a letter to Petr Vyazemsky (August 3, 1831). The version in the letter resembles Baranov's story most closely: "He acted fearlessly, even daringly; having scolded the murderers, he bluntly declared that he could not forgive them and demanded that the instigators be handed over. They promised and submitted."[20] Discussing the episode in his diary, Pushkin stresses the tsar's ability to impress with words, his "gift of words" (*dar slova*), as the main component of his power

---

[19]   Ivan Dmitriev, *Vzgliad na moiu zhizn'* (Cambridge, UK: Oriental Research Partners, 1974), 15–16.

[20]   Pushkin, *Polnoe sobranie sochinenii v 16-ti tomakh*, 14:205.

over the rebels.[21] The question remains whether the similarity in Nicholas's and Derzhavin's behavior drew Pushkin's attention to Baranov's anecdote or whether his own accounts of Nicholas's heroic actions affected the way he recorded Baranov's.

Despite the fact that Derzhavin's name is mentioned neither in the final text of *The Captain's Daughter* nor in the rough drafts, Pushkin's interest in Derzhavin in the *History of Pugachev* suggests that his adventures in the Volga region were very much on Pushkin's mind at the time he was working on the novel—which he conceived before beginning his research for the *History* and which he finished in September 1836, after his treatise on Pugachev had been published. I would argue that Shvabrin's unexplained apprenticeship to Trediakovsky comprises a vestige of Pushkin's unrecorded thoughts concerning the main character in *The Captain's Daughter* and that in contemplating the personality of his protagonist, Pushkin might have been considering not only the fates of Shvanvich, Basharin, Grinevs, and other historical figures who served as prototypes for Grinev's and Shvabrin's characters, but that of Derzhavin as well.[22]

The outlines and rough drafts for the novel show that Pushkin initially intended to portray a single protagonist, a young nobleman who had sided with Pugachev, was court-martialed after the uprising's suppression, and then forgiven (or partly forgiven) by the Empress. Pushkin split his original character, the renegade nobleman, in two—into the virtuous Grinev and the scoundrel Shvabrin—only at a late stage in his work. The writer called his original protagonist first Shvanvich and later Basharin, after the two officers who joined Pugachev's army. His final choice, Grinev (first used for a character who later became Zurin), was also a historical name: two unrelated Grinevs took part in suppressing the

---

21   Pushkin, *Polnoe sobranie sochinenii v 10-ti tomakh*, ed. B. V. Tomashevskii (Leningrad: Nauka, 1977–79), 8:20.

22   For a recent discussion of the historical background of the novel and the prototypes of its characters, see Aleksandr Ospovat, "Istoricheskii material i istoricheskie alliuzii v *Kapitanskoi dochke*," in *Tynianovskii sbornik*, vol. 10, *Shestye-Sed'mye-Vos'mye Tynianovskie chteniia*, ed. M. O. Chudakova and E. O. Toddes (Moscow: 1998), 40–67.

Pugachev uprising. One was Colonel Petr Grinev, an acquaintance of Derzhavin; the other was Second Lieutenant A. M. Grinev, who, like Derzhavin, was accused of being Pugachev's accomplice and had to clear his name. Pushkin knew the names of both Grinevs from the historical documents relating to the uprising.[23]

The prototypes of Pushkin's characters in *The Captain's Daughter*, as well as the characters themselves and their predecessors in the rough drafts, share a number of features with Derzhavin. Not every trait is shared by all members of the group, and therefore only the composite image can serve as a basis for including Derzhavin among the historical figures Pushkin contemplated while working on the novel. Some of the common features are biographical, such as service in the Guards in St. Petersburg before being transferred to the Volga region, a real or alleged alliance with Pugachev, the necessity of clearing one's name, a subsequent pardon or lenient punishment, and knowledge of the German language (which Derzhavin shares with Shvanvich). Others are similarities in opinions. Thus, Grinev's conviction, expressed during the war council of Orenburg, that "offensive actions" against Pugachev would be far more effective than defensive ones, closely resembles the view of Derzhavin that led to his conflict with Colonel Boshniak, which Pushkin describes in chapter 8 of his *History of Pugachev*. Yet other traits suggest a similar psychological makeup. Thus, Grinev's final predecessor in the rough drafts of the novel, Bulanin from the "omitted chapter," displays an irrational interest in executions, which, in Dmitriev's

---

23   Pushkin also used the names of Bulanin and Valuev for the main character of his future novel. The names reflect different stages of the novel's development and different concepts of the protagonist, which are largely irrelevant for my argument. For a fairly complicated history of Pushkin's work on *The Captain's Daughter*, the evolution of the protagonists, and their prototypes, see Iu. G. Oksman, "Pushkin v rabote nad romanom 'Kapitanskaia dochka,'" in A. S. Pushkin, *Kapitanskaia dochka* (Moscow: Nauka, 1964), 149–208; N. N. Petrunina, "U istokov 'Kapitanskoi dochki,'" in *Nad stranitsami Pushkina*, ed. N. N. Petrunina and G. M. Fridlender (Leningrad: Nauka, 1974), 73–123; Paul Debreczeny, *The Other Pushkin: A Study of Alexander Pushkin's Prose Fiction* (Stanford, CA: Stanford Univ. Press, 1983), 239–43, 250, and 253–55. Petrunina revises the date of Pushkin's first conceiving the novel, moving it from the previously accepted early 1833 to "not later than August 1832, perhaps even earlier" (74).

opinion as recorded by Pushkin, also characterized Derzhavin. Crossing the Volga River, Bulanin sees a raft carrying a gallows with three bodies and experiences an inexplicable urge to examine their faces more closely: "A morbid curiosity seized me. I wanted to look into the hanged men's faces" (8:375–76; 442). Grinev, too, experiences a similar emotion the night after the executions in Belogorskaya: having been forced to listen to the rebels singing a folk song about gallows, he is stricken with "poetic awe" (*piiticheskii uzhas*; 8:331; 317). Finally, while Grinev's ability to write poetry makes him Derzhavin's colleague, an apprenticeship to Trediakovsky unites him, Shvabrin, and Derzhavin.

Such "literary" features—a "poetic" curiosity about executions, an ability to experience "poetic awe," a propensity to write love couplets, and an apprenticeship to Trediakovsky—could be transmitted onto the novel's protagonist only by Derzhavin: no one else among Pushkin's prototypes was involved with literature. Shvabrin's connection to Trediakovsky can thus be explained: when the initial character in *The Captain's Daughter*, who was partially modeled on Derzhavin, split in two in the novel's final version, his characteristics, including his apprenticeship to Trediakovsky, also split. Consequently, both antagonists became Trediakovsky's disciples. Significantly, Grinev is oblivious to his kinship with the wretched versifier, while Shvabrin, like Derzhavin, is fully aware both of the connection and of its negative implications.

Shvabrin's and Grinev's connections to Trediakovsky, however, can lead us further in exploring Pushkin's poetic motivations. Pushkin's interest in Dmitriev's characterizations of Derzhavin's behavior as "poetic," his attention in the *History of Pugachev* to Derzhavin's literary activities, and his portrayals, however marginal, of Grinev and Shvabrin as poets suggest that the events of the Pugachev uprising attracted him as an opportunity to explore not only the figure of a renegade nobleman but also that of a poet taking part in social unrest. The fact that during his work on the *History of Pugachev* Pushkin tried to obtain Derzhavin's account of the events and also turned for information to two other poets who had witnessed the Pugachev rebellion, Ivan Krylov and Dmitriev, supports my suggestion.

The information supplied by Krylov and recorded by Pushkin under the title "Testimony by Krylov (a poet)" gives yet another example of a (future) poet confronted and fascinated by violence during the Pugachev uprising. The fabulist tells about an unusually cruel game popular among his young friends:

> After the rebellion, Iv[an] Krylov returned to Iaik settlement, where the game of *pugachevshchina* emerged. The children would divide into two groups: the town and the rebels, and there were significant fights [among them]. Krylov, as a captain's son, was the leader of one side. They thought up a rule: while exchanging captives, they would flog the remaining ones, which produced such a frenzy in the kids, among whom were also some grown-ups, that the game had to be banned. Someone named Anchapov (who is still alive) nearly fell victim to it. Mertvago, having caught him in one of the raids, hung him on a tree by a belt. A soldier passing by took him down.[24]

The motifs of flogging and hanging connect Krylov's account with Baranov's story about Derzhavin's confronting the Malykovka rebels, with the appropriate passages of *The Captain's Daughter*, and with "the omitted chapter."

Dmitriev too was not merely an informant for Pushkin; he actually rivals Derzhavin as a prototype for Grinev. In addition to the fascination with executions that Grinev (as well as his predecessor Bulanin) shares with Dmitriev, Pushkin incorporates other features of Dmitriev's life into his character's biography: like Dmitriev, Grinev owns land in Simbirsk *guberniya*, witnesses the execution of Pugachev, and writes about it in his memoir. Composing love poetry also links Grinev more to Dmitriev than to Derzhavin. The Karamzinians, as a group, tried to ignore their indebtedness to Trediakovsky, even though the latter had, in the 1730s, first developed many of their cherished ideas, including giving the theme of love a prominent place among literary subjects. Pushkin was aware of the Karamzinians' vulnerability in this respect already

---

24   Pushkin, "Pokazaniia Krylova (poeta)," in his *Polnoe sobranie sochinenii v 16-ti tomakh*, 9:492.

in 1825, when, in his essay "On Mr. Lemontey's Preface to the Translation of I. A. Krylov's Fables" ("O predislovii g-na Lemonte k perevodu basen Krylova"), he portrayed Trediakovsky as an awkward predecessor of the Karamzinians and the first proponent of literature for the "fair sex." In this context, Pushkin's portrayal of Trediakovsky as an unsuccessful writer of love poetry, rather than the pedantic author of *Tilemakhida*, as well as Grinev's ignorance of his kinship with Trediakovsky, underscores the similarity between Grinev and Dmitriev.[25]

The theme of "the poet and social unrest" was central for Pushkin throughout his life. For evidence of this one needs only recall his profound interest in the fate of André de Chénier or his fascination with the life and death of Lord Byron. The life of Derzhavin—a budding poet actively participating in the stormy events of 1773–75, a person for whom, as Pushkin suspected, "poetic" impulses could have been more important than moral imperatives—offered a perfect case study. However, even if Pushkin did consider such an exploration in *The Captain's Daughter*, he never carried it out, and in my opinion he sidestepped this opportunity for personal reasons.

The question of what constitutes a poet's possible role and mode of behavior during times of social upheaval certainly had a personal dimension for Pushkin. He often contemplated his own possible participation in such events. While in Kishinev, he thought about joining the Greek insurgents: he began to study Turkish and asked his friends to stop attempting to help him return to St. Petersburg. In May or June of 1824, on the rough draft of the poem about Napoleon, Pushkin drew two portraits of himself dressed as a French revolutionary.[26] In January of 1826, upon receiving news of the Decembrist uprising, he drew a portrait of himself with the

---

[25]   On the presence of Derzhavin, Krylov, and Dmitriev in the *History of Pugachev*, see Michael Finke, "Figures for History in *Kapitanskaia Dochka* and Poets as Historical Figures in *Istoriia Pugacheva*," *Pushkin Journal* 1, no. 2 (1993): 179–80.

[26]   Abram Efros, *Avtoportrety Pushkina* (n.p.: Goslitmuzei, 1945), 97; for the portraits, see 51 and 53.

distinct features of Robespierre.[27] The personal aspect was especially relevant in respect to the Decembrist uprising. The Pushkin/Robespierre portrait (drawn next to portraits of Mirabeau, Voltaire, Pavel Pestel, and Kondraty Ryleev), several other self-portraits of the same time (drawn next to portraits of Ivan Pushchin, Wilhelm Küchelbecker, Ryleev, and other Decembrists), and especially the famous line written next to the November 1826 drawing of the five hanged Decembrists, "And I also could, like a jester..." (*I ia by mog kak shut...*), bear testimony to that. Anna Akhmatova, in her essay "Pushkin and the Neva Seashore," argues that Pushkin sought to uncover the place of the five executed Decembrists' secret burial. She concludes her essay with a comment on the deeply personal impulse behind his efforts: "And the anonymous grave at the Neva seashore must have seemed to him almost his own grave."[28]

The question of a poet's reaction to social unrest acquired new importance in the fall of 1830, when Pushkin, confined to Boldino, found himself in the midst of a cholera epidemic and facing the threat of peasant riots. When actual riots broke out in the summer of 1831, cholera, violence, and the question of personal courage took a prominent place in Pushkin's correspondence, equal in importance to his discussions of the Polish rebellion. Around this time, Pushkin wrote a fragment about his personal encounter with cholera. Describing his 1830 trip to Boldino, he analyzed the emotions aroused in him by the threat of death: "To return seemed cowardly to me; I proceeded; perhaps you have had occasion to go to a duel in like manner: with vexation and great unwillingness."[29] Nonetheless, the poet preserved his composure and busied himself with reading Coleridge and writing. In fact, this time turned out to be the famous "Boldino autumn," the most prolific of Pushkin's autumn seclusions. Returning to Moscow in late November, Pushkin encountered barriers manned by local peasants to enforce the quarantine. Several years later, describing the rebels' pickets

---

[27]   Ibid., 102; for the portrait, see 29.

[28]   Anna Akhmatova, "Pushkin i Nevskoe vzmor'e," *Prometei* 10 (1975): 225.

[29]   Pushkin, *Polnoe sobranie sochinenii v 16-ti tomakh*, 12:309.

in chapter 9 of *The Captain's Daughter* as well as in the "omitted chapter," Pushkin found his 1831 notes handy.[30]

Descriptions of pickets and barriers are by no means the only personal element in the narrative of *The Captain's Daughter*. Pushkin regularly lends Grinev the memoirist his authorial voice, introducing passages from his own works into his character's memoir. Oksman points out that on two occasions in the novel Pushkin paraphrases passages from his *History of Pugachev*. He also moves a fragment from a rough draft of the essay "Journey from Moscow to Petersburg" into chapter 6 of the novel.[31] Furthermore, the Pushkin scholar Inna Almi suggests that Grinev's ability to experience "poetic awe" is also an autobiographical feature. She argues that "at a certain stage Pushkin simply replaces Grinev as the narrator with himself."[32]

Grinev's authorship of the memoir is, of course, a device; and one can argue that since the voice behind every character in *The Captain's Daughter*, including Grinev's, is ultimately Pushkin's, it is only natural for him to disregard occasionally the difference between himself and his protagonist. However, there are indications that Pushkin did more than just endow Grinev with his narrative skill— that he actually "tried on" the roles of both Grinev and Shvabrin, infusing them with aspects of his own personality.

Grinev, a poet (however minor) amidst social turmoil, is by far Pushkin's favorite alter ego. For example, in one of his usual ways of inserting personal notes into his fiction, Pushkin introduces his own ancestor into the action, making him Grinev's ancestor as well. As Oksman points out in his commentary to the novel, Pushkin gave Grinev's father the biography of his own grandfather, Lev Alexandrovich Pushkin, who, like Andrey Grinev, did not want to

---

30   Iu. G. Oksman, "Pushkin v rabote nad romanom 'Kapitanskaia dochka,'" in
      A. S. Pushkin, *Kapitanskaia dochka* (Moscow: Nauka, 1964), 152.

31   Ibid., 164 and 183–84.

32   Inna Almi, "'Evgenii Onegin' i 'Kapitanskaia dochka.' Edinstvo i poliarnost'
      khudozhestvennykh system," in *Boldinskie chteniia* (Gorky: Volgo-Viatskoe
      knizhnoe izdatel'stvo, 1987), 89. Almi credits Marina Tsvetaeva with pointing
      this out in "Pushkin i Pugachev," in her *Proza* (Moscow: Sovremennik,
      1989), 549–50.

serve the usurper and left military service after Catherine's coup d'état.[33] However, there is possibly an even more personal feature in Grinev's story.

Almi suggests that Pushkin modeled Grinev's conversation with Pugachev in chapter 8 after the circumstances of his own meeting with Nicholas I in 1826. Using the reconstructions of Pushkin's conversation with Nicholas made by N. Ya. Eidel'man and L. A. Sheiman, Almi exposes similarities in the basic plots of the two exchanges: a dangerous question by a monarch or an alleged monarch is answered daringly but sincerely; the monarch then displays magnanimity and rewards the candidness. Almi, however, points to a crucial difference between the conversations: Grinev declines Pugachev's invitation to pledge loyalty to him, whereas Pushkin, albeit with hesitation, accepts Nicholas's invitation. In replaying the situation in his novel, Pushkin ensures that his alter ego retains his independence.[34]

Finally, Pushkin shared a fascination for gallows and hangings with Grinev and with his predecessor, Bulanin. Following the execution of the five Decembrists on July 13, 1826, the theme of hangings crops up time and again in Pushkin's drawings, poetry, and letters. Beginning with the November 1826 drawings of gallows with five bodies and the line "And I also could, like a jester," hangings in one form or another recur throughout his work in the late 1820s. In *Eugene Onegin*, chapter 6, stanza 38 — represented only by its number in the final version — the poet mentions, among other possible fates

---

[33] For a detailed analysis of Pushkin's use of historical sources, see Ospovat, "Istoricheskii material i istoricheskie alliuzii v *Kapitanskoi dochke*," 40–55; for Pushkin's misreading of historical sources, see Mark Altshuller, *Mezhdu dvukh tsarei* (St. Petersburg: Akademicheskii proekt, 2003), 186–89, 196–98.

[34] Inna Almi, "Ob avtobiograficheskom podtekste dvukh epizodov v pro-izvedeniiakh A. S. Pushkina," in *Pushkinskie chteniia: Sbornik statei*, ed. S. G. Isakov (Tallinn: Eesti Raamat, 1990), 64–69. For a discussion of Pushkin's various reports on his meeting with Nicholas, see I. V. Nemirovskii, "Dva 'voobrazhaemykh' razgovora Pushkina," in his *Tvorchestvo Pushkina i pro-blema publichnogo povedeniia poeta* (St. Petersburg: Giperion, 2003), 203–15. Nemirovsky suggests that Pushkin inserted the theme of Fate in his stories about his meeting with the tsar: a theme that is central for *The Captain's Daughter* in general and for Grinev's relations with Pugachev in particular.

for Lensky, death by hanging: "[He could] . . . have been hanged like Ryleev." He makes a joke about rope and hints at the execution of the Decembrists in his March 2, 1827, letter to Anton Delvig. He includes a similar joke in his June 10, 1827, letter to P. A. Osipova. Numerous sketches of gallows and the hanged (including the five Decembrists) appear in the rough drafts to *Poltava*.[35] Pushkin can neither forget about five executed Decembrists nor stop thinking that execution could have also been his fate. Grinev, who narrowly escapes death by hanging and who is consumed by "poetic awe" and "pathological" curiosity about gallows, mirrors this obsession.[36]

Pushkin's kinship with Shvabrin might seem less likely, but it is nonetheless unmistakable: Pushkin lends the renegade his own appearance. Describing his first meeting with Shvabrin, Grinev writes: "The door opened and a young officer, not very tall, with a swarthy face that was strikingly unattractive but exceptionally lively, came into the room" (8:296; 283). A dark complexion, an animated or lively expression, and a small or very small stature are mentioned in virtually all descriptions of Pushkin left by his contemporaries. In his self-portraits (both in sketches and verbal portrayals), Pushkin frequently emphasized his African features and ugliness.[37]

---

[35]   One of these sketches is so expressive that a student of Pushkin's drawings suggests that it should be interpreted as a graphic commentary to humorous, but characteristic, autobiographical remarks in Pushkin's post-1826 poetry, such as "Will you sigh for me / If I am hanged?" ("To Ushakova," 1827) and "If God spares us, / If I am not hanged, / I will be at your feet" ("To Poltoratskaya," the younger sister of Anna Kern, 1829). See Abram Efros, *Risunki poeta* (Moscow: Academia, 1933), 374–75.

[36]   For a summary of the gallows theme and the analysis of Pushkin's preoccupation with it, see Tatiana Tsiavlovskaia, "Otkliki na sud'by dekabristov v tvorchestve Pushkina," in *Literaturnoe nasledie dekabristov* (Leningrad: Nauka, 1975), 202–14. The change of a narrative mode from comic to tragic in the description of the executions in Belogorskaya, discussed by Paul Debreczeny, also reflects Pushkin's preoccupation with the gallows theme; see Debreczeny, "The Execution of Captain Mironov: A Crossing of the Tragic and Comic Modes," *Alexander Puškin: Symposium II*, ed. Andrej Kodjak, Krystyna Pomorska, and Kiril Taranovsky (Columbus, OH: Slavica, 1980), 67–78; see also Debreczeny, *The Other Pushkin*, 258, 266–73.

[37]   See "Avtoportrety," in Tatiana Tsiavlovskaia, *Risunki Pushkina* (Moscow:

Shvabrin is not the only character to whom Pushkin attributes his own looks. Almi points out that Grigory Otrep'ev, as described in his arrest warrant in *Boris Godunov*, resembles Pushkin himself. She argues that Pushkin emphasizes his own features in the description of Otrep'ev's appearance, borrowed from Karamzin's *History*: small stature, broad chest, and reddish hair. This self-portrait differs from the one in *The Captain's Daughter*: it reflected Pushkin's interest at the time in his Russian roots and thus required, as Almi puts it, "a common [*prostonarodnyi*] Russian masquerade" and an emphasis on the Slavic features of his appearance.[38] Remarkable, however, is not the discrepancy in the two portraits, but the consistency of the device. In both cases Pushkin attributes his appearance to a character who carries out what Pushkin did not actually do but considered doing. Grigory flees Russia, realizing Pushkin's dream at the time of his exile in Mikhailovskoe. Shvabrin turns against the monarch, offering one possible response to a question that had great importance and personal significance for Pushkin: the extent of a nobleman's loyalty to the throne.

Over the years, Pushkin contemplated different answers to this question, but he never doubted a nobleman's right to preserve his independence and disagree with a monarch.[39] He cherished the memory of his ancestors who, he believed, dissented and were imprisoned or executed for that. In *Boris Godunov*, he exaggerates the rebelliousness of the Pushkins and portrays them as greater supporters of the imposter than they were in reality.[40] In "My

---

Iskusstvo, 1980), especially 340–44. Characteristically, in contrast to Walter Scott's Rashleigh, whom Shvabrin resembles with his combination of ugliness and expressiveness, his appearance is not repulsive. For a comparison of Rashleigh and Shvabrin, see Mark Altshuller, "*Rob Roi* Valtera Skotta i *Kapitanskaia dochka* A. Pushkina," *Russian Language Journal* 44 (1990): 96–98.

38 Almi, "Ob avtobiograficheskom podtekste," 61–63.

39 For an analysis of Pushkin's views of the problem, see Sam Driver, *Puškin: Literary and Social Ideas* (New York: Columbia Univ. Press, 1989), esp. chap. 3.

40 A. M. Gurevich, "Istoriia i sovremennost' v 'Borise Godunove,'" *Izvestiia AN SSSR: Seriia literatury i iazyka* (1984), 3:204–14.

Genealogy," he fondly remembers his grandfather, Lev Pushkin, who, as he believed, refused to serve Catherine the Great.[41] The very fact that the initial protagonist in *The Captain's Daughter* gave birth not only to the vicious Shvabrin but also to the virtuous Grinev testifies that Pushkin's interest in the figure of a renegade nobleman was not fed by the desire to condemn a state criminal, but rather by the urge to explore a personality with whose social and psychological make-up he could identify and in whose shoes he could imagine himself.

Shvabrin's reference to Trediakovsky as his own and Grinev's teacher thus acquires additional meaning as the signal for a possible autobiographical subtext in the portrayals of the novel's main characters. This is the more likely since in the 1830s Pushkin not only came to appreciate Trediakovsky's services to Russian literature, but also felt a certain kinship with the unfortunate poet, a feeling sharpened by Pushkin's own unpopularity with the reading public and his humiliations at court.[42] Significantly, using Trediakovsky's name as a polemical tool, Shvabrin, like Pushkin himself, has no difficulty in accepting his own kinship with the unpopular poet.

I believe that Pushkin's decision not to eliminate from the final text of *The Captain's Daughter* the seemingly unnecessary reference to Trediakovsky as Shvabrin's teacher constitutes an integral part of his narrative strategy in the novel: it is a way to introduce a personal element in his portrayals of the two antagonists without laying the device bare. Pushkin deliberately created ways for an attentive reader to discover information that he preferred to leave out. This information might seem to Pushkin both too personal and too dangerous to develop explicitly; even more importantly,

---

[41]   Significantly, in Pushkin's portrayal, the same Lev Alexandrovich also resembles Shvabrin in his cruel attitude to his first wife: as Pushkin reports, his grandfather locked his wife up in a homemade jail, where she died of extreme deprivation ("on the straw," *na solome*)—a fate that certainly would have been Masha Mironova's had not Grinev and Pugachev rescued her. See Pushkin, "Nachalo avtobiografii," in his *Polnoe sobranie sochinenii v 16-ti tomakh*, 12:311.

[42]   On Pushkin's feelings of affinity with Trediakovsky, see Reyfman, *Vasilii Trediakovsky*, 215–16, 221–22.

the very ambivalence he felt toward the ideas and situations that he was contemplating while working on the novel (creativity and death, creativity and cruelty, a nobleman's duty to the monarch and his right for independence) could also contribute to his decision to make them accessible only to the sagacious reader. Trediakovsky's name—rich in cultural connotations, inherently ambivalent, both base and heroic, ridiculous and tragic—was a suitable key to such a sly literary strategy.

6. *Kammerjunker in "Notes of a Madman":*
Gogol's View of Pushkin

The debate about the nature of Pushkin's and Gogol's relationship has been long and thorough, but scholarly agreement on the subject has still not been reached. The two main trends are aptly described by G. A. Grishin, in the synopsis of his 2006 dissertation, "Pushkin and Gogol: A Dialogue of Scholarly Versions in Literary Criticism of the Nineteenth to Twenty-First Centuries":

> In the entire spectrum of scholarly interpretations of Pushkin's and Gogol's relations, two main trends can be observed. The first one is fairly canonical and is the basis of the common textbook image of the two writers' relations imprinted in mass consciousness. [This image] presents a relationship of teacher and disciple, is based on the notions of friendship and mutual understanding, and presumes the idea of literary continuity. The second trend is not as well entrenched in the public consciousness. Its definitive property is an effort to see the patterns of Pushkin's and Gogol's biographies that define their individual characteristics and are most evident in their dealings with each other. The vector of scholarly interest in this case is directed toward finding disagreements in the relations between two classics of Russian literature.[1]

---

[1]   G. A. Grishin, "Pushkin i Gogol: Dialog issledovatel'skikh versii v lite-raturnoi nauke XIX-XXI vekov," avtoreferat dissertatsii na soiskanie stepeni kandidata filologicheskikh nauk (Saratov: Saratovskii universitet im. G. N. Chernyshevskogo, 2006), 3.

Given the continuing dominance of the first trend, it seems productive, at least for the time being, to test it by drawing scholarly attention to the disagreements mentioned by Grishin. This is particularly important because, as Grishin wisely points out in his overview of the scholarly picture of the writers' interactions, we should keep in mind Gogol's penchant for mystification as well as the fact that Gogol's relationship with Pushkin was "one of the focal points of his life-creating activities and an important element in creating his public image."[2]

It is also of crucial importance to remember that almost everything we know about the two writers' relations comes from Gogol and, furthermore, that the majority of Gogol's statements on this subject were made after Pushkin's death. It is therefore somewhat naïve to take the picture painted by Gogol at face value. I would not go as far as Yuri Druzhnikov in his informative and witty article "Hitting It Off with Pushkin," and deny any meaningful relationship between the two writers. This would present Gogol as a veritable swindler, who coldly and calculatedly used first Pushkin himself and then, after the poet's death, his name to advance his own career as a writer, while Pushkin barely acknowledged his existence.[3] Without a doubt, there was quite a bit of the manipulator in Gogol, as numerous memoirists testify and many scholars demonstrate, and he used this talent to portray his relations with Pushkin. It is also clear that for Pushkin Gogol meant far less than Gogol would have liked.[4] But it is still reasonable to acknowledge that not everything in Gogol's behavior with Pushkin was calculation, and that even though his artistic principles were very different, he did value Pushkin as a writer. Likewise, Pushkin

---

[2]   Ibid.

[3]   Yuri Druzhnikov, "Hitting It Off with Pushkin," in his *Contemporary Russian Myths: A Skeptical View of the Literary Past*, Studies in Slavic Languages and Literature (Lewiston, NY: Edwin Mellen Press, 1999), 14:31–52.

[4]   For an excellent and fair deconstruction of Gogol's manipulation of the public image of his relations with Pushkin in 1831–34, see A. S. Dolinin, "Pushkin i Gogol (K voprosu ob ikh lichnykh otnosheniakh)," in his *Dostoevskii i drugie* (Leningrad: Khudozhestvennaia literatura, 1989), 55–72.

too was not just a high-society snob entirely uninterested in what the young man from the provinces was publishing. His attention to Gogol's literary production, transitory as it apparently was, and his occasional helpful advice are both documented.[5]

It seems to me that the assessment of Gogol's and Pushkin's relations by Pavel Nashchokin, one of Pushkin's closest friends, is pretty much on the mark. In his conversations with Petr Bartenev in the early 1850s, he told his interviewer that even though Pushkin "received Gogol at his home, extended his protection to him, took care to bring him to the attention of readers [*zabotilsia o vnimanii k nemu publiki*], personally promoted the staging [*khlopotal o postanovke na stsenu*] of The Inspector General, in a word, *helped him to launch his career* [*vyvodil v liudi*, emphasis in the original]," nonetheless "Gogol was never close to Pushkin [*nikogda ne byl blizkim chelovekom k Pushkinu*]."[6] The information provided by Nashchokin is considered unreliable by some.[7] Bartenev himself expressed doubts about the veracity of Nashchokin's statement on the absence of a close friendship between Gogol and Pushkin. Bartenev blamed what he considered to be an unfair judgment on Nashchokin's ill disposition toward Gogol: "Nashchokin, while respecting Gogol's talent, doesn't respect him as a person." Curiously, he also rejects Nashchokin's assertion on the grounds that it would make Gogol a liar: "Otherwise what kind of a liar would Gogol have been before

---

5   See, for example, Pushkin's positive reviews of Gogol's *Vechera na khutore bliz Dikan'ki* in "Pis'mo k izdateliu 'Literaturnykh pribavlenii' k *Russkomu invalidu*," in Pushkin's *Polnoe sobranie sochinenii v 16-ti tomakh* (Moscow: Izdatel'stvo Akademii Nauk SSSR, 1937-59), 11:216; and "Vechera na khutore bliz Dikan'ki," ibid., 12:27. For the only documented advice Pushkin offered to Gogol, see Pushkin's letter to Gogol about "Nevskii prospekt," written in the fall of 1834, ibid., 15:198. As is well known, Pushkin initially invited Gogol to collaborate on The Contemporary—with rather disastrous results (see Druzhnikov, "Hitting It Off with Pushkin," 46–48).

6   P. V. Nashchokin and V. A. Nashchokina, "Rasskazy o Pushkine, zapisannye P. I. Bartenevym," in *A. S. Pushkin v vospominaniiakh sovremennikov v dvukh tomakh* (Moscow: Khudozhestvennaia literatura, 1985), 2:233.

7   See, for example, N. N. Petrunina and G. M. Fridlender, "Pushkin i Gogol' v 1831–1836 godakh," in *Pushkin: Issledovaniia i materialy*, Institut russkoi literatury (Pushkinskii dom) (Leningrad: Nauka, 1969), 6:536n14.

the public!"[8] What Bartenev has in mind here, first of all, are Gogol's numerous assertions about his extremely close friendly relations with Pushkin, the doubtful veracity of which I have discussed earlier in this chapter. However, by extension, Bartenev's remark also casts a shadow of doubt on Gogol's repeatedly expressed admiration for his older colleague's talent as well as on his acknowledgements of Pushkin's primacy among Russian poets and of the superiority of Pushkin's talent over his own. Was Gogol's praise of Pushkin always sincere, and if not, how can we know? Did Gogol remain unwounded by Pushkin's offering patronage but not friendship? How did Gogol signal his possible disagreements with Pushkin and his quite-probable hurts?

In her article "Equivocal Praise and National-Imperial Conundrums: Gogol's 'A Few Words about Pushkin,'" Edyta Bojanowska attempts to answer some of these questions, detecting the ways Gogol delivers his disagreements with Pushkin in the form of praise. She analyzes Gogol's 1832 article, "A Few Words about Pushkin" ("Neskol'ko slov o Pushkine"), included in his 1835 collection *Arabesques* (*Arabeski*). She convincingly demonstrates that Gogol's praise of Pushkin as the first and only Russian national poet can hardly be accepted at face value.[9] Bojanowska's careful reading of Gogol's article reveals that

> in the course of discussing Pushkin's strategies of encoding nationality in literature, Gogol develops his own conception of national literary expression, by which he aims to affix the stamp of nationality to his own writings, rather than Pushkin's.[10]

Bojanowska's analysis makes it clear that Gogol's attitude to Pushkin was much more complex and less positive than Gogol tried to claim. At the same time, she demonstrates that his criticism and dis-

---

[8]   Nashchokin and Nashchokina, "Rasskazy o Pushkine," 233.

[9]   Edyta Bojanowska, "Equivocal Praise and National-Imperial Conundrums: Gogol's 'A Few Words about Pushkin,'" *Canadian Slavonic Papers / Revue canadienne des slavistes* 51, nos. 2–3 (June-September 2009): 175–201.

[10]   Ibid., 178.

agreements were delivered in such a form that to this day, those who want to see them as praise can easily do so.[11]

I propose that the ambiguity of Gogol's attitude toward Pushkin also manifests itself in his story "Notes of a Madman" ("Zapiski sumasshedshego"), included in *Arabesques*, under the title "Scraps from the Notes of a Madman" ("Klochki iz zapisok sumasshedshego"). As we remember, in "Notes of a Madman," Gogol mentions Pushkin directly. Poprishchin copies a poem by Nikolay Nikolev and comments: "Pushkin's work, no doubt [*Dolzhno byt', Pushkina sochinenie*]."[12] Poprishchin's comment is usually interpreted as a sign of his ignorance and bad literary taste, but it is possible to see in it Gogol's mockery—very mild, but still mockery—of Pushkin's poetry and especially of his reputation as a poet. In this connection, it is essential that in his article "A Few Words about Pushkin," Gogol discusses the widespread problem of literary works falsely attributed to Pushkin. While talking about the rapid spread and breadth of Pushkin's fame, he notes that Pushkin's name by itself guarantees a work's success and is used for this purpose by "idle scribblers [*dosuzhimi marateliami*]." Gogol affixes a footnote to this allegation, in which he says the following:

> A multitude of the most ludicrous poems were disseminated under Pushkin's name. This is the usual fate of a talented man who enjoys great renown. At first it seems funny, but then it becomes aggravating, when one ceases to be young [*vykhodish' iz molodosti*] and sees that this nonsense doesn't stop. In this way they began to attribute to Pushkin "Medicine for Cholera," "The First Night," and the like.[13]

---

11   For the most recent example, see V. D. Denisov, "Kommentarii," in Nikolai Gogol', *Arabeski*, Seriia Literaturnye pamiatniki (St. Petersburg: Nauka, 2009), 411–14.

12   Nikolai Gogol', "Zapiski sumasshedshego," in his *Peterburgskie povesti*, ed. O. G. Dilaktorskaia, Seriia Literaturnye pamiatniki (St. Petersburg: Nauka, 1995), 113. In the 1835 edition of *Arabeski*, the poem quoted was different.

13   Gogol', "Neskol'ko slov o Pushkine," in his *Arabeski*, 84. In his comments to Gogol's article (ibid., 412–13), Denisov asserts that the anonymous poem "First Night" (*Pervaia noch'*) was circulated in the early 1830s as a mockery of Pushkin's family life. He cites A. V. Dubrovsky, senior fellow

A question arises: who is the butt of Gogol's joke here? The ignorant readers, the sly usurpers of Pushkin's name—or Pushkin himself, whose reputation somehow allowed the most absurd works, whether literary or not, to be attributed to him? One may suggest that the vexation shown here by Gogol is not quite sincere: as with Poprishchin's comment, Gogol's footnote leaves in doubt both the quality of Pushkin's real works and the actual worth of his literary fame.

My contention is that a somewhat critical (or, at least, ironic) attitude toward Pushkin manifests itself in "Notes of a Madman," not only in Poprishchin's mistaken remark about the authorship of Nikolev's poem but also in Gogol's play with the relative worth of the rank of titular councilor and the title of kammerjunker. I would like to argue that the joke is, at least partly, aimed at Pushkin, mocking his rank and, especially, his well-known vexation over receiving the title of kammerjunker.

As we know, in his service career Pushkin didn't rise beyond the rank of titular councilor, which he was granted on December 6, 1831, soon after he was reinstated at the College of Foreign Affairs in the rank of collegiate secretary, the very same rank he had received upon graduation from the Lyceum and kept throughout his service and retirement. On December 31, 1833, the court title of kammerjunker was bestowed on the poet, to be used alongside the rank of titular councilor.[14] We know from his diary and letters that he found the title insulting. Many contemporaries testified that Pushkin also expressed his indignation publicly, pulling no punches. For example, his brother, Lev Pushkin, told Yakov Polonsky the following about Pushkin's reaction to the news of his receiving the title:

---

in the Manuscript Division of the Institute of Russian Literature (Pushkin House), as his source. Dubrovsky's sources are not provided. Denisov also suggests that Pushkin himself asked Gogol to include this footnote in order to protect his good name—an assertion for the veracity of which Denisov alone stands surety.

[14]   Beginning in 1809, kammerjunker, originally a court title of the ninth class (equal to titular councilor), became an honorary title (*zvanie*); and its bearers were obliged to have a position in the military or civil service.

My brother . . . first learned about his kammerjunker's title at a ball in the house of Count Alexey Fyodorovich Orlov. It infuriated [*vzbesilo*] him to such a degree that friends had to take him to the Count's study and there calm him down in every possible way. I cannot comfortably repeat here everything that the enraged poet, foaming at the mouth, said about his appointment.[15]

Nashchokin told Bartenev a very similar story:

His friends, Viel'egorsky and Zhukovsky, had to throw cold water on the newly-minted kammerjunker, so agitated he was by this appointment! If not for them, he, beside himself, flaring up, his face burning, would have gone to the palace and said rude things to the tsar himself.[16]

Ultimately, Pushkin moderated his public expressions of displeasure and accepted the fact that, strictly speaking, his court title corresponded to his service rank.[17] Pushkin's discontent could have been justified only by the fact that kammerjunker titles were usually bestowed on younger men, most often between the ages of sixteen and thirty-nine, with the majority receiving them between the ages of twenty and twenty-five.[18]

"Notes of a Madman" was written in the late summer—early autumn of 1834, that is, about six to eight months after Pushkin received his supposedly insulting title. The event, therefore, had to be fresh in Gogol's memory. An additional argument in support of my contention that "Notes of a Madman" relates to Pushkin is provided by Gogol's manuscript of the story, as described by N. S. Tikhonravov: "In Gogol's notebook ... 'Notes of a Madman' is

---

[15]   "Rasskazy L. S. Pushkina v zapisi Ia. P. Polonskogo," in *A. S. Pushkin v vospominaniiakh sovremennikov*, 1:57.

[16]   Nashchokin and Nashchokina, "Rasskazy o Pushkine," in *A. S. Pushkin v vospominaniiakh sovremennikov*, 2:231.

[17]   For an illuminating analysis of Pushkin's place in the group of his fellow kammerjunkers, see S. A. Reiser, "Tri stroki dnevnika Pushkina," *Vremennik Pushkinskoi komissii, 1981* (Leningrad: Nauka, 1985), 146–52.

[18]   Ibid., 150.

on pages 208 through 220. There is no title. Instead of that, there is written 'O P.,' that is 'o Pushkine' [about Pushkin]."[19] Tikhonravov surmises that this is an indication that Gogol wrote his article "A Few Words about Pushkin" earlier than "Notes of a Madman"—which is, of course, true, but doesn't mean that Gogol didn't use "O P." as a temporary substitute title to indicate the story's theme. My supposition is made more likely by the fact that "A Few Words about Pushkin" is found earlier in the same notebook, beginning on page 136, where the article is also entitled "O P."[20] It is quite logical to my mind that the two works about Pushkin included in *Arabesques* have the same temporary title, indicating their similar subject matter.[21]

I believe that the Pushkin connection explains Gogol's choice of Poprishchin's rank (titular councilor) and his rival Teplov's title (kammerjunker). As we remember, the story culminates in a conflict over Sophie's hand between Poprishchin and Teplov—a conflict entirely imagined by the former. In this imaginary conflict, Poprishchin loses, and the loss plunges him irreversibly into madness. Poprishchin explains his defeat by the insurmountable vertical rift in status between a titular councilor and a kammerjunker. In his opinion, the status of a kammerjunker is equal to that of a general. As we remember, having found out about Sophie's engagement, he complains:

> Always either a kammerjunker, or a general. Everything that is best in this world, everything falls either to kammerjunkers, or to generals. The moment you find a poor little treasure [*bednoe bogatstvo*] for yourself, you think you can reach toward it [*dumaesh' dostat' ego rukoiu*]—but a kammerjunker or a general filches it from you [*sryvaet u tebia*].[22]

---

19   For Tikhonravov's commentary, see Gogol', *Sochineniia*, ed. Nikolai Tikhonravov, 10th ed. (Moscow: Naslednyki br. Salaevykh, 1889), 5:610.

20   Gogol', *Polnoe sobranie sochinenii v 14-ti tomakh* (Moscow: Izdatel'stvo Akademii Nauk SSSR, 1938), 3:697.

21   Neither Tikhonravov nor V. L. Komarovich, the editor of vol. 3 of Gogol's *Polnoe sobranie sochinenii*, comes to such a conclusion; both relate the "O P." title to "A Few Words about Pushkin" only.

22   Gogol', "Zapiski sumasshedshego," 119.

Poprishchin is, of course, mistaken: according to Reiser's analysis, Teplov's rank could not have differed very much from that of Poprishchin's (ninth class), whereas generals belong to the first four classes. Curiously, Poprishchin's mistake is a reversal of Pushkin's assessment of the title of kammerjunker: whereas Titular Councilor Poprishchin considers the kammerjunker's title much higher than his own, Titular Councilor Pushkin considers it much lower. Their behavior, nonetheless, is similar: as we remember, Pushkin's contemporaries described his reaction to receiving the kammerjunker's title as the actions of a person who had lost his mind: "beside himself, flaring up, his face burning," "foaming at the mouth." According to Nashchokin, the treatment Poprishchin gets in the insane asylum—cold water poured on his head—was applied to Pushkin by his friends to calm down the poet, who had lost his temper. It is not impossible that Gogol heard these stories about Pushkin's rage and his friends' actions prior to his work on "Notes of a Madman."

I believe that Poprishchin's insistent claims that only noblemen can write well and therefore he, as a true nobleman, is an exceptionally good writer, whereas non-nobles, especially tradesmen (or bourgeois, *meshchane*), can never be good writers also signal Pushkin's implicit presence in the story. These claims are likely to refer to Pushkin's poem "My Genealogy" (1830), especially to the repeated phrase "I am a tradesman/bourgeois," *Ia meshchanin*. They may also allude to debates about the so-called literary aristocracy in general, which are reflected in "My Genealogy."[23]

As William Mills Todd III points out in his *Fiction and Society in the Age of Pushkin*, Gogol held an ambivalent position in this debate: while he attempted to adopt the modes of behavior accepted

---

23   For a succinct and penetrating analysis of "My Genealogy" in the context of the debate about "literary aristocracy," see David M. Bethea, *Realizing Metaphors: Alexander Pushkin and the Life of the Poet* (Madison: Univ. of Wisconsin Press, 1998), 199–201. Of course, "My Genealogy" was not published in Pushkin's lifetime, but, as is evident from his letter to Benkendorf of November 24, 1831, it was broadly disseminated in manuscript, apparently, with Pushkin's blessing. See Pushkin, *Polnoe sobranie sochinenii v 16-ti tomakh*, 14:241–42.

in Pushkin's circles and even "joined in the polemics of Pushkin's associates against such rivals as Sękowski and Bulgarin," both his precarious societal position and his literary innovations placed him outside the behavioral and literary conventions shared by Pushkin and his friends.[24] Todd does not develop this point, whereas Bojanowska, in her analysis of Gogol's article "A Few Words about Pushkin," detects Gogol's concrete, albeit tacit, disagreements with Pushkin as an esthete and literary aristocrat. She points out Gogol's rejection of what he considers to be Pushkin's stance as a "poet's poet" as well as his "elitist esthetics," "refined hermeticism," and "disjunction from the current Russian reality."[25] She justly points out that the concluding lines of Gogol's article clearly portray Pushkin as a poet's poet, whose elitist position in literature is not acceptable for Gogol himself:

> The more a poet becomes a poet, the more he depicts the feelings that are familiar to poets alone—the more visibly the crowd that surrounds him diminishes and in the end it becomes so small that [the poet] can count his true admirers on his own fingers.[26]

The "literary aristocrats'" view of literature and the writer's role was not only unacceptable for Gogol aesthetically but may also have piqued him personally. I have already pointed out that in "Notes of a Madman," Gogol apparently mocks Pushkin's provocative self-definition as *meshchanin* in "My Genealogy." Bojanowska suggests that "My Genealogy" could have been directly offensive to Gogol, specifically with its assertion that the clearly autobiographical lyrical persona's ancestors "did not jump over to the princes from the Ukrainians [*v kniaz'ia ne prygal*

---

24   See William Mills Todd III, *Fiction and Society in the Age of Pushkin: Ideology, Institutions, and Narrative* (Cambridge, MA: Harvard Univ. Press, 1986), 171.

25   Bojanowska, "Equivocal Praise and National-Imperial Conundrums," 195, 196.

26   Gogol', "Neskol'ko slov o Pushkine," 87. I use Bojanowska's translation here (196).

iz khokhlov]."[27] This line, directed at Alexander Bezborodko, who made a breathtaking career under Catherine the Great, could have offended Gogol, as Bojanowska suggests, with its use of the word *khokhol*, a pejorative name for Ukrainians. Gogol may have felt the offense even more keenly, however, because the person derided was the founder of Gogol's alma mater, the Nezhin Gymnasium. In this connection, it is noteworthy that the theme of rapid social ascent, "jumping" from "tradesmen/bourgeois" or "even peasants" to grandees and sometimes even sovereigns, is so prominent in "Notes of a Madman."[28]

As a newcomer and upstart in the literary arena, Gogol needed help and support from writers with status and reputation, especially "literary aristocrats." At the same time, his incomplete acceptance by the circle of his benefactors, his provincialism, his marginal position among the members of the high society to which his benefactors belonged complicated his relations with them. The writer felt awkward among them and resented his dependence upon people whose views he did not always share and whose jokes and comments may have hurt his feelings, both as an author and as a social outsider. As Bojanowska puts it, "Gogol was acutely aware of his status as an impoverished parvenu in the circles of 'literary aristocrats' and resented his reliance on their patronage in equal measure as he craved it."[29]

One of the ways Gogol used to smooth out the awkwardness of his relations with his friends of higher rank was the exaggeration of his closeness to this social circle in general and to Pushkin in particular. As many scholars point out, Gogol used this method especially vigorously after Pushkin's death, when the late poet could not refute his assertions. Robert Maguire writes of the letters Gogol wrote in reaction to Pushkin's death:

> On the evidence of these letters alone, we could not guess that the two men had been anything but the most intimate

---

[27]   Bojanowska, "Equivocal Praise and National-Imperial Conundrums," 198.

[28]   Gogol', "Zapiski sumasshedshego," 119.

[29]   Bojanowska, "Equivocal Praise and National-Imperial Conundrums," 199.

> friends. The familiar terminology is restated, only now in
> overwrought and hyperbolized form . . . More important,
> Gogol's identification with Pushkin is now explicit, and so
> close that the two become virtually indistinguishable.[30]

It is at this time that Gogol speaks especially assertively and frequently about Pushkin's passing along to him the plots of *The Inspector General* and *Dead Souls*.[31]

Gogol's other way of dealing with the problem is less obvious and requires a close reading of his works. It involved including in his works implicit disagreements with the views of his "sworn friend" or even stealthy mockery of him. As Bojanowska's analysis demonstrates, Gogol uses this method in his article "A Few Words about Pushkin." I contend that in "Notes of a Madman," Gogol makes one of his characters a titular councilor and another a kammerjunker as a reference to Pushkin's relatively low service rank and, especially, to his public chagrin concerning the title of kammerjunker, and he does it not only to mock Pushkin's membership in the circle of "literary aristocrats" but also to ease to some degree his own social inferiority complex. This stealth strategy worked particularly well while Pushkin was alive, since Gogol could be reasonably sure his benefactor was smart enough not to acknowledge that he recognized himself in Gogol's portrayals. He would never "shriek out of stupid shock: that's me!"[32]

Pushkin's tacit presence in "Notes of a Madman" as kammerjunker and titular councilor invites us to study not only Gogol's position in the "literary aristocracy" debate or his true attitude toward Pushkin, which, obviously, was far from idealizing: both subjects have been studied more than thoroughly; instead, I propose, it invites us to study the specific strategies that Gogol used to express disagreement with Pushkin or even to ridicule him on the sly.

---

[30]   Robert A. Maguire, *Exploring Gogol* (Stanford, CA: Stanford Univ. Press, 1994), 111.

[31]   See ibid.; also, Yuri Druzhnikov, "Hitting It Off with Pushkin," 48–49.

[32]   Alexander Pushkin, *Eugene Onegin*, trans. James E. Falen (Carbondale: Southern Illinois Univ. Press, 1990), 158.

7. Death and Mutilation at the Dueling Site:
Pushkin's Death as a National Spectacle

> *What pleasure is to be found in looking at a mangled corpse, an*
> *experience which evokes revulsion? Yet wherever one is lying,*
> *people crowd around to be made sad and to turn pale. They even*
> *dread seeing this in their dreams, as if someone had compelled*
> *them to look at it when awake or as if some report about the beauty*
> *of the sight had persuaded them to see it.*
>
> —St. Augustine, *Confessions*[1]

Early Russian fictional dueling accounts are not guilty of "the lust of the eyes" that St. Augustine repeatedly condemns in the pages of his *Confessions*: they consistently avoid describing the bodily damage that dueling inflicts. The reader does not witness the physical suffering of the wounded or dying duelist. The protagonist in Mikhail Sushkov's epistolary novella *The Russian Werther* (written in the early 1790s, first published in 1801) briefly informs his correspondent about the death of his dueling opponent: "He was felled by my hand."[2] The narrator of the story about dueling interpolated into the 1802 anonymous travelogue *A New Sentimental Traveler* is equally reticent: "An ill-fated shot! Berngeim is no more!"[3] The narrator is only a little less abstract in his description of the death of Berngeim's daughter, Amalia, that immediately follows: "Amalia runs in frenzy, her knees give way, and, hardly having reached the body of her parent, she falls on him, and her soul and spirit unite with him."[4]

---

[1]   Saint Augustine, *Confessions*, trans. Henry Chadwick (New York: Oxford Univ. Press, 1992), 211.

[2]   M. Sushkov, "Rossiiskii Verter," in *Landshaft moikh voobrazhenii: Stranitsy prozy russkogo sentimentalizma* (Moscow: Sovremennik, 1990), 122.

[3]   K*. G*., "Novyi chuvstvitel'nyi puteshestvennik, ili Moia progulka v A***," in ibid., 409.

[4]   Ibid.

In contrast, the author of *A New Sentimental Traveler* devotes considerable attention to the psychological consequences of the incident for Franz, the victorious duelist. He describes in detail the torments that seize Franz immediately after the duel:

> Despair, frenzy, love—all passions produced the most powerful effect on his feelings. He dashed and rushed about, he threw himself against the ground, cursing the very hour when he met this ill-fated family whose misfortune he, and he alone, had caused.[5]

Franz escapes abroad to avoid punishment for the duel, but he is unable to escape the ghosts of the dead that haunt him: "The shadows of Amalia and Berngeim always followed him, reproached his cruelty . . . at night violent dreams showed the same ghosts and . . . his conscience mercilessly tore his soul."[6] The remorseful Franz eventually dies of self-inflicted starvation.

A similar pattern—an understated description of the fallen duelist followed by a detailed account of the victor's subsequent inner torment—can be found in the 1809 "Ode on Duels," which some scholars attribute to the fourteen-year-old Alexander Griboedov:

> Там вижу юноша, страдая,
> В крови, лишенный жизни, пал!

(There I see a youth fallen, suffering, in blood, deprived of life!)

Nothing more is said of the victim. Retribution for the victor, however, is promised to follow swiftly and inevitably:

> Наполнит сердце трепетанье,
> И тайной совести страданья,
> Как змеи, будут грудь терзать,
> Мечтами будешь ты томиться,
> И тень кровавая явится
> Тебя в убийстве укорять!

---

5   Ibid.

6   Ibid., 410.

. . . .
В ушах стенанья повторятся,
И будет кровь в очах метаться,
Пролитая твоей рукой! [7]

(Your heart will fill with trembling, and secret torments of
your conscience will torture your breast like snakes! Dreams
will oppress you, and a bloody shadow will appear to
reproach you for the murder! . . . Your ears will hear repeated
moans, and the blood spilled by your hand will appear before
your eyes!)

The poem goes on in the same vein for another five stanzas.

No doubt there were remorseful duelists in early-nineteenth-
century Russia (although, in contrast to Franz, they most likely
refrained from having hysterical fits on dueling sites). The
Decembrist Evgeny Obolensky is a frequently cited example. One
contemporary compared his mental anguish to the sufferings
experienced by Orestes pursued by the Furies.[8] Yet Obolensky's
case appears to be exceptional; at least, I am unaware of any other
reports of a duelist's public remorse. It is more likely, therefore, that
in their literary accounts of post-dueling remorse, Russians painted
not so much from life as from literature. One powerful model was
Jean-Jacques Rousseau's *La Nouvelle Héloïse*. Julie d'Étange, in her
letter to St. Preux against dueling (part 1, letter 57), tells of her
father's tortured memories of a friend he had killed in a duel:

> That fatal blow, which deprived the one of life, robbed the
> other of his peace of mind forever. From that time has the
> most cruel remorse incessantly preyed on his heart: he is
> often heard to sigh and weep in private: his imagination still
> represents to him the fatal steel, thrust by his cruel hand into
> the heart of the man he loved: his slumbers are disturbed by
> the appearances of his pale and bleeding friend: he looks with

---

[7]   Aleksandr Griboedov, *Sochineniia* (Moscow: Khudozhestvennaia literatura, 1988), 377, 378.

[8]   See V. A. Olenina, "Pis'ma k P. I. Bartenevu, 1869," in *Dekabristy*, ed. Nikolai Chulkov, Letopisi gosudarstvennogo literaturnogo muzeia 3 (Moscow: Gosudarstvennyi literaturnyi muzei, 1938): 488 (cf. also 491).

terror on the mortal wound: he endeavours to stop the blood
that flows from it: he seizes with horror and cries out, Will
this corpse never cease pursuing me?[9]

The pattern is the very same one used by the Russians I have quoted:
a brief statement of the opponent's death followed by a lengthy and
detailed description of psychological consequences for the victor.[10]

Alexander Bestuzhev-Marlinsky, the codifier of Russian
dueling discourse and its most prolific practitioner, also made use
of Rousseau's formula. In his 1824 short story "Novel in Seven
Letters," he frames the account of the fatal duel as the desperate
letter of a remorseful victor who focuses on his own pain more than
on that of his dying opponent:

> I killed him, I killed this noble, magnanimous man! . . . At six
> paces, I do not know why, I do not know how, I pulled this
> fateful trigger, and the shot resounded in my heart!.. I saw
> how Erast flinched... When the smoke was blown away, he
> was already lying on the snow, and the blood rushing from
> his wound froze on him with a hiss. Take away, take away
> this picture from my eyes, remove from my heart the memory
> of it![11]

But of course, he is no more successful in getting rid of the awful
visions than Julie's father, or Franz:

> It is night, everything is in slumber, but the worm of my heart
> is not sleeping. Days pass in pangs of conscience, night fills
> the darkness with monsters . . . If I doze from fatigue, terrible

---

[9]   Jean-Jacques Rousseau, *Eloisa, or a Series of Original Letters,* trans. William
Kenrick (1803; repr., Oxford: Woodstock Books, 1989), 1:266.

[10]   On the influence of Rousseau's novel on Russian dueling discourse see Irina
Reyfman, *Ritualized Violence Russian Style: The Duel in Russian Culture and
Literature* (Stanford, CA: Stanford Univ. Press, 1999), 30–31 and 156–57. The
influence of Rousseau is also suggested in the commentary to the "Ode on
Duels"; see Aleksandr Griboedov, *Sochineniia,* 696.

[11]   A. A. Bestuzhev-Marlinskii, "Roman v semi pis'makh," in his *Vtoroe
polnoe sobranie sochinenii,* 4th ed. (St. Petersburg: v Tipografii ministerstva
gosudarstvennykh imushchestv, 1847), vol. 2, bk. 4, p. 126.

dreams agitate my heart: the fateful shot resounds, a deathly moan tears my hearing.[12]

In contrast, the injuries sustained by the narrator of the interpolated story in Bestuzhev's "Evening at a Bivouac" (1823) are reported parenthetically:

> Some Spanish author—I do not remember his name and patronymic—said that the first sound of an apothecary mortar is the death-knell: the bullet went in and out close to the lung; gangrene threatened to burn the heart, but, contrary to Le Sage and Molière, I recovered, with the help of physicians and plasters, in a month and a half.[13]

The description is not only utterly concise, but also buried in a lengthy mockery of the medical profession.

In *Eugene Onegin*, Pushkin adds irony but still works with Rousseau's model in mind: even though the reader is spared the detailed description of ghosts and bloody visions, the inevitable psychological torment in store for Onegin is clearly suggested in stanzas 33–35 of the dueling chapter. Even Lermontov's portrayal of the highly irregular Pechorin-Grushnitsky duel presupposes the reader's knowledge of Rousseau's formula: the reader is expected either to be horrified by Pechorin's apparent lack of remorse or else to suspect that Pechorin will not actually be spared the usual torment. In fact, Lermontov subtly indicates that this is likely to be the case; there are clear signs that Pechorin is affected by Grushnitsky's death and in all probability will be visited by bloody ghosts:

> On my way down the trail, I noticed, among the crevices of the cliffs, Grushnitski's bloodstained body. Involuntarily, I shut my eyes. I untied my horse and set out for home at a walk. A stone lay on my heart. The sun seemed to me without luster; its rays did not warm me.[14]

---

[12] Ibid., 128.

[13] A. A. Bestuzhev-Marlinskii, *Sochineniia v dvukh tomakh* (Moscow: Gosudarstvennoe izdatel'stvo khudozhestvennoi literatury, 1958), 1:51.

[14] Mikhail Lermontov, *A Hero of Our Time*, trans. Vladimir Nabokov in

In Rousseau's novel, the account of Baron d'Étange's postdueling suffering serves a practical purpose: it helps avert the looming duel between St. Preux and Milord Eduard. Julie uses this emotionally charged description to reinforce the lengthy anti-dueling diatribe addressed to her lover. She begins with logical arguments and concludes by having "the passions and humanity" speak to St. Preux of her father's experience, hence the emphasis on physical sensations and visual impressions in her description ("the fatal steel, thrust by his cruel hand into the heart of the man he loved," "he looks with terror on the mortal wound," "he endeavours to stop the blood that flows from it").[15] In her appeal to humanity, Julie aims at the very core of dueling ethos. The duel, after all, is a test, which tests a duelist's ability to disregard both his own and his opponent's physical vulnerability. Failure to do so renders him incapable of withstanding the danger as well as harming his opponent. The first, of course, is dishonorable within the code of honor; the second replaces the code of honor with a different value system—the system that acknowledges the opponent's capacity for suffering.

Julie is successful in her appeal to St. Preux's humanity: her letter makes him receptive to Milord Eduard's apology offered shortly thereafter. The adversaries make up. In early Russian fictional dueling accounts, however, nothing of this sort ever happens. While Russians—both writers and their characters—seem to be affected by the emotional power of Rousseau's argument, they remain unresponsive to its call to renounce the code of honor. The dueling ethos prevails, and early Russian fictional duelists, while knowing very well the consequences of their actions, still proceed with their duels.[16] In the Russian context, Rousseau's formula for moral change remains a mere literary topos.

---

collaboration with Dmitri Nabokov (Ann Arbor, MI: Ardis, 1998), 171.

[15]   For Julie's letter, see Rousseau, *Eloisa*, 1:235–67.

[16]   For discussions of this feature of the early Russian literary duel, see William Mills Todd III, *Fiction and Society in the Age of Pushkin: Ideology, Institutions, and Narrative* (Cambridge, MA: Harvard Univ. Press, 1986), 128; Monika Greenleaf, *Pushkin and Romantic Fashion: Fragment, Elegy, Orient, Irony*

By the mid-nineteenth century, Russian writers had used Rousseau's formula to its full extent. The last, ironic reference to it can be seen in an aborted impulse by Dostoevsky's underground man to write an exultant letter to an officer who has offended him and with whom he fails to fight a duel. The letter parodies the series of letters that dissipate the duel between St. Preux and Milord Eduard—the series in which Julie's letter quoted above is the first. The underground man's "letter was composed in such a way that if the officer had even the slightest notion of 'the beautiful and the lofty,' he could not fail to come running to [him], to throw himself on [his] neck and offer [him] his friendship."[17] This is precisely what Milord Eduard does: a letter from Julie affected him so much that he arranged a meeting with St. Preux, "fell upon his knee," and refused to get up until his apology was accepted. Milord Eduard's gesture averted the duel and restored the men's friendship.[18] The underground man, of course, misreads his original, overlooking the crucial fact that it is not one of the opponents but Julie—a woman and thus someone not bound by the code of honor—who initiates the reconciliation. He also misreads Russian literary tradition, ignoring its aversion to the idea of the duelists' making peace. Dostoevsky's parody thus not only exposes the underground man as an inept (and, perhaps, dishonorable) duelist, but also underscores the fact that, for all its popularity with Russians, Rousseau's recipe for the

---

(Stanford, CA: Stanford Univ. Press, 1994), 276–79; and Reyfman, *Ritualized Violence Russian Style*, 30–31.

[17] Fyodor Dostoevsky, *Notes from Underground*, trans. Richard Pevear and Larissa Volokhonsky (New York: Alfred A. Knopf, 1993), 51; for the original, see Fedor Dostoevskii, *Polnoe sobranie sochinenii v 30-ti tomakh* (Leningrad: Nauka, 1972–90), 5:129.

[18] Rousseau, *Eloisa*, 1:273–74. Notably, Rousseau uses the device twice: in part 2, St. Preux becomes suspicious of the relations between Julie and Milord Eduard and once again wants to duel with him. A letter from Julie to Milord Eduard that he reads convinces him of the lofty nature of those relations. Deeply touched, he throws himself at Milord Eduard's feet and, "struck with admiration, affliction, and shame: [St. Preux] embraced his knees with the utmost humiliation and concern, but could not utter a word" (2:22). Milord Eduard forgives him, and friendship reigns again. Dostoevsky clearly makes a collage of the two episodes.

prevention of dueling was not supposed to work for an honorable Russian literary duelist.

With the Rousseau formula all but dead, a new literary mode of portraying death and mutilation on the dueling site had gradually emerged. It focused to a much larger degree on the physical suffering of the victim rather than on the psychological torment of the victor. The shift in literary paradigms, from the Romantic disregard for the body to the Natural School's keen interest in it, no doubt contributed to this change. In the sciences, the retreat of *Naturphilosophie*, with its distrust of analysis and anatomy, and the advent of positive sciences, with their emphasis on observation and experiment, also fostered the interest in the body. I contend, however, that while the new mode of portraying the injury and death of a duelist took shape in the atmosphere of heightened general interest in the body and its physicality, the concrete forms of such a portrayal developed under the influence of documentary accounts of Pushkin's duel and his death agony. Pushkin's emerging status as a cultural icon lent those accounts particular power.[19]

Before Pushkin's death, eyewitness accounts of what took place at dueling sites were as reserved as literary ones. Nor was the public admitted into the wounded duelists' death chambers. Contemporaries could mention the gravity of injuries, but they focused mostly on the duelists' behavior, not on the damage done to their bodies and even less on the pain their bodies suffered. If early Russian eyewitnesses mentioned a duelist's body part at all, it was to supply technical details. For example, in his letter to Yakov Tolstoy about Kondraty Ryleev's 1824 duel with Prince Konstantin Shakhovskoy, Alexander Bestuzhev mentions Ryleev's heel wound: "The first shot went through Ryleev's [heel]."[20] The interest, however, lay in the unusual nature of this duel that led to the

---

19   Coincidentally, the first Russian book in physiology advancing an experimental approach was published in 1837 by A. M. Filomafitsky. See Alexander Vucinich, *Science in Russian Culture: A History to 1860* (Stanford, CA: Stanford Univ. Press, 1963), 337.

20   Aleksandr Bestuzhev to Iakov Tolstoi, March 3, 1824, *Russkaia starina* 11 (1889): 375–76. The word "heel" is marked by the publishers as "unreadable" and is reconstructed from other accounts.

unusual wound. The duel's conditions were insanely harsh: there was no barrier (that is, the minimal distance between the opponents was not determined), and the duelists had to shoot simultaneously at a second's command. The opponents agreed to shoot as many times as it would take to kill or seriously wound one of them. They exchanged two shots at a distance of three paces. By sheer luck, both times the bullets hit the opponents' pistols. One of the bullets ricocheted and wounded Ryleev. The wound thus testified to Ryleev's fortitude, not to his physical vulnerability. Its description reinforced rather than undermined the dueling ethos.

Against this background, the number and, especially, the nature of accounts of Pushkin's duel and death are truly astonishing. Just to cite the most important documents—all eyewitness accounts—generated during the last days of the poet's life and the first two weeks after his death: we have the reports of both seconds, Auguste d'Archiac and Konstantin Danzas; Alexander Turgenev's letters to different members of his extended family and to Alexander Bulgakov; Petr Vyazemsky's three letters (of February 5 to Bulgakov, of February 9 to Denis Davydov, and of February 14 to Grand Duke Michael); Vasily Zhukovsky's letter to Sergey L'vovich Pushkin; and no less than three accounts by physicians: Wilhelm Scholz, the first physician to examine the wounded poet upon his arrival at home; Ivan Spassky, Pushkin's personal physician; and Vladimir Dahl, who took an informal yet active part in his care.

All accounts pay special attention to the physical damage that Pushkin's body sustained. They describe the wound and the injuries the bullet inflicted on the internal organs; many offer particulars of the poet's medical care in minute, often gory, detail. Frequently these accounts give the impression that the witnesses were actively seeking to examine and assess the damage. For example, Turgenev wrote to his cousin, Alexandra Nefed'eva, on January 30: "When they washed the body, I closely examined [*rassmotrel*] the wound, seemingly insignificant."[21] Shockingly, Dahl's memoir includes an autopsy report.

---

[21]   "Novye materialy dlia biografii Pushkina (Iz Turgenevskogo arkhiva)," in *Pushkin i ego sovremenniki: Materialy i issledovaniia* (SPb: AN, 1908), 6:57.

Even the seconds, traditionally reluctant to share their
knowledge of what took place at the dueling site, abandoned
their reticence. In fact, it was the account by d'Archiac, d'Anthès's
second, in a letter to Vyazemsky (February 1, 1837) that became the
master document for the subsequent narratives of the duel proper.
I translate from the French original:

> The two enemies prepared to shoot. In a few moments the shot
> resounded. Mr. Pushkin was wounded, which he declared
> himself as he fell on the overcoat that marked the barrier;
> he remained still, his face to the ground. As the seconds
> moved toward him, he raised himself into a sitting position
> and said: "Wait." The weapon that he held in his hand was
> covered in snow; he took another. I could have protested, but
> Baron Georges Heeckeren's [d'Anthès's] sign stopped me.
> Mr. Pushkin propped himself by his left arm, aimed with
> a firm hand and shot. Immobile until the shot, Baron Hee-
> ckeren was wounded and fell to his side.
>
> Mr. Pushkin's wound was too serious to continue; the affair
> was over. Having fallen again after the shot, [Pushkin] half
> fainted twice and was in a daze for several moments. He
> came to and remained conscious. In the sledge, being jolted
> during the half-mile trip on a very bad road, he suffered
> without complaint.[22]

The number of details concerning the body and pain is
substantial: his face to the ground, wound, fainted twice, came to,
in a daze, suffered without complaint.

Pushkin's second, Konstantin Danzas, in his own letter to
Vyazemsky written on February 6 (Vyazemsky asked him to verify
d'Archiac's account), was most of all concerned with the implied
allegation of irregularity (the replaced pistol) and therefore devoted
his letter almost entirely to defending Pushkin's right to a pistol not
damaged by snow. As far as the rest of d'Archiac's account, Danzas
confirmed its correctness, adding only one new detail: Pushkin's

---

[22]   *Duel' Pushkina s Dantesom-Gekkerenom: Podlinnoe voenno-sudnoe delo 1837 g.*
(1900; reprint, St. Petersburg: Russlit, 1992), 53.

words indicating that he had enough strength to continue the duel and make his shot—again underscoring Pushkin's physical condition.[23] Danzas did not provide any new written accounts until 1863, when Alexander Ammosov wrote down and published his story. Danzas, however, was at Pushkin's deathbed and no doubt shared his story with those present—and they, in turn, passed it along. Turgenev, for example, in his January 28 letter to Nefed'eva, shows a detailed knowledge of what took place at the dueling site; as do the Karamzin sisters, Ekaterina and Sophia, in their January 30 letter to Andrey Karamzin; Alexey Voeikov in his February 4 letter to a friend in Warsaw; and even Mariya Mörder, a maid of honor at court who knew Pushkin only socially and quite superficially, in the January 29 entry in her diary.[24]

Along with the particulars of the duel, Turgenev's January 28 letter to Nefed'eva also gives a detailed description of Pushkin's wound: "Heeckeren shot first and hit Pushkin in the stomach; the bullet passed through the entire body and stopped under the skin so that the doctors could feel it."[25] Turgenev's description includes the kind of information that could only be gained from the doctors who took care of the dying poet. Indeed, further in the letter, Turgenev demonstrates detailed familiarity both with the diagnosis and the prognosis:

> They sent for Arendt [the court physician who supervised Pushkin's care], but even before that the patient was attended by his friend, the skillful Doctor Spassky. Surgery would be useless; they had to leave the wound without surgery even though it would be easy to cut the bullet out. But that would needlessly increase bleeding. His intestines are not affected,

---

[23]   Ibid., 54.

[24]   See "Novye materialy dlia biografii Pushkina," 49; *Pushkin v pis'makh Karamzinykh 1836–1837 godov* (Moscow: Izdatel'stvo Akademii Nauk SSSR, 1960), 168 (Russian translation) and 298 (French original); B. Modzalevskii, pub., "Smert' Pushkina (Piat' pisem 1837 goda)," in *Pushkin i ego sovremenniki*, 6:108; and *Russkaia starina* 8 (1900): 385–87. Mörder presents two versions of the events, both imprecise but generally correct.

[25]   "Novye materialy dlia biografii Pushkina," 49.

but inside the blood nerves [*krovavye nervy*] are disrupted, and the wound has been declared lethal.[26]

The specifics of Pushkin's care were also described by the doctors themselves. As many as five physicians attended the wounded Pushkin, and three of them left written accounts. Wilhelm Scholz, an obstetrician who, together with the surgeon Karl Zadler, was the first to examine the wound, is brief and factual. Most interestingly, his account preserves Pushkin's own description of his condition: "What do you think of my wound?" the poet asked. "After the shot, I felt a strong blow [*udar*] to my side and a stabbing hot pain in my lower back. On the way [home] the bleeding was heavy. Tell me honestly, how do you find my wound?"[27] Ivan Spassky, Pushkin's family doctor, is less factual in his descriptions (his memoir has obvious literary pretensions: it opens with a quote from *Eugene Onegin* and closes with a quote from Zhukovsky's poem on Pushkin's death; it also pays considerable attention to Pushkin's moral condition, such as his alleged eagerness to receive the last rites). Still, Spassky registers the illness's progression, notes Pushkin's good behavior as a patient (several times he remarks, "He followed all medical prescriptions"), and describes his suffering—in particular, the terrible paroxysm of pain that Pushkin experienced in the early hours of January 28:

> Around four the pain in his stomach began to grow and by five o'clock it became significant. I sent for A[rendt] who came without delay. The pain in his stomach increased to the highest degree. This was real torture. P[ushkin]'s face changed; his gaze became wild; it seemed that his eyes were about to pop out of their sockets; cold sweat covered his forehead, his hands were cold, the pulse had disappeared. The patient felt terrible torment.[28]

---

26   Ibid., 50.

27   P. E. Shchegolev, *Duel' i smert' Pushkina* (1916; repr., St. Petersburg: Gumanitarnoe agentstvo "Akademicheskii proekt," 1999), 186.

28   Ibid., 188.

The third doctor who left accounts of Pushkin's death agony was Dahl, the writer and future lexicographer whom Pushkin had known socially for several years. He arrived at Pushkin's side a day after the duel, in the afternoon of January 28, and stayed to the end. He authored three narratives. One is an untitled account of everything he witnessed in the twenty-four hours between his arrival and Pushkin's death (he calls these hours Passion, *strastnýe*, or terrible, *stráshnye*). During this time he effectively fulfilled the duties of an attending physician, with Spassky and Arendt visiting. The two other narratives are a document entitled "An Autopsy of A. S. Pushkin's Body" and a strictly medical account entitled "The Course of Pushkin's Illness." The first of the three narratives is factual and detailed, with the focus on the course of the illness and the patient's condition. The other two are highly technical and thus especially graphic.[29]

The autopsy report is of particular interest as far as spectacles of death go. The Military Ministry *ukaz* of 1779 required autopsies to be performed on all victims of violent deaths. This included deaths in duels, and accordingly Pushkin's body was examined — in general view, by Spassky, with Dahl writing down his findings:

> The autopsy of the abdominal cavity showed that the intestines all were very much inflamed; only one spot, about the size of a coin, was gangrenous. This is the point where, in all probability, the intestines were bruised by the bullet.
>
> The abdominal cavity contained no less than a pound of black coagulated blood, which probably came from the injured abdominal artery.
>
> In the pelvic cavity, at the right side, numerous small bone fragments were found, and, finally, the lower part of the sacrum was shattered.

The next two paragraphs describe the bullet's path and speculate on the immediate cause of death.[30] Boris Shubin, in his analysis of Pushkin's care from the point of view of modem

---

[29]   Ibid., 191–96.

[30]   Ibid., 194–95.

medicine—citing Dahl's comment, "Time and circumstances did not allow a more detailed investigation to continue"—argues that the autopsy was done in a hurried and perfunctory manner.[31] The relative thoroughness of Dahl's account, however, becomes evident in comparison with Lermontov's autopsy report (the autopsy was performed by a doctor at the Piatigorsk Military Hospital):

> The examination showed that the pistol bullet, having entered the right side below the last rib, at the point where the rib is joined with cartilage, pierced the right and left lungs and, going up, exited between the fifth and sixth ribs at the left side and on the way cut through the soft tissues of the left shoulder. Lieutenant Lermontov died of this wound immediately at the site of the duel.[32]

Even more important than the report's relative thoroughness was the fact that Dahl freely shared the information gained in the autopsy with friends and acquaintances. Turgenev, for example, wrote to Nefed'eva on February 1: "The autopsy of the lower body [*nizhnei chasti*] showed that his rib was shattered."[33] Likewise, Voeikov's February 4 letter demonstrates a thorough knowledge of the internal injuries that Pushkin sustained:

> [D'Anthès] was wounded lightly in the right arm, Pushkin in *bas ventre*; the bullet traveled from the right side to the left and stopped under the skin, not having injured either the bladder, or intestines, or the spleen, but it bruised and paralyzed all the interior.[34]

Voeikov was not present at Pushkin's deathbed, and his knowledge could only be secondhand, originating directly or indirectly with Dahl's written or oral accounts. Dahl's openness, thus, made

---

31   B. M. Shubin, *Skorbnyi list ili Istoriia bolezni Aleksandra Pushkina*, in his *Dopolnenie k portretam* ([Moscow]: Znanie, 1989), 115.

32   A. D. Alekseev, comp., *Duel' Lermontova s Martynovym: Po materialam sledstviia i voenno-sudnogo dela, 1841* (Moscow: Russlit, 1992), 14–15.

33   "Novye materialy dlia biografii Pushkina," 57.

34   Modzalevskii, pub., "Smert' Pushkina," 108.

the information normally available only to a restricted number of officials—and perhaps relatives—open to public scrutiny. In particular, all of Dahl's accounts were available to Zhukovsky when he wrote his February 15 letter to Sergey L'vovich.

Zhukovsky, in fact, had the accounts of all three physicians in his possession while working on his letter to Sergey L'vovich.[35] He knew Dahl's memoir in its original, more detailed and graphic form: when Dahl published it in 1860, he abridged the autopsy and medical sections. Zhukovsky, understandably, did not include the autopsy report in his letter to Sergey L'vovich; he also removed all references to the actual cause of Pushkin's death not only from the version that he published in *The Contemporary* but also from versions that he allowed to circulate. It was forbidden to mention dueling in print, and Zhukovsky cautiously self-censored the circulating manuscript versions as well.[36] Only one original version speaks openly about the duel and the cause of Pushkin's death. In the censored versions, Zhukovsky writes about an illness; the readers, of course, easily reconstructed the censored information. Furthermore, even without mentioning Pushkin's wound directly, Zhukovsky still pays considerable attention to the body in pain and its physiology.

Zhukovsky meticulously reports everything that had to do with Pushkin's deteriorating physical condition: level of pain and discomfort, pulse and temperature, appetite, thirst, and the

---

[35]   Zhukovsky drew on many eyewitness accounts of the poet's death, both written and oral. Shchegolev cites Vyazemsky's testimony in his February 5 letter to Bulgakov about the joint effort to collect all eyewitness accounts for Zhukovsky; see Shchegolev, *Duel' i smert' Pushkina*, 146–47. I. Borichevsky argues that Zhukovsky solicited memoirs from everyone present at the time of Pushkin's death; see his "Zametki Zhukovskogo o gibeli Pushkina," *Pushkin: Vremennik Pushkinskoi kommissii* 3 (1937): 371-392, esp. 375-76 and 388-89.

[36]   Shchegolev thoroughly analyzes Zhukovsky's misrepresentation of facts in his final version of the letter in his *Duel' i smert' Pushkina*, 146–60. In Borichevsky's formulation, "Pushkin's friends consciously, and in an organized way, created a legend about the poet's death" (see his "Zametki Zhukovskogo o gibeli Pushkina," 392). For my purposes, however, only distortions that concern the duel and the wound are important.

particulars of medical care. For example, he reports on the paroxysm of pain that Pushkin suffered in the early hours of January 28. His account is less graphic than that of Spassky, but not much so. I quote from the version published in *The Contemporary*:

> Until five o'clock Pushkin suffered, but bearably. But around five o'clock the stomach pain became intolerable, and its strength overpowered the strength of his soul; he began to moan; they sent again for Arendt. Upon his arrival, it was determined necessary to give him an enema, but it did not help, and only increased his sufferings to the highest degree, which continued until seven o'clock in the morning.[37]

The same level of detailed description continues throughout the letter. By focusing on pain and bodily functions and dysfunctions, Zhukovsky emphasizes Pushkin's stoicism and prepares a suitable background for his portrayal of the poet's peaceful Christian death. Thus, even the versions that avoided references to the duel and the wound provided the public with graphic images of physical suffering.

Virtually all eyewitness accounts of Pushkin's illness and death became widely known right away. I have already cited evidence that Dahl's narratives immediately became available to the public. Private letters also began to circulate at once. Turgenev's correspondence is a good example. He spent the days of January 27–29 in Pushkin's Moika apartment, writing several letters a day, and those letters were intended for immediate circulation. Turgenev writes in his diary on January 28: "I have described everything in a letter to my cousin [Nefed'eva, *sestritsa*, as he calls her] and asked Bulgakov to send a copy to [Turgenev's cousin Ivan] Arzhevitinov." On January 29, he writes: "I have described the entire day and Pushkin's death in two letters to my cousin [*sestritsa*]."[38] Turgenev used Bulgakov as an intermediary in his correspondence with Nefed'eva and Arzhevitinov, which meant that every letter was

---

[37]   Shchegolev, *Duel' i smert' Pushkina*, 170 and notes *d*, *e*, and *zh*.

[38]   A. I. Turgenev, "Iz 'Dnevnika,'" in *A. S. Pushkin v vospominaniiakh sovremennikov v dvukh tomakh* (Moscow: Khudozhestvennaia literatura, 1985), 2:215.

read by at least two people, but often by many more. Bulgakov's—
often sinister—role in disseminating information that came his way
is well known, and Vyazemsky also counted on him to make his
letters public. He wrote to Bulgakov in his February 5 letter:

> Please show my letter to Iv[an] I[vanovich] Dmitriev and
> Solntsev or, better, give them copies and in general show the
> letter to everyone you find necessary . . . Read it to Vladimir
> Pushkin and, if you can find him, to Pavel Voinovich
> Nashchokin, the friend of the late Pushkin.[39]

Therefore, despite the fact that only one document, Zhukovsky's
letter to Sergey L'vovich, was published at the time (it appeared
in the 1837 volume of *The Contemporary*), and the rest of the documents were published decades later, descriptions of Pushkin's
pain and suffering immediately entered the public domain.

Dmitry Bantysh-Kamensky, the author of the first biography
of Pushkin published in 1847, was familiar with the eyewitness
accounts circulating in manuscript and, perhaps, in oral tradition.
His main source for the story of the poet's duel and death appears to
be Zhukovsky's letter to Sergey L'vovich, to which he refers, but he
also quotes Vyazemsky's February 5 letter to Bulgakov.[40] In addition,
the biography reveals the author's familiarity with accounts in oral
circulation. For example, he offers a description of the poet's wound
that echoes numerous epistolary and, no doubt, oral reports:
"Pushkin was wounded in his right side, above the liver: the bullet
pierced the gut and stayed inside."[41]

While less specific in his representations of the poet's pain,
Bantysh-Kamensky nonetheless emphasizes the physical distress
that Pushkin's last illness inflicted on him. The biographer not only
repeats words like "torment" (*múka*) and "suffering" (*stradanie*)
throughout his account but also includes a description of the
paroxysm of pain that the poet suffered early in the morning on

---

[39]   V. V. Kunin, ed., *Poslednii god zhizni Pushkina* (Moscow: Pravda, 1988), 517.

[40]   D. N. Bantysh-Kamenskii, *Slovar' dostopamiatnykh liudei russkoi zemli,
Dopolneniia* (St. Petersburg: A. Shiriaev, 1847), 2:99 and 92.

[41]   Ibid., 92n.

January 28. The description is more cursory than those of Spassky or Zhukovsky, but it mentions the "insufferable pain," "violent pain," and the poet's moaning. Bantysh-Kamensky's biography was the first published account of Pushkin's death that openly mentioned its real cause. It was thus the first to connect the themes of dueling and mutilation in print.

The unprecedented candor of the accounts of Pushkin's death agony affected Russian documentary dueling narratives almost immediately: already in the early 1840s, they began to pay much closer attention to the fallen duelist's bodily damage and pain. This is evident, for example, in accounts of the 1817 duel between Vasily Sheremetev and Alexander Zavadovsky that Griboedov's friend D. A. Smirnov wrote down in 1842. In this duel—in which Griboedov took part as a second—Sheremetev was gravely wounded and died several days later. One of the witnesses, the physician B. I. Ion, gives a graphic account of Sheremetev's wound and pain:

> [Zavadovsky] made a shot, the bullet punctured [She-remetev's] side and went through his stomach, only it did not exit but stopped in his other side. Sheremetev fell on his back on the snow and began to dive in the snow like a fish. It was a pity to watch.[42]

Andrey Zhandr (Griboedov's friend, to whose house he went immediately after the duel) is equally explicit: "Zavadovsky took a shot. The shot was fatal: it wounded Sheremetev in the stomach. Sheremetev jumped several times on the spot, then fell and began rolling on the snow."[43] These accounts, written down in 1842 (that is, after the reports of Pushkin's post-dueling agony had entered the national consciousness), were in sharp contrast with contemporary 1817 factual and understated accounts of the duel:

> The bullet hit him in the side; according to other reports, it went through his stomach and stopped in his side. Sheremetev

---

[42]   D. A. Smirnov, "Rasskazy ob A. S. Griboedove, zapisannye so slov ego druzei," in *A. S. Griboedov v vospominaniiakh sovremennikov* (Moscow: Khudozhestvennaia literatura, 1980), 213.

[43]   Ibid., 243.

fell down at once, but then stood up and remained standing until they laid him down to dress the wound.[44]

Contemporary accounts of Lermontov's duel with Nikolay Martynov (July 15, 1841) are still relatively reticent. Yet even though Lermontov's death was instantaneous and thus provided little material for portrayals of physical suffering, these accounts do offer substantial details about the nature of the poet's wound and the manner of his death. An account by Alexander Traskin (which is believed to be based on conversations with the seconds) is representative in this respect. He wrote in a letter (July 17, 1841): "Martynov shot first, and Lermontov fell down. The bullet punctured his body from the right to the left and went through his heart. He lived for only five minutes, and did not have time to utter a single word."[45]

The new interest in death spectacles is even more vividly evidenced by the unseemly attention that the Piatigorsk public paid to Lermontov's dead body. In her memoir, Emiliya Shan-Girey reports on the unprecedented curiosity that sent the inhabitants of this spa town to view the poet's body on the day he was killed: "A duel was an unheard-of thing in Piatigorsk! Many went to look at the slain poet out of curiosity . . . This movement back and forth continued until midnight."[46] Shan-Girey's choice of words makes it clear that this was not a Christian respectful viewing of the body but precisely the type of curious staring that St. Augustine condemned as "the lust of the eyes."

---

[44]   V. Sheremetevskii, ["O V. V. Sheremeteve"], in *A. S. Griboedov v vospominaniiakh sovremennikov*, 271. Sheremetevsky's account, written for Sheremetev's biography, in *Sbornik biografii kavalergardov* (St. Petersburg: Ekspeditsiia zagotovleniia gos. bumag, 1906), 3:241–43, reproduces the materials of the official inquiry into the duel. The materials have since been lost, and Sheremetevsky's account thus preserves the voices of the original reporters.

[45]   A. S. Traskin, "Iz pis'ma k P. Kh. Grabbe," in *M. Iu. Lermontov v vospominaniiakh sovremennikov* (Moscow: Khudozhestvennaia literatura, 1989), 444–45.

[46]   E. A. Shan-Girei, "Vospominanie o Lermontove," in ibid., 434.

Eventually, heightened attention to the body began to undermine the dueling ethos, making it difficult for duelists to disregard their opponents' physical vulnerability. In an 1857 duel, an officer, Kozlov, wounded another officer, Korsakov. According to a contemporary account, Korsakov was a very unwilling duelist. Repeatedly he voiced his reluctance to fight, citing his fear he would kill Kozlov: "Korsakov did not want to fight, because he knew for sure: he would kill the other."[47] At the dueling site, Korsakov found it impossible to aim at his opponent and shot on the air, again evoking his reluctance to kill: "Korsakov had to shoot first. When he took the pistol and lifted it, he turned pale and said: 'I cannot shoot, because I will kill him for sure,' and he shot upward."[48] It is crucial that Korsakov did not forgo his shot out of contempt for Kozlov (which was the usual reason for shooting on the air and which was warranted in this case since the duel was over Kozlov's cheating at cards), but precisely because he did not want to kill his opponent. Kozlov, however, exercised his right to a shot and wounded Korsakov in the side; Korsakov survived.

The new attitude toward the body and its potential for suffering and death affected literary dueling accounts as well. Tolstoy and Dostoevsky in particular displayed interest in the suffering body of the duelist. In some cases, I believe, their explorations were directly influenced by narratives of Pushkin's duel and his death. I will examine two such cases: Tolstoy's portrayal of Pierre's duel with Dolokhov and Aglaya's and Prince Myshkin's lengthy discussion of the Pushkin-d'Anthès duel in part three of *The Idiot*. The former, I will argue, suggests Tolstoy's familiarity with accounts of the Pushkin-d'Anthès duel; the latter refers to the duel directly and clearly shows Dostoevsky's knowledge of its particulars. It is significant that the most important accounts of Pushkin's duel and death—those by Spassky, Dahl, and Danzas—were published in the

---

47   See *Mikhail Semenovich Shchepkin: Zhizn' i tvorchetsvo* (Moscow: Iskusstvo, 1984), 1:277. The author of the account is the actor's wife, E. D. Shchepkina.

48   Ibid. For an analysis of this duel, see Reyfman, *Ritualized Violence Russian Style*, 27.

late 1850s and early 1860s and thus had to be fresh in the writers' memory when they worked on their novels.

In the *War and Peace* dueling episode, Tolstoy draws attention to the duelist's body open to violence. He describes Pierre's defenseless posture as he awaits Dolokhov's shot. To underscore Pierre's vulnerability, the writer focuses on the different parts of his body:

> "Sidewise! Cover yourself with your pistol!" ejaculated Nesvitsky.
>
> "Cover yourself," even Denisov cried to his adversary.
>
> Pierre with a gentle smile of pity and remorse, his arms and legs helplessly spread out, stood with his broad chest directly facing Dolokhov and looked sorrowfully at him.[49]

One is tempted to contrast Pierre's defenseless posture with d'Anthès's expert cover mentioned in all accounts of the Pushkin-d'Anthès duel. I quote from Danzas's reports: "He returned to his spot, having positioned himself sidewise and covered his chest with his right hand" (letter to Vyazemsky) and "d'Anthès stopped by the barrier and waited, having covered his chest with his right hand" (the 1863 account to Ammosov).[50]

Tolstoy's portrayal of the wounded Dolokhov also concentrates on his body. It uses every opportunity to underscore Dolokhov's suffering, repeatedly mentioning his paleness, his quivering face, his visible efforts to overcome pain:

> He was pressing one hand to his left side, while the other clutched his drooping pistol. His face was pale. Rostov ran towards him and said something.

---

[49]   Leo Tolstoy, *War and Peace*, trans. Louise and Aylmer Maude, rev. and ed. Amy Mandelker (Oxford, UK: Oxford Univ. Press, 2010), 338; Lev Tolstoi, *Voina i mir*, in his *Polnoe sobranie sochinenii v 90 tomakh* (Moscow: Gosudarstvennoe izdatel'stvo khudozhestvennoi literatury, 1928–64), 10:26.

[50]   *Duel' Pushkina s Dantesom-Gekkerenom*, 55; K. K. Danzas, "Poslednie dni zhizni i konchina Aleksandra Sergeevicha Pushkina v zapisi A. Ammosova," in *A. S. Pushkin v vospominaniiakh sovremennikov*, 2:373.

"No-o-o!" muttered Dolokhov through his teeth, "No, it's not over." And after stumbling a few staggering steps right up to the sabre [marking the barrier], he sank on the snow beside it. His left hand was bloody; he wiped it on his coat and supported himself with it. His frowning face was pallid and quivering . . . Dolokhov lowered his head to the snow, greedily bit at it, again raised his head, adjusted himself, drew in his legs and sat up, seeking a firm centre of gravity. He sucked and swallowed the cold snow, his lips quivered, but his eyes, still smiling, glittered with effort and exasperation as he mustered his remaining strength. He raised his pistol and aimed . . . "Missed!" shouted Dolokhov, and he lay helplessly face downwards on the snow.[51]

The general scenario of Dolokhov's duel with Pierre strikingly resembles that of Pushkin's encounter with d'Anthès: one opponent shoots before reaching the barrier; the other is wounded in his side, falls, yet insists on making his shot, and faints right after. The passage reads very much like Danzas's account of the duel to Ammosov—one, however, that has absorbed the physiological details from Pushkin's death narratives. It seems that Tolstoy was not merely familiar with the documents concerning Pushkin's duel, but actively modeled his fictional duel upon it. Strangely, it is the unsympathetic Dolokhov who plays the role of the martyred poet.

After the duel, Dolokhov continues to behave like Pushkin: he not only stoically endures pain but also shows extreme concern for his mother—in great similarity to Pushkin's taking care not to frighten his wife. Many accounts mention this circumstance. In his 1863 story to Ammosov, Danzas reports: "On the way home, Pushkin was particularly concerned about not scaring his wife on arrival; he gave special instructions to Danzas on how to act so that this would not happen." In fact, Pushkin did exactly what Tolstoy makes his character do: he sent his second ahead to prepare the unsuspecting woman.[52]

---

51   Tolstoy, *War and Peace*, 338; *Voina i mir*, 10:26.

52   Danzas, "Poslednie dni zhizni i konchina Pushkina," 374.

On his way back to town after the duel, the wounded Pushkin also spoke of his friend, the famous *bretteur* Rufin Dorokhov. Ammosov writes down after Danzas:

> Pushkin recalled the duel that their common acquaintance, Shcherbachev, had with Dorokhov; in this duel Shcherbachev was mortally wounded in the stomach. Complaining of pain, [Pushkin] said to Danzas: "I am afraid that I may be wounded like Shcherbachev."[53]

Dorokhov is believed to be Tolstoy's chief model for Dolokhov.[54] This connection not only provides yet further evidence of Tolstoy's familiarity with the narratives of Pushkin's duel but also explains why he attributes the behavior of Russia's most beloved poet to a character whose integrity is at best ambivalent. Dolokhov is a collective portrait of the generation of which both Dorokhov and Pushkin were members. Dolokhov, the ruthless and merciless *bretteur*, is psychologically much closer to Pushkin than the reflective and hesitant Pierre is.

The dueling episode is the only one in the novel in which Dolokhov is portrayed sympathetically: the readers see him in the unexpected role of a loving son. His human qualities become apparent largely thanks to his revealed physical vulnerability:

> Rostov and Denisov drove away with the wounded Dolokhov.
>
> The latter lay silent in the sledge with closed eyes, and did not answer a word to the questions addressed to him. But on entering Moscow he suddenly came to, and lifting his head with an effort, took Rostov, who was seating beside him, by the hand. Rostov was struck by the totally altered and

---

[53]   Ibid.

[54]   Kathryn B. Feuer names Rufin's father, the 1812 war hero Ivan (1762–1815), as Tolstoy's model (see her *Tolstoy and the Genesis of "War and Peace,"* ed. Robin Feuer Miller and Donna Tussing Orwin [Ithaca, NY: Cornell Univ. Press, 1996], 237n27). While chronologically Ivan Dorokhov might seem a better-fitting model, psychologically he is not: it is the *bretteur* Rufin, twice reduced to the ranks for his duels and debauchery, who is Dolokhov's real original.

unexpectedly rapturous and tender expression on Dolokhov's
face.

"Well? How do you feel?" he asked.

"Bad! But it's not that, my friend—" said Dolokhov with
a gasping voice. "Where are we? In Moscow, I know. I don't
matter, but I have killed her, killed... She won't get over it! She
won't survive..."

"Who?" asked Rostov.

"My mother! My mother, my angel, my adored angel-
mother," and Dolokhov pressed Rostov's hand and burst into
tears.[55]

Dolokhov's affinity to Pushkin—as a duelist, a family man, and
a suffering human being—underscores his humanity. Tolstoy's
allusions to the narratives of Pushkin's fatal duel allow him to reveal
the aspects of Dolokhov's personality that the ruthless *bretteur* hides
so effectively.

Dostoevsky, in his dueling narratives, is extremely attentive to
the human body's vulnerability to physical violence. I use the term
"dueling narratives" to cover not only dueling scenes proper but
also numerous—and far more typical for Dostoevsky—situations
when a conflict over honor takes place but a duel does not—and
often cannot—occur. These situations are invariably marked by
extreme, grotesque violence: Dostoevsky's actual or potential
duelists either inflict disfiguring wounds on their opponents or beat
their faces to a pulp, or even bite them.[56] These violent and often
repulsive scenes demonstrate Dostoevsky's willingness to develop
the idiosyncrasies of post-Pushkin dueling discourse to the limit.

In one instance, Dostoevsky directly connects Pushkin's name
to the issue of violence to the human body—and a particularly
grotesque, brutal violence at that. Part 3, chapter 3 of *The Idiot*
features a curiously technical discussion between Aglaya and
Prince Myshkin in which the Pushkin-d'Anthès duel is mentioned

---

[55]   Tolstoy, *War and Peace*, 338–39; Tolstoi, *Voina i mir*, 10:27.

[56]   For a discussion of violence against the human body, especially against the
         face, in Dostoevsky's dueling narratives, see Reyfman, *Ritualized Violence
         Russian Style*, 228–55.

directly. At a time when Myshkin is under the threat of a challenge but naively does not suspect this, Aglaya covertly instructs him in the art of dueling. In the course of this instruction, they argue about the probability of being killed in a duel. Myshkin maintains that death in a duel is a rare occurrence and that d'Anthès wounded Pushkin by chance, but Aglaya disagrees:

> "I don't suppose that they often hit each other at duels."
>
> "Not often? But they killed Pushkin."
>
> "That may have been an accident."
>
> "It was not an accident. It was a duel to the death, and he was killed."
>
> "The bullet struck him so low down that Danthes [sic] probably aimed higher, at his chest or his head. No one aims so low, so that the bullet must have hit Pushkin by accident, by mere fluke. I've been told that by people who are experts in that sort of thing."
>
> "But a soldier I talked to once told me that, according to the army regulations, when spreading out for an attack, they are ordered to fire half way down [*v polcheloveka*]—that's the expression they use, 'half way down' [*v polcheloveka*]. So that, you see, they are ordered to fire not at the chest or the head, but half way down [*v polcheloveka*]. I asked an officer about it afterwards, and he told me it was quite true."[57]

The term *v polcheloveka*—literally, "at half a person"—is bluntly, brutally anatomical. It sounds worse than "at the chest" or "at the head," not only because it suggests dismemberment but also because it turns a human body into an effigy, a target for practicing marksmanship. Moreover, a duelist who aims *v polcheloveka* is detached from his victim. As Myshkin explains the meaning of the military order to shoot halfway down, "I expect that's because they shoot from a great distance."[58] Unlike Julie's father, a duelist shooting from afar cannot feel the blade entering his opponent's flesh and

---

[57]   Fyodor Dostoevsky, *The Idiot*, trans. David Magarshack (London: Penguin, 1955), 340; Dostoevskii, *Idiot*, in his *Polnoe sobranie sochinenii v 30-ti tomakh*, 8:294.

[58]   Ibid.

cannot see the blood rushing from his wounds. He therefore cannot be haunted by visions of the violence that he has inflicted and thus cannot experience remorse. He cannot learn from his experience, and this experience cannot be used to instruct others.

Dostoevsky seems to imply that violence involving physical contact, ugly as it is, might still be better than the detachment of a duelist who aims *v polcheloveka*.[59] Physical contact can force the aggressor to see the inflicted damage close-up—which, in turn, can interfere with his ability to inflict violence and thus make dueling problematic. This brings us back to Rousseau, who explores the consequences of seeing and feeling the damaged body of one's dueling opponent. Unlike the authors of earlier Russian dueling narratives who used the Rousseau formula to portray their characters' post-dueling remorse but rejected it as a recipe for avoiding dueling, Dostoevsky wants the spectacle of the damaged body to work as Rousseau envisioned it: not just punitively but also preventively. Contrary to Rousseau's, however, Dostoevsky's duelists cannot learn from others' experiences: they have to confront the consequences of their own violent actions.

Dostoevsky was the first Russian writer to explore in earnest ways for his fictional duelists to decline a duel. In doing so, he was keenly aware of Russian literature's traditional hostility to the very idea of backing out of a duel. He was also aware of the moral problems that the rejection of the honor code could pose. The best of Dostoevsky's characters, however, find ways to decline dueling without loss of honor. Prince Myshkin—a saintly fool, an *idiotes*—does it several times in the course of the novel. His sensitivity to human suffering, particularly to the violence done to the human

---

59   For this reason, biters are the least problematic of Dostoevsky's duelists. Apart from Stavrogin, whose biting the governor's ear is part of his image as a frivolous duelist, a parody of a *bretteur*, there are three biters in Dostoevsky's works: the underground man, who plans to bite Zverkov in order to force him to duel; the anonymous sub-lieutenant in *Demons*, who bites his superior after he humiliates him in front of his subordinates; and Ilyusha in *The Brothers Karamazov*, who bites Alyosha's finger to avenge his father's dishonor. All of them bite out of sheer desperation because no other recourse is available to them. For a treatment of the biting episode in *The Brothers Karamazov*, see Reyfman, *Ritualized Violence Russian Style*, 250.

face, enables him to do it spontaneously and gracefully.[60] Others, like the Elder Zosima, however, require special instruction, and Dostoevsky instructs them by making them aware of the human body's capacity to suffer. Zosima's conversion is preceded (and precipitated) by such a lesson. As a young and arrogant officer, Zosima slaps his orderly, Afanasy, and then suddenly acquires the ability to see his bloody beaten face. This experience not only leads him to apologize to Afanasy but also teaches him how to reconcile with his opponent in the upcoming duel. The fact that Afanasy is not—and cannot be—Zosima's dueling opponent is of secondary significance: Afanasy's beaten face teaches Zosima about the vulnerability of the human body in general, and this knowledge allows him to see that any violence, including the violence of the duel, is wrong. It also teaches him how to forgo dueling without disgracing himself.

In Dostoevsky's dueling narratives, Rousseau's argument regains its original power. However, it became useful for Russians only after the narrative of Pushkin's death had been absorbed by the Russian dueling discourse. It was the sight of the suffering body of the poet—who, ironically, until our days survives in the Russian cultural imagination as a paragon of dueling behavior—made them aware of the ambiguities of the duel. St. Augustine thus was not quite on the mark in his condemnation of "the lust of the eyes": spectacles of death can be morally instructive.

---

[60]   For a discussion of Myshkin's sensitivity to the human face, see Leslie Johnson, "The Face of the Other in *Idiot*," *Slavic Review* 50, no. 4 (1991): 867–78.

8. *The Sixth Tale of Belkin:*
Mikhail Zoshchenko as Proteus

Mikhail Zoshchenko wrote his "Sixth Tale of Belkin" in the fall of 1936, in the midst of general preparations for the Pushkin Jubilee, and published it in January of 1937. This was his contribution to the celebrations honoring "the luminous [*presvetlyi*] poet and philosopher Pushkin."[1] It is an unusual contribution, in that the story is an imitation of the stories included in Pushkin's collection *The Tales of Belkin* (1830). In post-classical, highbrow literature, imitation as an independent project, without additional aesthetic goals such as parody or stylization, has virtually disappeared, and unintentional imitation was regarded as a feature that lowered a work's literary value.

Zoshchenko, however, seemed unafraid to acknowledge his love for imitation. He begins his introduction to "The Sixth Tale of Belkin" with the following admission:

> In the days of my literary youth I felt something like envy toward those writers who were lucky enough to find a re-markable subject for their works . . .
>
> Even now there are a good many such subjects belonging to others [*chuzhikh siuzhetov*], to which I am not indifferent [*nespokoen*].
>
> I would like, for example, to use L. Tolstoy's topic—"How Much Land a Man Needs?"[2] This is an amazing topic, and it is executed by Tolstoy with colossal power. Nevertheless,

---

1   Mikhail Zoshchenko, *Golubaia kniga*, in his *Izbrannye proizvedeniia* (Leningrad: Khudozhestvennaia literatura, 1978), 2:73. "The Sixth Tale of Belkin" is on 1:507–20 of this edition. Hereafter, references to this publication are given in the text.

2   Zoshchenko distorts the title of the original: instead of Tolstoy's "Mnogo li cheloveku zemli nuzhno," he renders the title as "Skol'ko cheloveku zemli nuzhno."

I would like to approach it anew and in my own way [*zanovo i po-svoemu*].

I would like to write on some subjects of Maupassant's, Mérimée's, and so on. (507)[3]

As is well known, Zoshchenko not only declared his desire to imitate but, like Molière, freely "took his goods where he found them." For example, he recycled preexisting titles: "Confession," "Dangerous Liaisons," "Intrigue and Love," "Crime and Punishment," and many others.[4] By the time Zoshchenko began working on "The Sixth Tale," he had already "approached anew and in his own way" many of Tolstoy's topics, including the story "How Much Land Does a Man Need?": one of the stories included in his *Blue Book* (1934) is entitled "How Much Does a Man Need?"[5] However, Zoshchenko's use of these works is far from purely imitative: the title (even in a distorted form) raises certain expectations in an educated reader, which then clash with Zoshchenko's way of telling these stories on levels of both language and plot. The effect produced is comical.[6]

Pushkin, however, was not among the writers Zoshchenko parodied—at least, so he claimed: "But with respect to Pushkin I always had a special attitude [*osobyi schet*]. Not only some of

---

3   Throughout, Zoshchenko uses the word *siuzhet*, or plot, which I here translate as "subject" but consequently will translate as "plot." Whether Zoshchenko was aware of the Formalists' distinction between *siuzhet* and *fabula* and was willfully disregarding it by following a common usage is worth considering but would take me too far afield.

4   For more examples, see Kornei Chukovskii, "Iz vospominanii," in *Mikhail Zoshchenko v vospominaniiakh sovremennikov* (Moscow: Sovetskii pisatel', 1981), 66.

5   On this topic, see Alexander Zholkovsky, "Through Revolution's Looking Glass: Tolstoy into Zoshchenko," in his *Text Counter Text: Rereadings in Russian Literary History* (Stanford, CA: Stanford Univ. Press, 1994), 44.

6   The fact that the comic effect depends on the reader's knowledge of the original works reminds us that we should take Zoshchenko's claim that his prose is "accessible to the poor" with a grain of salt. For this claim see Mikhail Zoshchenko, "O sebe, o kritikakh i o svoei rabote," in *Mikhail Zoshchenko: Stat'i i materialy* (Leningrad: Academia, 1928), 11.

Pushkin's plots, but his manner, form, style, and structure were always significant [*pokazatel'ny*] for me" (507). In other words, Zoshchenko presents Pushkin as a model for imitation, not an object of parody: "It seemed to me (and also seems now) that Pushkin's prose is a precious standard [*obrazchik*] which should be studied by the writers of our time" (507).

Marietta Chudakova, in her book *The Poetics of Mikhail Zoshchenko*, suggests that Zoshchenko's close attention to Pushkin's prose in the mid-1930s was brought about by the writer's contemplation of his own development as a prose writer. She points out that "Zoshchenko, like Pushkin long ago, is interested in reforming prose as a whole—its genres, its language."[7] She compares Zoshchenko's attraction to documentary genres— biography, autobiography, scientific prose, what Vera Zoshchenko calls "the provenance of fact" —with Pushkin's interest in historical genres.[8]

From this point of view, *The Tales of Belkin* were an attractive object of imitation for Zoshchenko. The author who pretends to be the publisher of the supposedly real-life stories collected by an allegedly real-life narrator was a device used by Zoshchenko himself in *Sinebriukhov's Stories* (1922) and *Sentimental Tales* (1922–29). In "The Sixth Tale of Belkin," however, the situation is more complicated: instead of two- or three-member chains ("writer M. Z.—Sinebriukhov in *Sinebriukhov's Stories*," "Mikhail Zoshchenko—I. V. Kolenkorov in *Sentimental Tales*," or "publisher A. P. —Belkin—Belkin's

---

7   Marietta Chudakova, *Poetika Mikhaila Zoshchenko* (Moscow: Nauka, 1979), 150. Cf. Zoshchenko's opinion in the late 1920s about his contemporary prose writers: "And I want to say something about the language. It is now difficult for me to read the books of the majority of contemporary writers. For me their language is almost like Karamzin's. Their turns of phrase are like Karamzin's [rhetorical] periods." At that time, Zoshchenko assigned Pushkin's role to Viktor Shklovsky: "He was the first to rip apart the old form of literary language. He shortened the phrase. He 'introduced air' into his essays. It made reading easy and comfortable." Zoshchenko claims that he follows Shklovsky: "I have done the same" (Zoshchenko, "O sebe," 11).

8   Chudakova, *Poetika Mikhaila Zoshchenko*, 131; for Vera Zoshchenko's phrase, see her "Tvorcheskii put' Zoshchenko," in *Neizdannyi Zoshchenko*, ed. Vera von Wiren (Ann Arbor: Ardis, [1976]), 146.

informants in *The Tales of Belkin*"), Zoshchenko promises to create a far longer and more complicated chain: "Mikhail Zoshchenko—pseudo-Pushkin—pseudo-Belkin—pseudo-Belkin's sixth informant (non-existent in Pushkin's collection)." Zoshchenko himself points out the difficulty of the task:

> The complexity of such an imitation is particularly great because all five of Pushkin's tales are written as if by different narrators. Therefore I could not imitate a common manner (which would be easier), but had to introduce a truly new story, a story that could have existed among the tales of Belkin. (508)[9]

At the same time that he presents it as an imitation of Pushkin, Zoshchenko also pretends that his story is documentary, suggesting that the reader can ignore the complicated game of stylization: "In conclusion, I would like to say that my tale is based on a real fact, and thanks to this the exacting reader can read my work without projecting it onto the works of Pushkin" (509). This disclaimer, however, echoes the assertion of Belkin's anonymous friend, quoted in the publisher's preface, that the tales "are mostly truthful and were heard by him from various persons."[10] Thus Zoshchenko presents the reader with a multi-layered literary game that is far more complex than either a story based on reality or an imitation of his alleged model, Pushkin, with the purpose of studying his literary devices.[11]

---

[9]   Zoshchenko's count is inaccurate: Belkin's five tales are told to him by four narrators. Furthermore, as is well known, Pushkin does not follow the rules of his own game and does not develop separate narrative voices for his narrators. This is especially obvious in "The Shot," which is narrated by someone closely resembling Belkin instead of by Lieutenant Colonel I.L.P. as promised. This was pointed out by the tales' first readers. See Evgenii Toddes, "Neizvestnye teksty Kiukhel'bekera v zapisiakh Iu. N. Tynianova," in *Pushkin i russkaia literatura* (Riga: Latviiskii gos. universitet im. P. Stuchki, 1986), 90.

[10]   Aleksandr Pushkin, *Povesti Belkina*, in his *Polnoe sobranie sochinenii v 16-ti tomakh* (Moscow: Izdatel'stvo Akademii Nauk SSSR, 1937–59), 8:61. Hereafter, references to this volume are given in the text (8:61).

[11]   Walter Schamschula argues that "The Sixth Tale of Belkin" is an example

Let us examine the clues Zoshchenko offers us to help decipher his literary game. Most noticeable are the references to Pushkin's works, especially to *The Tales of Belkin* and to "The Shot," in particular. Zoshchenko's story resembles "The Shot" in many ways, both general and specific. Both are stories about the military officers that feature an enigmatic main character, two duels (one of which does not take place), a conflict with the regimental commander, and an affair with a married woman. Their narrative devices are also similar: both present a story within a story, use several first person narrators, create tension by introducing a mystery, and give "an unexpected incident" (*nechaiannyi sluchai*) a special role.[12] Zoshchenko's story also quotes Pushkin's story directly. Below are some examples:

Zoshchenko	*Pushkin*
унылое местечко (bleak little town)	бедное местечко (poor little town)
глухое местечко (remote little town)	

---

of "apocryphal narrative," in which the reader is offered an "apocryphal Pushkin," and a meaningful reading of the work is possible only if the reader knows the model. See his "On the Type of Historiographical Narrative in Slavic Literature," *A Journal for Descriptive Poetics and Theory of Literature* 6 (1979): 133–43. Even though this interpretation is fruitful, one should remember that, in contrast to real apocrypha or literary imitations of apocrypha (such as Bulgakov's "gospel" in *Master and Margarita*), Zoshchenko's tale is presented not as an original (a newly discovered work of Pushkin, for example), but as an apprentice's imitation. The relations between the primary and secondary texts are therefore different. Zoshchenko is playing a different game than Bulgakov. I would like to thank Walter Schamschula for bringing his article to my attention.

12   The common motifs have a different importance in Pushkin's story and in Zoshchenko's. For example, the dueling theme, pivotal in Pushkin's story, plays an auxiliary role in Zoshchenko's. An affair with a married woman is simply mentioned by Pushkin (Silvio's rival attracts the attention "of all the ladies, and especially the hostess herself," who had an affair with Silvio; 8:69) but is central for Zoshchenko. Similarly, a conflict with the commanding officer, just alluded to in Pushkin's story, becomes crucial in Zoshchenko's.

Zoshchenko	Pushkin
злоречие гусарского поручика Б. (Hussar Lieutenant B.'s sharp talk)	злой язык Сильвио (Silvio's sharp tongue)
ротмистр почел себя крайне обиженным (the cavalry captain regarded himself to be utterly insulted)	офицер . . . почел себя жестоко обиженным (the officer . . . regarded himself to be bitterly insulted)
поручик . . . страшно побледнел (the lieutenant . . . became terribly pale)	Сильвио встал, побледнев от злости (Silvio rose, pale with rage)
собеседники хотели схватиться за сабли (the interlocutors wanted to grab their swords)	мы бросились к саблям (we rushed to our swords)

More examples are easy to find. Moreover, Zoshchenko quotes some expressions many times. For example, he uses variations of Pushkin's phrase about "an unexpected incident [*nechaiannyi slu-chai*]" that "astonished everyone" (8:66) three times: "An incident helped us to fulfill our evil plan"; "However, an unfortunate incident [*neschastnyi sluchai*] interrupted these plans"; "An unexpected incident [*nechaiannoe proisshestivie*] changed everything" (510, 511, 513).

"The Blizzard" is another source. Zoshchenko's story is connected with it through the theme of the 1812 war with Napoleon, which Zoshchenko introduces using expressions similar to those of Pushkin (Zoshchenko, 512: "At the beginning of the year 1812, in a time [*v epokhu*] that was, as everyone knows, so stormy because of military events [*stol' burnuiu voennymi sobytiiami*], there served [*sluzhil*]—"; Pushkin, 8:77 and 85: "At the end of the year 1811, in a time that is memorable to us [*v epokhu nam dostopamiatnuiu*], there lived [*zhil*]—" and "At the beginning of the year 1812—").[13] The

---

13   Cf. also the opening of Pushkin's fragment of 1829: "At the beginning of the year 1812 our regiment was stationed in a small provincial town, where we

hero's name in "The Sixth Tale," designated by the letter *B*, can refer both to the character of Burmin, "a wounded Hussar Colonel with the St. George Cross in his buttonhole" (8:83), from "The Blizzard," and to "his Excellency Count B***" of "The Shot."[14]

Quotations from Pushkin's works establish a connection with *The Tales of Belkin* in the reader's mind. However, the most prevalent method of signaling Pushkin's presence in the story is not quoting, but "pushkinisms," more general imitations of the peculiarities of Pushkin's stylistics and usage, and perhaps, of Pushkin's poetics in general. One example of such stylization is the title of the "Sixth Tale of Belkin," "Talisman." It refers to Pushkin's poems "Guard me, my talisman" (1825) and "Talisman" (1827). Even though there are no direct connections between Zoshchenko's tale and these two poems, the title serves as a reference to Pushkin's oeuvre in general. Furthermore, it also creates a Pushkin-style paradox: the first talisman in Zoshchenko's work does not save its owner, the unfortunate cavalry captain, from a horrible death, but the owner of the second one is saved despite the fact that he has lost the magic object.[15]

Zoshchenko also reproduces Pushkin's poetics by supplying his tale with an epigraph. The use of an epigraph itself refers to Pushkin, but the fact that it is taken from an ode by Mikhail Kheraskov makes it unmistakably Pushkinian: most of Pushkin's epigraphs are drawn from eighteenth-century Russian poets, including Kheraskov. Furthermore, Zoshchenko attempts to imitate the way Pushkin plays with his epigraphs, which never relate directly to the piece they introduce. To do so, Zoshchenko cuts the

---

spent our time very merrily" (8:402). The fragment was published in 1931.

[14]   In the inserted story, the protagonist's name is K., similar to the "jurist K.," with whom Zoshchenko himself had a duel in Kislovodsk in 1913 (see Valentin Kaverin, "Molodoi Zoshchenko," in *Zoshchenko v vospominaniiakh sovremennikov*, 92). I will discuss the importance of the St. George Cross in Zoshchenko's story later in this chapter.

[15]   Cf. the paradoxes in Pushkin's poems: in the first one, the talisman guards the hero from life's cruelty even when he does not value his life anymore. In the second poem, the talisman wards off only infidelity, nothing else.

two last lines of the quoted quatrain and thus hides from the reader the part that relates to his story. The full quatrain reads:

> Не титла славу нам сплетают,
> Не предков наших имена—
> Одни достоинства венчают,
> И честь венчает нас одна.[16]

(It is not our titles that create our glory, / Not the names of our ancestors— / Only merits crown us, / Only honor crowns us.)

Together with the title, the epigraph refers the reader of "The Sixth Tale of Belkin" to Pushkin's poetics, to his love for play and paradoxes.

In his choice of language Zoshchenko also prefers stylization, not direct quoting. Chudakova points out some expressions that, in her view, constitute "successful approximations [*sblizheniia*] of Pushkin's prose." Other cases she describes as "a more naïve decoration of his style with 'Pushkinian' little words, repeated multiple times."[17] I refer the reader to her examples, but would like to point out one device that Zoshchenko particularly favors: using the conjunction "and" to connect words that normally are not used in coordinating constructions, both non-homogeneous parts and pairs of words that are semantically very close, almost synonymous: *sluchainye i neschastnye obstoiatel'stva* (accidental and unfortunate circumstances), *sluchaino i oshibochno poluchennyi krest* (the cross that was received accidentally and mistakenly), *prostrelennaia i izurodovannaia ruka* (shot-through and maimed hand), *neprilichno i chudovishchno* (improperly and monstrously), *polozhenie bylo neprilichno i skandal'no* (the situation was improper and scandalous). Pushkin also uses such expressions: *chestnye i blagorodnye roditeli* (honest and noble parents), *krotkii i chestnyi molodoi chelovek* (gentle and honest young man), *molodaia i prekrasnaia devushka* (young and beautiful girl), *mutnaia i zheltovataia mgla* (murky and yellowish haze/ darkness), *vnezapnoe i reshitel'noe ob''iasnenie* (sudden and decisive

---

16   Mikhail Kheraskov, *Izbrannye proizvedeniia* (Leningrad: Sovetskii pisatel', 1965), 95.

17   Chudakova, *Poetika Mikhaila Zoshchenko*, 151.

declaration). However, for the most part Pushkin's expressions are formulaic; furthermore, their frequency is negligible in comparison with Zoshchenko's. Such insistently repeated stylistic elements create an illusion of Pushkinian style that ultimately becomes onerous. The thrice-repeated expression "unexpected incident" and the twice-mentioned "clasping / squeezing of hands" (*pozhimanie ruk*) amplify the effect.[18] It seems as if Zoshchenko is intentionally overloading his tale with an excess of Pushkinian elements and thus violating stylistic verisimilitude.

The Pushkinian style is further compromised by Zoshchenko's use of stylistic anachronisms. In "Talisman," he consistently employs the stylistic elements of *skaz* that we normally encounter in his popular stories about contemporary Soviet life. One such device is using the conjunction "and" at the beginning of a sentence: "My soglasilis'. I utrom dolzhny byli peredat' poruchiku vyzov" ("We agreed. And in the morning we had to convey the challenge to the lieutenant"). Another is the frequent use of the adverb *dazhe* (even), particularly in a position characteristic of colloquial (non-standard) usage: *esli dazhe ego zhizn' ne byla sberezhena talismanom* instead of *esli ego zhizn' ne byla sberezhena dazhe talismanom* ("if even his life wasn't saved by the talisman" instead of "if his life wasn't saved even by the talisman"). Yet another incongruent stylistic feature is the use of highly colloquial expressions, such as *kuda devat'*, *vykhodil iz etogo s chest'iu*, or *i chto pust' etot talisman* ("where to shove it," "came out of this with honor," or "and that let this talisman"). Finally, Zoshchenko freely uses colloquialisms nonexistent in Pushkin's time: *prekrasno obespechennyi i izbalovannyi s nezhnogo vozrasta molodoi gusar* ("a young hussar, well provided for and spoiled from a tender

18   "The lieutenant gratefully began to clasp / squeeze our hands" and "We began to clasp / squeeze his hands" (511, 519). Cf. Pushkin's "The Stationmaster," in which the ostensibly sick Minsky "squeezes" (not clasps) Dunya's hand every time she offers him lemonade (8:101). The use of plural for the hands in Zoshchenko's story strongly suggests squeezing, not clasping. Consider the comical effect of using this gesture to describe the relations between nineteenth-century military men. This gesture is mentioned in a similar situation in Zoshchenko's *Sinebriukhov's Stories* (*Rasskazy Sinebriukhova*), in *Izbrannye proizvedeniia*, when the prince thanks Sinebriukhov for saving him during the gas attack (1:34). I will show that this coincidence is significant.

age"), *eshche v dostatochnoi stepeni molodaia i na redkost' krasivaia zhenshchina* ("a still young to a sufficient degree and exceptionally beautiful woman"), *do kontsa boevoi obstanovki* ("to the end of the battle situation"), *ne terial raspolozheniia dukha* ("didn't lose his disposition"), *nekotoroe kolichestvo georgievskikh krestov* ("some number of St. George Crosses"), *armeiskaia chast'* ("army unit").

Zoshchenko does not stop at using stylistic anachronisms: "Talisman" is full of violations of behavioral conventions of the epoch the story pretends to describe. To begin with, the tragic death of the hapless cavalry captain (who accidentally shoots himself while preparing his dueling pistols for an upcoming duel) seems not very probable in the light of dueling conventions. Prospective duelists were supposed to use unfamiliar weapons, and before the duel the seconds testified that the pistols had not been used by the opponents.[19] It is therefore unlikely that the cavalry captain would prepare his own pistols for the duel.

The young hussar's love affair with the wife of his commander also seems to be modernized. An open involvement with the wife of one's superior was not only "scandalous to the highest degree" (512) but most likely impossible. Such an affair cost Vronsky his career, even though it was not complicated by service relations between the cuckolded husband and the lucky lover. Furthermore, such a situation would dishonor the regimental commander and would require immediate action on his part. His complacent acceptance of his wife's improper behavior and her lover's offensive actions as described by Zoshchenko would surely mean the inglorious end of

---

[19]   Iu. M. Lotman, *Roman Pushkina "Evgenii Onegin": Kommentarii* (Leningrad: Prosveshchenie, 1980), 304; Aleksei Vostrikov, *Kniga o russkoi dueli* (St. Petersburg: Izd. Ivana Limbakha, 1998), 220–21. Both Lotman and Vostrikov refer to the early period in the history of dueling in Russia. In their dueling codes published in the early twentieth century, V. Durasov and A. A. Suvorin (A. Poroshin) state that if the offense is a physical assault (*oskorblenie deistviem*), the offended party has the right to use his personal weapon, and his opponent is allowed to do the same. In all other cases, the weapons had to be unfamiliar to the duelists. See V. Durasov, *Duel'nyi kodeks*, 4th ed. (St. Petersburg: [n.p.], 1912), 89; A. A. Suvorin (A. Poroshin), *Duel'nyi kodeks* (St. Petersburg: Knigoizdatel'stvo "Novyi chelovek," [1913]), 18. There is no physical assault in Zoshchenko's story.

his career.[20] Finally, it is unlikely that the unfaithful wife could so easily have married again so soon after her cuckolded husband's death—but she did, as we are told in the epilogue, and was "immeasurably happy" in her second marriage (520).[21]

It can be argued that our ideas about early nineteenth-century behavioral norms idealize the actual situation, and that, in fact, people of that time didn't necessarily behave as we imagine was proper. However, even in this case, my examples are "anachronistic" because Zoshchenko claims to be reconstructing the world of Pushkin's *Tales of Belkin*, and in this world, the behavior of Zoshchenko's characters is hardly possible.

As Chudakova points out, there is no doubt that such anachronisms and stylistic blunders constitute a consciously constructed device.[22] In his introduction to the story, Zoshchenko actually warns his readers that such inaccuracies are not only inevitable but simply necessary:

> Possibly, and even certainly, in my copy I have erred against style and, mostly, against character description [*obrisovki kharakterov*]; but in my copy I couldn't leave certain things [*koe-chto*] in their age-old fixity [*v vekovoi nepodvizhnosti*].
>
> It would be better to transmit every little feature of Pushkin's prose in the form in which it exists [*v tom vide, kak ona est'*], but the feelings of a writer of my time have probably added a different flavor, even though I have tried to avoid it. (508–9)

---

[20]   Regardless of the insulted husband's personal beliefs, the convention strongly suggested dueling. Tolstoy's Pierre and Karenin come to mind: the former cannot help but duel with Dolokhov and the latter seriously contemplates challenging Vronsky. True, in "Talisman" the rivals' inequality of rank made a duel awkward, but one way or another, the regimental commander was responsible for his wife's indecent behavior and had to put an end to the affair. Instead he promises her to petition the tsar to restore her lover's rank, of which he was stripped for dueling.

[21]   One wonders whether Zoshchenko could be referring to Pushkin's situation and Natalya Nikolaevna Pushkina's happy second marriage: after all, the story was written to commemorate Pushkin's death. Natalya Nikolaevna waited six years before she married Petr Lanskoy in 1843, however.

[22]   Chudakova, *Poetika Mikhaila Zoshchenko*, 151.

Zoshchenko attempts to present his errors as involuntary, but his usage of the pronoun *koe-chto* suggests intention: unintentional modernization would be described by the pronoun *vse* (everything). "Errors" are likely to signal that Zoshchenko's imitation of Pushkin's prose is only a sign, a reference to Pushkin that the writer needs for some more complicated purpose than an accurate reproduction of Pushkin's style.

It is crucial in this context that Pushkin's prose is not the only source of Zoshchenko's "Talisman": the epoch that the story describes refers the reader to Tolstoy. Granted, any literary work about the War of 1812 written after *War and Peace* is likely to be compared with Tolstoy's epic. However, "The Sixth Tale of Belkin" contains numerous specific references to Tolstoy's work. The main character of "Talisman," for example, is transferred into the *** Infantry Regiment from the Guards: a detail that is absent in Pushkin's tales. In *War and Peace*, however, a minor character, Lieutenant Teliatin, is transferred from the Guards to a less prestigious regiment; moreover, like Zoshchenko's character, Teliatin is disliked by his comrades. The circumstances of Lieutenant K.'s flight from captivity resemble Nikolay Rostov's escape from the French: for both it is marked by an injured hand or arm. Another similarity is Lieutenant K.'s temporary loss of his talisman, which resembles the episode in which Prince Andrey, wounded in the Battle of Austerlitz, is robbed by the French of the icon that his sister gave him to keep him safe, only to get it back after Napoleon notices him. The episodes of decorating soldiers who distinguished themselves in battle are also similar in the two works. In Tolstoy's description of the meeting of Alexander and Napoleon in Tilsit in 1807, Napoleon asks Alexander to name the bravest Russian soldier and personally awards a Legion of Honor medal to him. Likewise, in "Talisman," the Grand Duke asks the regimental commander "to name those who distinguished themselves the most on the battlefield" and personally "pins" (*prikalyvaet*) St. George Crosses to their uniforms. Lieutenant K.'s "elderly parent" (*prestarelyi roditel'*) suggests killing Napoleon by feeding him his own body parts, which resembles the style of the leaflets written by Rostopchin that Tolstoy quotes in the third book of his epic. In addition, this "elderly parent," who despises "Napoleonishka" and corresponds with his son's commander, looks like a parody of the elder Bolkonsky, who also despises "the contemptible little Frenchman" (*nichtozhnyi frantsuzishka*) and corresponds with his son's commander, Kutuzov. The demoted Guards Lieutenant K.—the troublemaker, gambler, and *bretteur*; the seducer of married women who talks back to his commander—closely resembles Tolstoy's Dolokhov. Furthermore, at some point both behave heroically: Lieutenant K. does so in order to be worthy of the St. George Cross that he has received by mistake, and Dolokhov, to regain his rank as a commissioned officer. Finally, the motif of the St. George Cross is common to both works: it is the most frequently mentioned decoration in Tolstoy's epic, and in Zoshchenko's story, it is at the center of the conflict of honor.

These common motifs and details allow us to consider *War and Peace* as one of the sources of "The Sixth Tale of Belkin." Zoshchenko's mentioning, in the introduction to the story, his desire to "borrow" from Tolstoy is thus not accidental: in his story, he in fact treats a Tolstoyan theme, the War of 1812, "anew and in his own way [*zanovo i po-svoemu*]." He does this, however, not directly, but using Pushkin as an intermediary.

Zoshchenko was not the first to come up with the idea of transposing the Tolstoyan rendering of the Napoleonic War into Pushkin's style: it was first suggested by Konstantin Leont'ev in his essay *Analysis, Style, and Atmosphere: About Count L. N. Tolstoy's Novels* (1890; first published in 1911). In the conclusion of his analysis, Leont'ev suggests conducting the following mental experiment:

> I will allow myself, to better clarify my critical idea, to imagine something that is already impossible as an actual event but which, as a *retrospective fantasy*, is, I think, quite natural. I will allow myself to imagine that D'Anthès missed his mark and that in the *1840s* Pushkin wrote a long novel about the year 1812.[23]

---

23   Konstantin Leont'ev, *Analiz, stil' i veianie. O romanakh gr. L. N. Tolstogo* (repr.; Providence, RI: Brown Univ. Press, 1968), 112. Emphases in the original.

Leont'ev needs this experiment to illustrate one of the crucial points of his essay—namely, the fundamental stylistic differences between what he calls the "Pushkinian" and "Gogolian" periods of Russian literature. Leont'ev gives credit to the Gogolian period (which, in his view, begins with *Dead Souls* and ends with Tolstoy's "What People Live By," 1882), particularly for psychological analysis, at which he considers Tolstoy to be a master. Nonetheless, Leont'ev generally believes that the Pushkinian period is superior: consistent in style, chaste, and healthy. In his introduction to "The Sixth Tale of Belkin," Zoshchenko offers a very similar picture of Russian literary history:

> Sometimes it even seemed to me that, together with Pushkin, there died the genuine national trend [*narodnaia linia*] in Russian literature that began with such an amazing brilliancy and which (in the second half of the past century) was replaced by psychological prose that is, in essence, alien to our nation's spirit. (507)

Leont'ev's and Zoshchenko's main points are the same: both value "national" principles in literature, both believe that after Pushkin Russian literary style deteriorated, both doubt the validity of psychological analysis in literature. Furthermore, Zoshchenko's praise for Pushkin's style, given in the introduction to "The Sixth Tale of Belkin" ("An ability to engage the reader [*zanimatel'nost'*], conciseness and precision in exposition, utter elegance of form, irony—these are the traits that make Pushkin's prose attractive," 507), is very similar to Leont'ev's characterization of Pushkin's style as concise, simple, and elegant. Finally, Leont'ev and Zoshchenko agree that Tolstoy concludes the Gogolian period, returning in his stories for the people to truly national literary principles: Leont'ev praises the story "What People Live By," and Zoshchenko admires "How Much Land Does a Man Need?"

Even more remarkable is that in his recasting of the Tolstoyan theme of the Napoleonic War, Zoshchenko not only conducts the experiment suggested by Leont'ev but also follows his prescriptions in doing so. In Leont'ev's opinion, to remove the stylistic anachronisms he finds disgraceful in Tolstoy's prose (that is, to reconstruct the spirit of the time he portrays), it is necessary to "strain" (*protsedit'*) the descriptions of the characters "through a special kind of mental *filter*":

> 1) *To simplify* (mentally, *in your own* mind) Tolstoy's language in general; to make it more like the language of Pushkin's prose or like the language of Tolstoy himself in his short tale "The Prisoner of the Caucasus" or in his other stories *purified of naturalism*.
> 2) To get rid of superfluous looking into [*podgliadyvaniia*] the characters' psyches entirely.
> 3) To cast out of the narrative all those expressions, turns of phrases, and epithets that are *too [clearly] in the spirit of the post-Pushkinian* school and all those repetitions of a special sort that are characteristic of Tolstoy himself (as a participant of that school): "strange," "strange" [*chuzhdyi*], "hands," "hands," "hastily," "sobbing" [*vskhlipyvaniia*], "luscious mouth" [*sochnyi rot*], the too frequent "tremor of the lower jaw" attributed to different people and because of different sorts of emotions, and so on.[24]

Zoshchenko has changed Tolstoy's style according to Leont'ev's suggestions: he gave the style a Pushkinian ring, having rejected both psychological analysis and what Leont'ev considered to be the stylistics of the Gogolian Natural School. A profoundly psychological description of Nikolay Rostov's escape from the French is reduced to several simple details: the character's running, the bullets' buzzing, the wounded hand, and eventual deliverance from danger among Russians. In addition, Zoshchenko avoids psychologizing epithets, using only factual and general ones. For example, a dramatic scene, in which the main character burns off

---

[24]   Leont'ev, *Analiz*, 132, 133 (emphases in the original). The fourth point suggests "reject[ing] the possibility of admiring Karataev" as an anti-historical manifestation of Slavophilism. "Hands" are in Leont'ev's interpretation an example of inappropriate naturalism (see 91, 92, 98). We may suppose that Zoshchenko introduced the burned hands as a prominent motif in his "Talisman" under the influence of Leont'ev's critique of Tolstoy: the frequency of this motif in the story seems to challenge Leont'ev's critique. At the same time, however, in Zoshchenko's story, the references to hands are included not for the sake of excessive verisimilitude (as, in Leont'ev's view, they are in Tolstoy's prose) but strictly as plot devices.

the ropes that bind his hands in a bonfire, is descriptive, not analytical:

> Barely restraining himself from crying out in hellish [*adskaia*] pain, K., using a furious effort of will, suppressed the incredible pain. Little by little, the red-hot coals burned through the rope, scorching his palms and fingers. (517)

As a result, his story actually begins to sound somewhat Pushkinian. One can even apply to it Tolstoy's definition of Pushkin's prose as lacking in psychology: "In the new trend the interest in the details of emotions replaces the interest of events. The tales of Pushkin look somehow bare."[25] In this respect Zoshchenko's attempt to imitate Pushkin's style is quite successful.

The question as to whether Zoshchenko knew Leont'ev's article cannot be answered with certainty. However, there are strong indications that he did. When Zoshchenko wrote "Talisman," Leont'ev's "experiment" caught the interest of Boris Eikhenbaum, with whom Zoshchenko was in close and frequent contact. Even more importantly, his story "Photograph" (1943) resembles Leont'ev's description of Tolstoy's creative method in *War and Peace*. Leont'ev compares Tolstoy's depiction of his material to overexposure in photography:

> One of my friends who was forty years old was photographed in the depths of the country [*v glushi*] and without good equipment [*bez udobstv*] by an inexperienced photographer. The features of his face, the expression of his eyes came out very accurately; but in the photograph instead of forty he looked about sixty . . . The photograph was taken on a bright day in bright sunlight, and all of his fine wrinkles became very deep and very black.[26]

This is exactly what happens to Zoshchenko's character in the 1943 story: photographed under harsh light, he looks much older in the picture than in real life.

---

[25] Lev Tolstoi, *Polnoe sobranie sochinenii v 90 tomakh* (Moscow: Gosudarstvennoe izdatel'stvo khudozhestvennoi literatury, 1928–64), 46:188.

[26] Leont'ev, *Analiz*, 127.

If my contention is correct and Zoshchenko indeed knew Leont'ev's essay, it follows that his artistic game is far more complicated than he claims in his introduction. He not only imitates Pushkin's style in *The Tales of Belkin* but, at the same time, realizes Leont'ev's "retrospective fantasy," using the critic's prescriptions to present a Tolstoyan theme in a Pushkinian manner.

However, the chain of identity changes doesn't stop here. While "imitation" of Tolstoy by Pushkin was possible only as a fantasy, imitation of Pushkin by Tolstoy is a recognized fact. Moreover, Tolstoy's imitation of Pushkin is similar to Zoshchenko's: Tolstoy "borrows" Pushkin's titles ("The Prisoner of the Caucasus") and plots (*The Cossacks* resembles Pushkin's *The Gypsies*; *Anna Karenina* refers both to *Eugene Onegin* and to the fragment "The Guests Were Arriving at the Dacha").[27] Finally, Tolstoy uses expressions very similar to those of Zoshchenko when he speaks of his admiration for Pushkin. On March 19, 1873, Sophia Tolstaya wrote down his words about Pushkin: "I am learning a lot from Pushkin; he is my father, and it is necessary to learn from him."[28] At the same time, Tolstoy writes about *The Tales of Belkin* to E. G. Golokhvastov: "Every writer needs to study them, and to study them again."[29] The number of imitators thus increases: not only does Zoshchenko imitate Pushkin and Pushkin "imitates" Tolstoy, but Tolstoy also imitates Pushkin.

Having outlined all the literary games Zoshchenko seems to be playing, I would like to remind the reader that he claims in his introduction that "Talisman" can also be read as a real-life story. Is this a reference to the introduction to *The Tales of Belkin*, which also claims that all the stories in the collection are the real-life stories, or does Zoshchenko means what he says?

The toponymy of "Talisman" may be useful here. The action

---

[27]   See Barbara Lönnqvist, "The Pushkin Text in *Anna Karenina*," in "Pushkin's Secret": Russian Writers Reread and Rewrite Pushkin, vol. 1 of *Two Hundred Years of Pushkin*, ed. Joe Andrew and Robert Reid, Studies in Slavic Literature and Poetics 37 (Amsterdam: Rodopi, 2003), 67–75.

[28]   S. A. Tolstaia, *Dnevniki*, vol. 1, *1862–1900* (Moscow: Khudozhestvennaia literatura, 1978), 500.

[29]   Tolstoi, *Polnoe sobranie sochinenii v 90 tomakh*, 57:22.

begins in a "bleak little town [*mestechko*]," a reference to Pushkin's *mestechko* *** in "The Shot." The action of the interpolated story about the unruly hussar begins, in all probability, in St. Petersburg or in its vicinity, since the character serves in the guards regiment and gambles for high stakes, and his behavior is being talked about "in every high society drawing room" (512), which sums up Petersburg high life. As the war begins, the regiment decamps and ends up in *mestechko* S***. In several days, the action moves "to the south of *mestechko* N."

Naming towns *mestechki* can reflect the fact that the military action in which the character participates is taking place in the western parts of the Russian Empire, at the very beginning of the 1812 campaign. Simple chronological calculations, however, don't support this supposition: as we know, Napoleon's army moved so fast within Russian territory that a regiment that left Petersburg at the beginning of hostilities should have met the enemy far to the east of the sort of places where the word *mestechko* was used. Even in the text of "Talisman," the swiftness with which the French moved is mentioned: "The French hordes swiftly approached the heart of our dear [*liubeznogo*] fatherland" (513). It seems that the place of action bifurcates: historical verisimilitude refers us to "the heart of our dear fatherland," the center of European Russia, Moscow; the toponymy, however, violating historical accuracy, detains the action on the border with Poland.

The western parts of Russia and Poland played a significant role in Zoshchenko's own life: it is there, in 1915–17, more than a hundred years after the events described in "Talisman," that the writer himself participated in World War I. It is known that in this period of his life Zoshchenko's behavior was brave to the point of recklessness. In 1913, as he wrote in his autobiography, he "went to the Caucasus. Had a duel with a lawyer [*pravoved*] K. After this I immediately felt that I was an exceptional person, a hero, and adventurer; I went to war as a volunteer."[30] In the war, he behaved heroically, was wounded three times, and received several decorations for bravery.

---

[30]   I quote from Kaverin, "Molodoi Zoshchenko," 92.

One of the most memorable events during this time was a gas attack on July 20, 1916, near the *mestechko* Smorgon. Zoshchenko writes about this event in his book *Before Sunrise* (1943) and, which is important for my argument, connects Smorgon with the War of 1812:

> I stand in the trenches and curiously look at the ruins of the *mestechko*. It is Smorgon. The right flank of our regiment is near the vegetable gardens of Smorgon.
> This is a famous *mestechko*, from which Napoleon fled, passing the command to Murat.[31]

Let us note that the word *mestechko* is used twice in this short passage.

World War I interested Zoshchenko long before he analyzed its impact on the psyche of his autobiographical hero in *Before Sunrise*; it is the subject of *Sinebriukhov's Stories* (1921). Furthermore, beginning in 1922 Zoshchenko repeatedly talked about writing another work on the same topic. Sometimes he called it a novel, sometimes a cycle of stories, and the tentative title was to be either *The Notes of an Officer* or *The Notes of a Former Officer*. We don't know much about Zoshchenko's plans for this work, but we can be fairly confident that it was to be based on his own life. Thus, the writer points out in his 1922 autobiography: "I was an officer. I will not say more, because this will lead me to steal from myself. Currently, I am writing *The Notes of a Former Officer*, not about myself, of course, but everything will be there."[32] As Mikhail Slonimsky recalls, Zoshchenko planned to write a "healthy" work: full of adventures, with "a mind-boggling plot," a positive main character, and a happy ending.[33]

Zoshchenko never wrote this work. However, an autobiographical basis can be easily detected in *Sinebriukhov's Stories*,

---

[31]   Mikhail Zoshchenko, *Pered voskhodom solntsa*, in his *Sobranie sochinenii v trekh tomakh* (Leningrad: Khudozhestvennaia literatura, 1987), 3:484.

[32]   I quote from Chudakova, *Poetika Mikhaila Zoshchenko*, 178.

[33]   See M. Slonimskii, "Mikhail Zoshchenko," in *Mikhail Zoshchenko v vospominaniiakh sovremennikov*, 122.

which, as Chudakova suggests, was the first part of a "diptych" about an orderly and an officer.[34] Thus, the characters of *Sinebriukhov's Stories*, Sinebriukhov and "prince, your Excellency" (*kniaz' vashe siiatel'stvo* is the appellation Sinebriukhov consistently uses for the officer to whom he is assigned), experience a gas attack, like Zoshchenko himself and his autobiographical hero in *Before Sunrise*. It is noteworthy that the aggregate behavior of Sinebriukhov and the prince is similar to that of the hero in *Before Sunrise*: the hero is in a dugout, hears some noise, realizes that a gas attack is in progress, alerts others, and gets a gas mask for himself.[35] In *Sinebriukhov's Stories*, these actions are divided between the orderly and the officer: the prince is in a dugout, while Sinebriukhov stands sentinel, hears the noise, realizes that the gas attack is in progress, alerts others, and gets a gas mask for the prince.[36] In *Before Sunrise*, the hero then lights the brushwood that was on hand in case of a gas attack. When the attack ends, the hero goes through a paroxysm of terrible vomiting. These actions are also distributed between Sinebriukhov and the prince: the former "makes a little fire according to the training manual [*kosterik razlozhil po ustavu*]" and the latter "puked a little bit [*malekhon'ko pobleval*]."[37]

But *Sinebriukhov's Stories*, "based on real life," are surprisingly similar to the other "real life" story by Zoshchenko, namely "The Sixth Tale of Belkin." In this respect the story "Viktoriya Kazimirovna" especially stands out. Its action takes place in the then-Polish (now Belorussian) *mestechko* Krevo, and, as in "The Sixth Tale," the word *mestechko* is persistently repeated. In "Talisman," five soldiers "step out" to receive their decorations. In "Viktoriya Kazimirovna," volunteers are called out for a reconnaissance mission, and the wording to describe the scene is similar: "Five people, I remember, stepped out, and I [stepped out] with them."[38]

---

[34]   Chudakova, *Poetika Mikhaila Zoshchenko*, 178.

[35]   Zoshchenko, *Pered voskhodom solntsa*, 484.

[36]   Zoshchenko, *Rasskazy Sinebriukhova*, in his *Izbrannye proizvedeniia*, 1:34.

[37]   Ibid.

[38]   Ibid., 47.

Furthermore, in "Talisman" the main hero also volunteers for a reconnaissance mission. His life is safeguarded by a talisman, given to him by Varen'ka L., who is in love with him, whereas Sinebriukhov is safeguarded by Fate, as was foretold to him in 1916 by a "learned/trained [*uchenaia*] bird."[39] During their mission, both characters kill an enemy and go through his pockets: the hussar finds his talisman, and Sinebriukhov procures a watch (*chasishki*) for his beloved Viktoriya Kazimirovna. Fleeing their enemies, both characters injure their hands: the hussar, as we remember, does this while burning through the rope that binds his hands together; and Sinebriukhov, while climbing over barbed wire. This detail is central in "Talisman," but it is also important in "Viktoriya Kazimirovna" and is mentioned several times. The characters also return to their regiments in a similar way: they run, the enemy shoots, and each is wounded in the shoulder; each hero faints as soon as he is among friends. Both characters are awarded St. George Crosses and both take them off in the presence of their rivals, albeit in different circumstances: Lieutenant K., in delirium, tears off the award and casts it to the feet of his beloved's husband, whereas Sinebriukhov's rival orders him: "Take off your St. George Cross, [because] it looks like I am going to hit you."[40] It is noteworthy that during the farewell scene between the hussar and Varen'ka in "Talisman," Varen'ka's husband, who interrupts the lovers, nearly strikes his rival with a whip (514).

The similarities between *Sinebriukhov's Stories* and "Talisman" go beyond analogous circumstances and adventures: even though these works are stylistically different, the literary devices used are often similar. Both works insist that they are "documentary," based on real-life events. To achieve the effect of authenticity, both works employ narrators who witness the narrated events. Furthermore, both works are attributed to fictitious authors: Sinebriukhov and pseudo-Pushkin, respectively. Finally, both works describe unusual, mind-boggling incidents. But all the devices listed are also used by

---

[39]   Ibid., 48.

[40]   Ibid., 51.

Pushkin in *The Tales of Belkin*, which makes *Sinebriukhov's Stories* itself a kind of copy of Pushkin's work. Rereading Zoshchenko's introduction to "Talisman" carefully, we notice that Zoshchenko refers to some earlier, not quite successful, attempt to imitate Pushkin: "In any case, in my literary youth, as hard as I tried, I could not produce a copy like this. I didn't understand the complexity of [Pushkin's] skill [*masterstva*] and didn't have the mastery of color that was needed" (508). We can even find references to Pushkin's works in *Sinebriukhov's Stories*: the beautiful proud Polish woman (*gordaia poliachka*) in "High Society Story"; an echo of the *Mermaid* plot in "Viktoriya Kazimirovna"; excessive repetition by Sinebriukhov of the title of his officer, "Prince, your Excellency," which recalls the analogous repetition of the title "Count, your Excellency" in the concluding passages of "The Shot."

The fact that both works by Zoshchenko refer to Pushkin strengthens the connection between them. It makes *Sinebriukhov's Stories* yet another source for "Talisman." It turns out that Zoshchenko is imitating not only Pushkin and Tolstoy, but also Nazar Sinebriukhov, the fictitious author of *Sinebriukhov's Stories*, and thus his own youthful self. At the same time, an imitation of Pushkin's work reveals itself as the realization of Zoshchenko's plan to write an adventure story about an officer. The documentary character of "Talisman" is thus of the same nature as that of *The Tales of Belkin* and *Sinebriukhov's Stories*.[41]

This chain of references and copies, in my view, is not the "bad infinity" of a scholar's associations. On the contrary, as the main structural principle of "Talisman," it provides a clue to understanding this seemingly unserious and marginal work. The story's objective, I believe, was far more significant than improving Zoshchenko's style by learning from a genius. Granted, Zoshchenko does speak about style in his introduction, and his possible realization of Leont'ev's "experiment" in "Talisman" also demonstrates his interest in literary stylistics. It is clear, however, that it was not in the naïve imitation of Pushkin's style (realized in "Talisman" with

---

41   Let us recall the autobiographical nature of "The Shot," which includes details of one of Pushkin's duels in Kishinev.

obvious laxity) that Zoshchenko searched for a means to renew the language of literature and, more broadly, literature in general.

Much more important than the imitation of Pushkin's style in "Talisman" was Zoshchenko's following Pushkin in recreating his artistic freedom as manifested in his well-known play with authorial masks—in the so-called Protean nature of his creativity. The free play that we find in "Talisman" is what Zoshchenko borrows from his predecessor. Most important in this respect is the fact that the persona of Zoshchenko, the author in "The Sixth Tale of Belkin," is as fictitious as his other characters. In the introduction, Zoshchenko presents himself as a modest admirer of established literary authorities who envies their ability to find good subjects for their works. He also insists that he is a respectful imitator of Pushkin. But Zoshchenko tricks his reader, not so much imitating Pushkin's style as transforming his own image as author: he appears not only in the promised mask of Pushkin as Belkin but also in the masks of Pushkin as Tolstoy and Zoshchenko as Sinebriukhov.[42] Zoshchenko himself uses the word "mask" in the introduction to "Talisman" (508). He stresses the playfulness of this device and asserts that Pushkin himself sanctioned the playful use of Belkin's mask:

> Pushkin was great in his work and, laughing, wrote (to Pletnev), that some literati are already using Belkin's name to their advantage [*promyshliaiut imenem Belkina*] and that this pleases him; but, at the same time, he would like to announce that the real Belkin has died and doesn't accept the sins of others as his own. (509)

Pushkin's letters to Pogodin (early May of 1835) and to Pletnev (October of the same year) show Pushkin being somewhat

---

42   It is useful to recall Zoshchenko's "An Incident in the Provinces" (1924), a story with an autobiographical narrator who, together with his fellow writers, is supposed to read his literary works in front of an audience. The audience, however, expects not a literary reading, but a performance by an actor capable of changing (transforming) his appearance. As each writer takes the stage, he is greeted with laughter by the audience, which admires the supposed actor's ability to transform his looks. Chudakova (*Poetika Mikhaila Zoshchenko*, 64) points out the importance of this story for understanding of Zoshchenko's views on the nature of art.

annoyed by Senkovsky's using the pen-name Belkin. He isn't laughing in these letters: Zoshchenko's interpretation is forced. It appears that it was important for Zoshchenko to stress that Pushkin wanted to resolve his conflict with Senkovsky playfully.[43] Crucially, it is Pushkin's ability to play and laugh that makes him "great" in Zoshchenko's eyes.

In my view, Zoshchenko's insistence on the writer's right to play, changing his "face" and style, was his response to the problems that Russian literature faced in the 1930s. It was his assertion that art was free, his refusal to fulfill any social mandate, his rejection of the simplified, "Jubilee" understanding of apprenticeship to the great predecessors. Finally, it was his response to the then-fresh official call for *narodnost'* in art. The writer chose an elegant way to remind his readers that it was Pushkin's ability to change his "masks," his ability to be playful, the versatility of his gift, and his ability to transform and to imitate creatively that allowed Dostoevsky in his "Pushkin Speech" to proclaim him as the people's (*narodnyi*) poet.

---

[43]   We can point out yet another mask used by Zoshchenko, that of Senkovsky, Baron Brambeus, the well-known master of mystifications: "A hundred years have past, and now I 'use the name of Belkin' ['*promyshliaiu' Belkinym*] for a different purpose" (509).

Part Three

TOLSTOY

Preface

This part is mostly devoted to Tolstoy's struggle with the inevitability of death—the struggle that often undermined his power over language. It also explores the ways he firmly guides the reader to accept his point of view, exercising precisely this very power. In the first article, I examine how Tolstoy's narrator in his story "Three Deaths" controls the reader's perception of the story's characters in such a way that the reader believes the unbelievable: that the dying young woman may be just pretending to be dying, even though the reader sees her dead body shortly after her energetic and lengthy egotistical outbursts. Tolstoy's narrator attempts to convince his reader not only that to die unfeelingly and unthinkingly is the best way to go, but also that such an attitude toward death can be achieved by a rational being. Tolstoy is determined to force the reader to accept his rigid view of a proper death, and he does so by rejecting not only the main points of Turgenev's story "Death" but also its narrative method, which allows the story's readers to form their own view of dying characters.

In the second article, on *Family Happiness*, I am also interested in how Tolstoy makes his reader accept the idea that it is the novella's heroine who is to blame for departure of eros from her marital relationship. Most importantly, by having the heroine narrate how it happens, Tolstoy is able to convince the reader that the view of female sexuality that he propagates in the novella is indeed accurate.

The next article, on Tolstoy's "Notes of a Madman," explores Tolstoy's use of Gogol's eponymous story. I argue that, among other things, Tolstoy is attracted by the similarity of his and Gogol's spiritual development, which led each of them to religious conversion and to rejection (at least partial, in Tolstoy's case) of the value of art, including verbal art. The theme of insanity, central to Tolstoy's narrative of conversion, was also instrumental in Tolstoy's attempt to use Gogol's story as his model.

The last article concentrates on Tolstoy's mostly unsuccessful post-conversion attempts to formulate the guidelines for a correct way to die. Likely inspired, among other sources, by "The Wanderer," Pushkin's poetic transposition of introductory passages from John Bunyan's *Pilgrim's Progress*, Tolstoy endeavors time and again to create a narrative of leaving home and sinful life in search of truth and of acceptance of death. In two of the three stories that I analyze ("Notes of a Madman" and "Posthumous Notes of the Elder Fyodor Kuzmich"), Tolstoy is unable to finish his narratives, at least in part because of the difficulty of putting in words the explanation of the correct way of accepting death. Apparently he is able to complete the third work, the biography of Buddha, because transposing the existing story offers less resistance. However, Tolstoy still doesn't succeed in convincingly verbalizing the rules for proper dying. The only "text" that Tolstoy brings to an end is his own reenactment of Pushkin's "The Wanderer," by leaving his home on the eve of his death and by dying in Astapovo.

9. Turgenev's "Death" and Tolstoy's "Three Deaths"

In his *Problems of Dostoevsky's Poetics*, Bakhtin presents Leo Tolstoy's 1858 story "Three Deaths" as an example of a quintessentially monologic work. The structure of the story, he argues, is intrinsically closed, and the three plotlines are isolated from one another, connected only in the author's perspective. The three main characters (the lady, the peasant Fyodor, and the tree) are not given their own voices but are judged *"in absentia"* (zaochno)—that is, are deprived of a chance to respond to the author's judgment. The author's point of view is the only one present and, as a result, the only correct one. Bakhtin concludes:

> Thus, despite the multiple levels in Tolstoy's story, it contains neither polyphony nor (in our sense) counterpoint. It contains only *one cognitive subject*, all else being merely *object* of its cognition. Here a dialogic relationship of the author to his heroes is impossible, and thus there is no "great dialogue"

in which characters and author might participate with equal rights; there are only the objectivized dialogues of characters, compositionally expressed within the author's field of vision.[1]

In her 1985 article "The Tolstoy Connections in Bakhtin," Caryl Emerson rightly argues that by applying his notions of polyphonic and dialogical discourses to Tolstoy's texts, Bakhtin ends up misreading Tolstoy: "Bakhtin's world is not designed to accommodate writers like Tolstoy. In it Tolstoy is a loser, the negative example." Emerson makes exceptions for "certain short pieces," acknowledging that interpreting them "Bakhtin does make some intoxicating generalizations and insightful comments."[2] The analysis of "Three Deaths," offered in *Problems of Dostoevsky's Poetics*, seems to be precisely such an exception.

In my view, however, what accounts for the readers' feeling of claustrophobia in "Three Deaths" is not so much the lack of any dialogue of ideas within the story, but rather the dominance of the author's/narrator's point of view, achieved through tight authorial control over the reader. Tolstoy uses his formidable narrative authority to guide his readers to certain conclusions and to discourage the readers' questioning these conclusions. There is thus no dialogue allowed between the author/narrator and the reader, and it is the absence of this kind of exchange that makes the text feel as hermetic as it does.

My interpretation runs contrary to that of Gareth Williams who, in his fundamental study *The Influence of Tolstoy on Readers of His Works*, argues that Tolstoy allows his readers some degree of freedom in "Three Deaths." He writes:

> The relative freedom of the reader of "Three Deaths," a rather didactic story, is made possible by three factors: firstly, the author's dialectical depiction of artistic reality, secondly, the

---

[1] Mikhail Bakhtin, *Problems of Dostoevsky's Poetics*, ed. and trans. Caryl Emerson, Theory and History of Literature 8 (Minneapolis: Univ. of Minnesota Press, 1984), 71 (emphasis in the original).

[2] Caryl Emerson, "The Tolstoy Connection in Bakhtin," *PMLA* 100, no. 1 (1985): 75.

strong role given in the narration to the character's point of
view, and, thirdly, the presentation of the three solutions of
the central problem, how to die.[3]

By dialectics Williams means "the fact that the characters are
conditioned by time, place, and circumstance." From this it follows
that "the author cannot make the lady behave like the peasant, or
vice versa. He must follow the rules of the dialectical relationship
between the individual and his environment which he himself
has established."[4] It is precisely in establishing these rules and
declaring them absolute that I see the author's commandeering of
the reader's freedom. Furthermore, the characters' points of view
are not really represented. Fyodor is depicted exclusively from
the outside; his inner thoughts and feelings are not presented. The
lady's thoughts are described only to show that they are selfish or in
conflict with the natural way of things. And the tree, of course, does
not have any thoughts. Finally, the three solutions to the problem
of how to die do not in fact constitute freedom of choice, since
only one of them is truly good. And this solution is not a solution
at all, because humans are not like trees in that they have consciousness.

My point about the tight control the narrator in "Three
Deaths" exercises over the reader is best illustrated by comparing
it with a story with which Tolstoy, in fact, was in a dialogue (or
rather a sharp disagreement) when he wrote his own story—Ivan
Turgenev's 1847 "Death." "Rewriting" Turgenev's story, Tolstoy
disagrees with his predecessor not only about the message but
also about the structure of the narrative and, particularly, about the
degree of the narrator's control over the reader. This dialogue was
one-sided: Turgenev never responded to Tolstoy's objections to his
story. Even when he wrote to Tolstoy, in his letter of February 11,
1859, about the mixed reception of "Three Deaths" in St. Petersburg,
he confined himself to mere reporting and kept his own opinion

---

[3]   Gareth Williams, *The Influence of Tolstoy on Readers of His Work* (Lewiston,
        NY: Edwin Mellen Press, 1990), 214.

[4]   Ibid., 214–15.

to himself: "'Three Deaths' generally has been accepted well here, but some find the conclusion strange and do not even wholly understand its connection with the two preceding deaths, and those who understand do not like it."[5]

Turgenev first published his story "Death" in 1848 in Nikolay Nekrasov's *The Contemporary* and then included it in *A Sportsman's Sketches* (1852), the book that brought him fame as a prose writer. Tolstoy, by his own account, read *A Sportsman's Sketches* in the summer of 1853, and the book made a strong impression on him.[6] Turgenev's story is narrated—as all stories in *A Sportsman's Sketches* are—in the first person and from the point of view of a young nobleman who wanders across the countryside with a gun and a dog, hunting and meeting different people along the way. In our story, the narrator witnesses the death of a contractor, Maksim, who is killed by a tree he and his workers are taking down. The incident prompts the narrator to meditate on how Russian peasants die: "Poor Maksim's death made me think. How amazingly [*udivitel'no*] the Russian peasant [*russkii muzhik*] dies!" The narrator is bewildered by the absence of fear, the calmness, and the simplicity with which the Russian peasant accepts his death: "His state of mind before death can be called neither indifference nor dullness. He dies as if he is performing a rite: coldly and simply."[7] Indeed, despite the unbearable pain, Maksim methodically takes care of his earthly affairs: he asks for a priest, begs his workers' forgiveness for making them work on Sunday, and gives detailed instructions concerning his finances. Only then does he die—before he can be taken to a doctor.

---

[5] Lev Tolstoi, *Perepiska s russkimi pisateliami*, 2nd ed. (Moscow: Khudozhestvennaia literatura, 1978), 1:168.

[6] Lev Tolstoi, *Polnoe sobranie sochinenii v 90 tomakh* (Moscow: Gosudarstvennoe izdatel'stvo khudozhestvennoi literatury, 1928–64), 46:170. Also see V. Savel'eva, "'Smert' I. S. Turgeneva i 'Tri smerti' L. N. Tolstogo," *Problemy stilia i vzaimodeistviia literatur: Sbornik nauchnykh trudov* (Alma-Ata: Kazakhskii gos. universitet, 1987), 8–9.

[7] Ivan Turgenev, "Smert'," in his *Sobranie sochinenii v dvenadtsati tomakh* (Moscow: Khudozhestvennaia literatura, 1954), 1:283. All subsequent references to this edition are given in the text.

The narrator perceives this extraordinary calmness in the face of death as a characteristic of every Russian peasant, not only the hapless Maksim. The contractor's death therefore forces him to recall other examples of such behavior. He speaks of another peasant, a burn victim, who, upon receiving last rites, waits calmly and patiently for death to end his sufferings—asking for nothing but an occasional sip of *kvass*.

The narrator's third example is particularly bewildering because the hero of this episode, a miller, rejects medical attention and chooses instead to set his affairs in order when there still seems to be some hope for a cure. "If I have to die, I'd better die at home," the miller says to the doctor's assistant who tries to persuade him to stay in the hospital for treatment. "Why would I want to die here? God knows what would happen at home" (285). He departs and dies three days later.

At this point the narrator repeats his maxim about the manner in which Russians die, but in an altered form: he now speaks of all Russian people, not only peasants: "In general, Russian people die in an amazing way" (286). He is ready to give many examples ("Many dead people come to my mind now"), but he chooses one—his "old friend, Avenir Sorokoumov, a student who never finished his studies, an excellent and most noble man" (286). The portrait that follows allows the reader to identify Avenir easily as a *raznochinets*, a member of the 1830s generation known for its idealism and Hegelianism. Unable to finish his university studies because of poverty, lack of either wit or diligence, and, finally, consumption, Avenir accepts a position as a tutor in the family of a provincial landowner, in whose home he eventually dies. The narrator visits him shortly before his death and finds him calm and more interested in the events of his youth and in new developments in the sciences and philosophy than in his own present sorry condition. Soon after their meeting, Avenir's master reports his death to the narrator and comments on his lack of emotion: "Your friend died fully conscious and, one could say, equally indifferent, without any signs of regret, even when our entire family bade him farewell" (289–90). (The master's frustrated expectations of an emotional parting are comical, since even though he did not throw the dying Avenir out of the house, he did not treat him very cordially either.)

Having finished this report, the narrator once again assures the reader that he could have offered many more examples of this kind of stoicism in the face of death, but confines himself to one last story about a dying old lady, a landowner, whose death he witnessed. Clearly on her way out of this world, the old lady still wants to make sure that everything is done properly. Even though her tongue barely obeys her anymore, she attempts to give guidance to the priest who administers the last rites and tries to pay for the service, right before breathing her last. The memory of this woman makes the narrator exclaim once again: "Yes, Russian people die in an amazing way!" (290). This is the last sentence of the story. The narrator offers no interpretation of what he observes, except for implying (by gradually making his statement about the manner in which Russians die more and more general) that calmness in the face of death is a Russian national feature, equally characteristic of all social classes.

Tolstoy's "Three Deaths" is connected to Turgenev's story by many obvious ties. Both stories examine a succession of deaths, and in both people die of consumption. Turgenev describes a dying wood, and Tolstoy depicts the death of a tree. Both writers choose an ash tree (*iasen'*) for their description of death in nature. Furthermore, both authors use personification in their descriptions of dying trees.

Tolstoy, however, rewrites Turgenev's story in a radical way. First of all, he restructures it. Turgenev offers the reader a loose, open-ended plot. The list of his examples of strange deaths is not complete, and it is possible to add to it indefinitely, all the more so in that all the deaths portrayed in the story amaze the narrator equally, and every new example only reinforces his initial point: Russians die in a remarkable way.[8] Tolstoy, in contrast, presents

---

[8]   These moments of apparent randomness and open-endedness are, of course, carefully constructed: in her article, Savel'eva reports that Turgenev's rough drafts show great attention to the arrangement of the episodes ("'Smert'' I. S. Turgeneva," 9–10).

a tight three-piece structure: he gives the reader one example of a bad death, one example of a good death, and one example of a perfect death.

Tolstoy also rejects both the nationalistic slant in Turgenev's interpretation of the amazing phenomenon and his sociology. For Turgenev, as I have noted before, the remarkably indifferent attitude toward death is a specifically Russian feature, equally characteristic of Russian peasants, Russian *raznochintsy*, and Russian nobility. The character of Gottlieb von der Kock, a German from the Baltic provinces, serves to emphasize the quintessentially Russian nature of this stoicism in the face of death. Von der Kock's regret for the dying wood (motivated both by sentiment and by economics) is in sharp contrast to the nonchalance with which the Russian peasant Arkhip observes the disaster:

> "Mein Gott! Mein Gott!" — von der Kock exclaimed at every step — "Vat a prank! vat a prank [*zhalost'* that the German pronounces as *shalost'*]" "What prank do you mean?" — remarked my neighbor, with a smile. "Dat is, vat a peety, I meanttt to zay." . . .
> The oaks lying on the ground particularly aroused his regret — and, indeed, any miller would have paid a high price for them. In contrast, Arkhip, the village foreman, maintained imperturbable composure, and did not grieve in the least; on the contrary, he leaped over them not without satisfaction, and lashed them with his whip. (281)[9]

Tolstoy dismisses Turgenev's thesis that all Russians, regardless of their social status, meet death in the same stoic manner. First of all, Tolstoy's view of Russian social structure differs from that of Turgenev: as is well known, *raznochintsy* hardly figure at all in Tolstoy's fictional world. Accordingly, whereas the *raznochinets* Avenir is, if not central, then certainly the most lovingly and minutely portrayed of all characters in Turgenev's "Death," Tolstoy omits the *raznochintsy* from his story altogether.

---

[9] I have based my translation of this passage on Ivan Turgenieff, "Memoires of a Sportsman," trans. Isabel F. Hapgood (New York: Charles Scribners Sons, 1907), part 14, 51–52.

Tolstoy's omission—and thus rejection—of Avenir's example is particularly remarkable, because Avenir's behavior is a mirror image of the lady's behavior in "Three Deaths": he does everything Tolstoy's narrator would want the lady to do but which she does not do. Like the lady, Avenir is dying of consumption, but, unlike her, he is fully aware that his life is ending, openly speaks about it, refuses to go abroad in search of a cure, and does not want to contact his family lest he burden them with his illness: "They cannot help me, and when I die they'll find out" (289). Nonetheless, Tolstoy chooses to disregard Avenir and his stoicism in the face of death. There are only two social classes in "Three Deaths": the nobility and the peasants.

And then there is the tree. The tree, while nonhuman, is portrayed as being on a par with the other two main characters in the story, the lady and the peasant. The personification used in its description ceases to be a mere trope, allowing Tolstoy to ascribe moral significance to the tree's allegedly good behavior in the face of death. Tolstoy's strategy disconcerted his contemporaries, as is evident in Turgenev's remark about "Three Deaths," quoted above. Apollon Grigor'ev, in his 1862 essay "Early Works by Count L. N. Tolstoy," also expresses his uneasiness about the tree's alleged superiority:

> The death of an oak <sic!> in "Three Deaths,"—the death that is placed by the [author's] consciousness above the death not only of the lady who is mentally developed, but also above the death of a simple man. It is only one step from here to nihilism.[10]

Among those who were disturbed by the ending of the story was Alexandra Tolstaya, Tolstoy's relative and friend, to whose criticism of the non-Christian philosophy of the story Tolstoy responded in his oft-cited letter of May 1, 1858. He concludes his exegesis of the story: "The tree dies calmly, honestly, and beautifully. Beautifully—because it does not lie, does not pretend,

---

[10]   Apollon Grigor'ev, "Rannie proizvedeniia gr. L. N. Tolstogo," in his *Sobranie sochinenii*, ed. V. F. Savodnik (Moscow: Tip. I. N. Kushnerev, 1916), 12:51–52.

is not afraid."[11] His choice of words emphasizes the moral beauty of the tree's behavior. The peasant is also praised, whereas the lady is condemned: "*Un brute*, you say, so how is [being] *un brute* bad? [Being] *un brute* is happiness and beauty, harmony with the entire universe, and not the discord that we see in the lady."[12]

It is obvious from these passages that the absence of any kind of moral judgment in Turgenev's story was one of the impulses for Tolstoy's rewriting it. In order to make his moral message clear, Tolstoy employs a narrative mode that allows the narrator a high degree of control over the reader.

As I mentioned earlier, Turgenev's first-person narrator entirely withholds his judgment. He occasionally displays his feelings (love for Avenir or, perhaps, a slight irritation with the burn victim's resignation: "I couldn't take it any more [*ne vyterpel*] and left," 283), but the reader is not told what he thinks about the way Russians die beyond the fact that they all die in an amazing way. Turgenev's narrator leaves it up to the readers to interpret these deaths and to give them—or not to give them—moral significance.

In contrast, Tolstoy's third-person omniscient and omnipresent narrator directs the reader to the correct interpretation of events. Tolstoy achieves this effect by various narrative techniques. One is to invest the narrator's voice with the highest authority by positioning him, at strategically crucial points in the story (such as the beginning of chapter 1, the beginning of chapter 3, and the conclusion), high above the depicted scenes and having him report on cosmic events: the change of seasons and the rising of the sun. "It was autumn," chapter 1 begins. "Spring has arrived," the opening of chapter 3 announces. The concluding paragraph of the story begins with a description of "the first rays of the sun, breaking through a partly transparent cloud" and moving "across the earth and the sky."[13] Placing the three deaths in the context of cosmic events endows

---

11   Lev Tolstoi to A. A. Tolstaia, May 1, 1858, in Lev Tolstoi, *Polnoe sobranie sochinenii v 90 tomakh*, 60:266.

12   Ibid., 60:265–66.

13   Tolstoi, "Tri smerti," in his *Polnoe sobranie sochinenii v 90 tomakh*, 5:53, 60, and 64. From now on, all references to this edition will be given in the text (5:53).

them with the highest philosophical and religious meaning, which they certainly do not have in and of themselves.

Tolstoy's narrator also firmly guides his readers in their perception and, most importantly, their judgment of the characters. This kind of narrative technique is most obvious in the depiction of the young lady and her incorrect way of dying. We know from Tolstoy's letter to Alexandra Tolstaya that he intended to portray the lady in the worst possible light: "The lady is pathetic [*zhalka*] and disgusting [*gadka*], because she has lied all her life and is lying before her death." Tolstoy repeats: "She is disgusting and pathetic."[14] In order to make his reader feel this way about this character, Tolstoy's narrator consistently portrays her in a manner that induces negative feelings. As a result, it is virtually impossible for the reader either to sympathize with her or to pity her (the pity in Tolstoy's letter is clearly scornful). The subtle suggestion of the lady's unpleasantness begins with her physical description. Among the signs of her illness, the narrator plants disagreeable little details that cumulatively create a feeling of loathing in the reader:

> Прямой ряд, уходя под чепчик, разделял русые, *чрезвы-чайно плоские напомаженные волосы*, и было что-то *сухое, мертвенное* в белизне кожи этого просторного ряда. *Вялая, несколько желтоватая кожа неплотно обтягивала* тонкие и красивые очертания лица и краснелась на щеках и скулах. Губы были сухи и *неспокойны, редкие* ресницы *не курчавились,* и дорожный суконный капот делал прямые склад-ки на впалой груди. Несмотря на то, что глаза были за-крыты, лицо госпожи выражало усталость, *раздражение* и привычное страдание. (5:53; emphasis added)

> (A straight parting, disappearing under the cap, divided her *extremely flat, pomaded blond hair*, and there was *a dry deathly whiteness in the skin of this spacious parting. The flabby and somewhat sallow skin was loosely drawn* over her fine and beautiful features, showing red on the cheeks and cheekbones. Her lips were dry and *restless,* her *thin* eyelashes *didn't curl,* and a cloth traveling overcoat made straight folds over her

---

14   Lev Tolstoi to A. A. Tolstaia, in Lev Tolstoi, *Polnoe sobranie sochinenii v 90 tomakh*, 60:265.

sunken chest. Although her eyes were closed, the lady's face expressed *irritation*, and habitual suffering.) [15]

One can argue that this is simply a realistic portrait of a sick person, and sick people are not pretty. The dying Nikolay Lyovin in part 5 of *Anna Karenina* is not pretty either. However, Nikolay's emaciation, thin hair, and unkempt mustache, while frightening (especially to his brother, who, as we remember, has a problem with the idea of mortality), do not produce a feeling of aversion, whereas the lady's "extremely flat pomaded hair," the "dry, deathly whiteness" of the "spacious parting" in her hair; her "flabby" (instead of faded or withered, *uviadshaia*) loose skin; her "restless" lips, her thin straight eyelashes—all work to produce an unpleasant impression in the reader. The fact that the imagery combines the signs of illness with signs of vanity reinforces the negative impression. The reader's dislike of the lady is further increased by the clear signs of her moral shortcomings: the irritable, even malicious (*zlaia ironiia*) expression of her face, her intolerance toward her maidservant, and her implied propensity to exaggerate her sufferings. Occasional references to the lady's beauty ("fine and beautiful features" of her face, "beautiful thin hand," and twice-mentioned "beautiful dark eyes") do not smooth away the unpleasant impression. On the contrary, they heighten the suspicion that she is not truly sick. The reader is left with the feeling that the lady's desire to go abroad in search of a cure is frivolous—not so much because such a trip would be useless, as the doctor and the lady's husband let the reader know, but because she is not as sick as she pretends to be.

To harm the lady even further in the eyes of the reader, Tolstoy presents her normal human desire to live and regain her health as petty and capricious:

"What is the use of being at home? . . . To die at home?" replied the invalid, peevishly. But the word "die" evidently frightened her, and she looked at her husband with supplication and

---

[15]   I have based my translation of this passage and of the next three indented quotations on E. R. DuMont's 1899 translation of the story, accessed January 19, 2011, http://en.wikisource.org/wiki/Three_Deaths.

inquiry. He dropped his eyes, and remained silent. The sick woman's mouth suddenly contracted in a childish fashion, and the tears flowed from her eyes. (5:57)

The young woman's wish to live is presented as a refusal to face the truth—that is, the fact that death, even when it is untimely, is a natural part of life. Her prayer for health is consequently pictured as petty and futile, because she is asking to change something that is as much a force of nature as the weather and should be accepted as such:

"No, I will go," said the invalid; and, lifting her eyes to the sky, she clasped her hands and began to whisper incoherent words. "My God! What for?" she said, and the tears flowed more violently. She prayed long and fervently, but still there was just the same sense of constriction and pain in her chest, just the same gray melancholy in the sky, in the fields, and on the road; just the same autumnal mist, neither thicker nor thinner but ever the same was falling on the muddy highway, on the roofs, on the carriage, and on the sheepskin coats of the drivers. (5:57)

In contrast, the description of Fyodor, the consumptive peasant in the same story, forces the reader to sympathize with him. The narrator leaves no doubt that Fyodor is truly dying. His portrayal as a dying man is brutally honest, his cough is horribly genuine (as opposed to the lady's "slight cough," *pokashlivanie*), and his efforts to take a drink or to speak clearly require all his strength. Unlike the lady, who has the energy to be angry with the maid and to rebuke her husband for not paying enough attention to her, Fyodor is oblivious to the conditions around him: he is too sick to care. Most importantly, he not only accepts but welcomes death.

Despite the lady's implied exaggeration of her sickness, she dies, and the description of her death reveals even tighter control on the narrator's part to ensure the reader's negative response to her behavior. To begin with, her death is in conflict with the natural cycle: unlike the peasant Fyodor, who dies in the fall, when the weather is gloomy and rainy, the lady dies in the spring, when the entire world is renewed and happy: "There was joy and youthfulness in the sky, on the earth, and in the human heart" (5:60). Furthermore, unlike Fyodor, who dies alone, in the middle of the night, and thus does not disturb anyone, the dying lady keeps the entire household of people busy: her immediate and extended family, a priest, a doctor, and numerous servants. She is capricious and selfish: she nags her husband and neglects her children. It is particularly telling that her death seems to mean nothing to her son and daughter, who continue to play both while she is dying and after she is dead. Crucially, the reader is informed that this is not due to a moral failing on their part (they are in harmony with nature, running around and pretending to be horses), but on hers: in the fall, she was ready to leave them in order to go abroad in search of a cure, and now she refuses to say goodbye to them so as not to upset herself.

Most surprisingly, the narrative not only explicitly portrays the lady as a hypocrite (right after receiving Christian last rites and expressing faith in God's mercy, she asks for a quack doctor, hoping for a miracle from pagan rites), but also subtly suggests that she is only pretending to be dying. She is supposed to be in a state of death-agony—and yet she is talkative and energetic. There is no mention of her coughing, and she is preternaturally alert and active even as her heart obviously begins to fail:

> The doctor came to her, and took her hand. Her pulse was evidently growing weaker and weaker. He winked at the husband. The sick woman observed this gesture, and looked around in fright. The cousin turned away and wept. "Don't weep, don't torment yourself and me," said the invalid. "That takes away from me my last comfort." "You are an angel," said the cousin, kissing her hand. "No, kiss me here, they only kiss the hands of those who are dead. My God! My God!" (5:63)

Nonetheless, right after this exchange, the reader learns that the very same evening the talkative and complaining not-so-sick lady "was already a dead body" (5:63).

For a moment it seems that at this point the narrator will finally allow the reader to sympathize with the lady since her portrayal in the coffin listening to a sexton's reading Psalm 104 (103 in Russian Orthodox tradition) is almost exalting: "The face of the deceased was severe and majestic. There was no movement either in her clear brow, or her firmly closed lips [*usta*]. She was all attention." But even in death this is pretense, and the lady lacks understanding: "But did she understand even now these grave words?" (5:63). It is crucial for the final condemnation of the dead lady that the psalm she fails to understand is about God's wisdom in creating Earth to be a home for all creatures, from plants to humans, and in including death as an integral part of the natural cycle. The quoted verses, significantly, apply as much to humans as they do to beasts and plants. The lady does not comprehend that she is just a link in the chain of beings and thus her death is as inconsequential as a death of a plant. This is the moral failing for which the author/narrator wants the reader to condemn her.

How is the reader made to accept this point of view? I believe that it happens because the reader is in thrall to Tolstoy's narrative skill. Williams, in his analysis of "Three Deaths," makes a perceptive observation that contradicts his initial statements about the story's narrative strategies and with which I wholly agree:

> When you read Tolstoy the authority with which he presents reality is usually so great that you may feel that you are being presented with a single, monolithic view of the world with which it is impossible to argue, from which nothing may be taken away and to which nothing can be added, what Bakhtin would term a monologic presentation of reality . . . Everything seems to cohere. The laws of cause and effect are constantly in evidence. Time and the environment constantly affect the characters, creating a pattern of change which we recognize as the pattern of our lives. The laws of Tolstoy's artistic universe are, so it seems, the laws of our universe. The reader is overwhelmed by his powers of mimesis, which are extraordinary.[16]

Williams points out, quite correctly, that "what Tolstoy achieves is not a mirror of reality, it is an illusion of a reflection of reality." I do not think, however, that "the reader is an active participant

---

[16]   For this and the two subsequent quotations, see Williams, *Influence of Tolstoy*, 216.

in the creation of this illusion"—at least as it applies to "Three Deaths." I believe that, on the contrary, the powerful illusion of reality constructed by Tolstoy's controlling narrator makes the reader suspend critical judgment and accept the author's doubtful philosophy and the questionable verdicts he pronounces on his characters.

There is, however, something in Tolstoy's story that betrays his own uneasiness with the proposed recipe for dying and ultimately calls the story's conclusion into question. Not only is the idea that a person's death is as inconsequential as that of a tree disconcerting (as it was to the story's first readers), but also the scene of the tree's death is not as peaceful and painless as Tolstoy implies in his letter to Alexandra Tolstaya. True, the surviving trees rejoice, celebrating their newly found freedom, but the tree that is chosen to die reacts with pain and fear: "The tree shuddered with all its body, bent and straightened up again quickly, shaking with fear on its roots" (5:64). How then can nature ignore suffering and death in its midst? It can do so because it lacks consciousness. It seems that at some level Tolstoy is aware of the difficulty his philosophy of death presents to a conscious being and lets this awareness out: the birds happily chirping over the dead tree are described as *poteriannye* (lost), a word that implies insanity—that is, the loss of the faculty of reason. By the narrator's logic, to accept death one must stop thinking. How can a human being stop thinking, except by going mad? In order to evade answering this question, Tolstoy does not let us in on Fyodor's thoughts. The reader does not learn how Fyodor, simple and uneducated as he is but still conscious, deals with his impending death and how he achieves his state of apparent acceptance and equanimity. The story thus fails as a recipe for correct personal behavior in the face of death.

Ironically, in this "Three Deaths" resembles Turgenev's story, which also leaves the reader with questions as to how the story's narrator would behave if personally facing death. True, the story does not pose the question of how to die—it just registers and depicts the puzzling phenomenon of Russians' indifference in the face of death. Yet the reader cannot help but wonder about the narrator's position vis-à-vis death. Is he one of the stoic Russians who accept death with calm and indifference? Perhaps not; he mourns the dying wood much more passionately than von der Kock does:

> I confess, it was not without a feeling of bitterness that I now rode into the forest which was but too familiar to me. The pernicious, snowless winter of [18]40 had not spared my old friends, the oaks and ash-trees... Well, I thought, as I looked at the dying trees: I think you must feel ashamed and bitter. (280)

The narrator's thrice-repeated surprise at Russians' behavior in the face of death is even more telling. It firmly places him outside the community of stoically dying Russians: one is not surprised by something that is one's own. One needs to be alienated from a behavior to be surprised by it.

While Turgenev was comfortable with leaving unanswered the question of what his own position on death and dying was, and thus allowing his readers to decide for themselves what theirs should be, Tolstoy felt compelled to offer a definite answer—both to himself and to his readers. He obviously failed in this task, because to do so he would have had to accomplish the impossible—namely, to resolve the "antinomy of nature and reason," the antinomy of the primitive state of existence, which he found beautiful and longed to be part of at this particular stage of his artistic and philosophical development, and the faculty of thought, which he would have liked to be without but could not suppress or ignore.[17]

---

[17]   Mikhail Gershenzon, "L. N. Tolstoi v 1855–1862 gg.," in his Izbrannoe, vol. 3, Obrazy proshlogo (Moscow: Universitetskaia kniga; Jerusalem: Gesharim, 2000), 639.

10. Female Voice and Male Gaze
in Leo Tolstoy's Family Happiness

Tolstoy's 1859 novella *Family Happiness* (*Semeinoe schast'e*) has not attracted much scholarly attention, perhaps because of its reputation as "an unexciting story of courtship, early married bliss, subsequent marital problems, and eventual compromise."[1] Just as its content has been judged unremarkable, so too has its form often been characterized as a failure.[2] In many respects, however, the novella is noteworthy, even paradoxical. To begin with, it is one of Tolstoy's few first-person works and the only one with a female narrator. Furthermore, in spite of its female narrator, the novella is autobiographical in nature and reflects its male author's 1856–57 love affair with V. V. Arsen'eva and his views on family life at the time, which he developed in semifictional form in several of his letters to her.[3] Remarkably, Tolstoy even continued to apply the

---

[1]   Victor Terras, *History of Russian Literature* (New Haven, CT: Yale Univ. Press, 1991), 354. For a more sympathetic analysis of the novella, see Ruth Crego Benson, *Women in Tolstoy: The Ideal and the Erotic* (Urbana: Univ. of Illinois Press, 1973), 23–44. An interesting Jungian interpretation of the novella can be found in Richard Gregg, "Psyche Betrayed: The Doll's House of Leo Tolstoy," *Slavic and East European Journal* 46 (2002): 269–82.

[2]   In addition to Terras, see Boris Eikhenbaum, *Lev Tolstoi: Kniga pervaia, 50-e gody* (Leningrad: Priboi, 1928), 360–63. Benson argues that it is male critics who tend to underappreciate the novella, whereas female readers (women students in the courses she has taught) find its female perspective fairly convincing and thus judge the novella as successful (*Women in Tolstoy*, 42). Given Tolstoy's less than sympathetic treatment of his heroine, this effect is remarkable, and I will return to it later in this chapter.

[3]   See Eikhenbaum, *Lev Tolstoi*, 345–48; and P. A. Zhurov, "L. N. Tolstoi i V. V. Arsen'eva," in *Iasnopolianskii sbornik* (Tula: Priokskoe knizhnoe izdatel'stvo, 1976), 119–35. For the letters, see Lev Tolstoi, *Polnoe sobranie sochinenii v 90 tomakh* (Moscow: Gosudarstvennoe izdatel'stvo khudozhestvennoi literatury, 1928–64), 60:97, 105, 108–9, 116–19, 122–23, 126–28. Benson, however, argues that since Tolstoy's treatment of Arsen'eva was "so abusive," *Family Happiness* could not have been imitating life; on the contrary, in his

novella's circumstances to his own life. Like Sergey Mikhailovich, the novella's male protagonist, the newly married Tolstoy quotes Lermontov's 1832 poem "The Sail" ("Parus") to explain his young wife's discontent. Tolstoy writes in his diary on March 3, 1863: "Today she feels bored, constrained. The madman seeks a storm [*Bezumnyi ishchet buri*]—not the madman but the young [person]."[4] Tellingly, both Sergey Mikhailovich and Tolstoy misquote Lermontov, substituting "the madman" (*bezumnyi*) for "the rebellious one" (*miatezhnyi*) of the original.

Finally, as some critics point out, the novella was written in response to vigorous discussion, both in Europe and in Russia, of the "woman question."[5] More precisely, it was a response to Jules Michelet's 1858 treatise *L'Amour* and was influenced by that book's ideas of marriage and womanhood.[6] Boris Eikhenbaum argues that Tolstoy follows Michelet's concept of the stages that love necessarily

---

relations with Arsen'eva, the writer was acting out "the novella that had already taken shape in his imagination" (*Women in Tolstoy*, 24–25). For my purposes, this is sufficient to establish the novella's autobiographical nature: either way, it had to do not only with Tolstoy's general views on marriage and women but also with his own desire to marry and his efforts to identify a suitable partner.

[4] Tolstoi, *Polnoe sobranie sochinenii v 90 tomakh*, 48:52. For Sergey Mikhailovich's quoting of the same lines, see 5:115.

[5] For useful recent overviews of Tolstoy's responses to the "woman question," see Hugh McLean, "A Woman's Place: The Young Tolstoy and the 'Woman Question,'" in *Word, Music, History: A Festschrift for Caryl Emerson*, ed. Lazar Fleishman et al., Stanford Slavic Studies 29 (Stanford, CA: Stanford University, Dept. of Slavic Languages and Literatures, 2005), 1:355–69; and Svetlana Slavskaya Grenier, "A Tale of Two Cities: Tolstoy's Gendered Moral Geography in *Anna Karenina*," in *Mapping the Feminine: Russian Women and Cultural Difference*, ed. Hilde Hoogenboom, Catharine Theimer Nepomnyashchy, and Irina Reyfman (Bloomington, IN: Slavica, 2008), 93–111.

[6] See Eikhenbaum, *Lev Tolstoi*, 349–59; and Marie Semon, *Les femmes dans l'oeuvre de Leon Tolstoi: Romans et nouvelles* (Paris: Institute d'études slaves, 1984), 88. Benson doubts Tolstoy's familiarity with Michelet's treatise (*Women in Tolstoy*, 23), whereas Amy Mandelker downplays its influence on Tolstoy; see Amy Mandelker, *Framing Anna Karenina: Tolstoy, the Woman Question, and the Victorian Novel* (Columbus: Ohio State Univ. Press, 1993), 21, 26.

undergoes in a marriage. Tolstoy also apparently subscribes to the idea, advocated by Michelet, that a woman's place is in the family, where she should be subjected to her husband's moral influence. The husband's duty is to form his wife's character: "Il faut que tu crées ta femme. Elle ne demande pas mieux," as one chapter title in Michelet's book declares. It is notable that Tolstoy employs a female narrator to develop Michelet's views, which are, if not outright misogynistic, then certainly gender-biased.

Tolstoy's use of a female narrator is even more striking because the text implies that Masha herself is to blame for her marital troubles.[7] Indeed, the conflict that propels the action originates in the heroine's failure to live up to her husband's ideal of marital life. Significantly, this conflict is not completely resolved even as the novella ends, for however satisfying Masha's future life with the father of her children may seem, it clearly does not measure up to the happiness of the first months of their marriage. The initial intense love is gone, and Masha is clearly the one to blame. Sergey Mikhailovich all but spells it out:

> And do you want me to tell you the whole truth, if you want frankness? Just as, that year when I first got to know you, I spent sleepless nights thinking of you, and created my own love, and that love grew and grew in my heart, so, in Petersburg and abroad, I spent dreadful nights awake destroying, breaking up that love that tormented me. I did not destroy it, I only destroyed what was tormenting me; I regained my peace of mind and I love you all the same, but with a different love.[8]

---

7   Benson suggests that both spouses are blameless and "are portrayed as victims of a doomed illusion" (*Women in Tolstoy*, 27). As I will argue, this balanced view is not supported by the text.

8   Tolstoi, *Polnoe sobranie sochinenii v 90 tomakh*, 5:141; Leo Tolstoy, "Family Happiness," in *"A Landowner's Morning," "Family Happiness," and "The Devil": Three Novellas by Leo Tolstoy*, trans. Kyril and April FitzLyon (London: Quartet Books, 1984), 150. All future references to both the original and the translation are given in the text: the first two numbers indicate the page of the original (5:141); the third number indicates the page of the translation. Here and elsewhere in the article, I have modified the FitzLyons' translation.

It is clear that the love he manages to salvage has suffered irreparable damage. He explains: "Love remains but is not the same love; its place remains, but the old love has disappeared through suffering, and there's no strength or sap in the new one; memories and gratitude remain, but..." (5:142; 151–52).

But what is lost? What is it that Sergey Mikhailovich was so busy destroying? I want to argue that he has been purging his marriage of eros.[9] In the novella's conclusion, Masha herself acknowledges the loss of the erotic dimension of their relationship: "Not a lover, but an old friend was kissing me" (5:142; 152). She even finds a way to accept it and perhaps to be reasonably happy in their new relationship:

> From that day my romance with my husband was over, the old feeling became a dear, irretrievable memory, and a new feeling of love for my children and for the father of my children laid the foundation for another, this time completely different, happy life, which I am still living at the present moment. (5:143; 153)

From now on familial love (*philia*) will be the basis of the marriage, whereas romance (eros) is gone.[10]

But why did Sergey Mikhailovich have to banish eros from his marriage in the first place? What did Masha do to cause the loss of her husband's erotic love? How did she misbehave? The novella presents Masha's life in society as not just reprehensible but outright sinful. The reader is left with the impression that she has seriously betrayed her husband. While no actual adultery occurs, its possibility is suggested; and although this possibility is never

---

[9] Gregg suggests that "eros seems to play—on Masha's side at least—no role at all" ("Psyche Betrayed," 274). As is clear from the rest of my paper, I strongly disagree with this point of view.

[10] Benson identifies this change as a "conversion" from "*eros* to *agape*" (*Women in Tolstoy*, 39). I believe that this formula fits the ideas of sex and family that Tolstoy developed after his religious crisis, when he began to advocate what Mandelker calls "radical chastity" (see her *Framing Anna Karenina*, 30–33). At the time *Family Happiness* was written, Tolstoy was still looking for ways to reconcile erotic desire with marital (familial) love.

realized, it is enough to condemn Masha in her husband's (and the readers') eyes.

Masha's sin apparently lies in her ability to excite and experience erotic feelings—that is, in being a sexual creature. Her initial fall consists of becoming the subject of another man's erotic desire. At the St. Petersburg ball, Prince M.'s lascivious gaze uncovers her sexuality both for herself and for her husband:

> As I got up [to greet the prince] I instinctively looked for my husband, and saw him look at me from the other end of the ballroom, and turn away. I suddenly felt so ashamed and hurt that I became painfully shy, and blushed all over my face and neck under the gaze of the prince. But I had to go on standing and listening to what he was saying as he looked down at me. (5:124; 132)

In a twisted reinterpretation of the New Testament commandment (Matthew 5:28: "But I say to you that everyone who looks at a woman with lust has already committed adultery with her in his heart"), Masha becomes sinful after she is looked at with lust by a man other than her husband. This eventually (and apparently inevitably) translates into her own ability to look at a man other than her husband with lust. Masha's erotic longing is evident in the scene with the Marquis D.:

> His burning, moist eyes close to my face looked at me strangely, at my neck, my breast; both his hands held mine above the wrist; his open lips were saying something—were saying that he loved me, that I meant everything to him, and his lips came closer to me, and his hands pressed mine harder, burning me. Fire ran in my veins, everything became blurred, I was trembling, and the words with which I wanted to stop him dried in my throat. Suddenly I felt a kiss on my cheek and, trembling and growing cold all over, I looked at him. Without strength to speak or move, terrified, I waited and wanted something . . . I hated, I feared him; he was so alien to me; but at that instant the emotion and passion of that hated stranger found such a powerful response in me I irresistibly longed to give myself up to the kisses of that coarse and beautiful mouth, to the caresses of those white hands with

fine veins, and with rings on the fingers; I felt impelled to throw myself headlong into the abyss of forbidden delights thus suddenly opening up in front of me! (5:131; 140)[11]

Breaking the spell, Masha runs away, and this is the extent of her misconduct. But she has clearly "already committed adultery" in her heart, and this is enough to make erotic love between her and her husband forever impossible. Sergey Mikhailovich will be her friend, he will father her children, but he will never be her lover as he used to be in the early days of their marriage.

The quasi-biblical reference draws our attention to the centrality of visual imagery in the novella. It can justly be said that the main mode of action in Tolstoy's novella is visual. Everything of importance that transpires in the novella is described through various forms of visual activity. Glances are exchanged, averted, stolen, and withheld. Most importantly, they express and excite sexual feelings.[12] This visual activity is disproportionately ascribed to males, with Masha for the most part serving as an object of the male gaze. In this way, her behavior conforms to the general rule formulated by John Berger in his *Ways of Seeing*:

> One might simplify this by saying: *men act* and *women appear.* Men look at women. Women watch themselves being looked at. This determines not only most relations between men and women but also the relation of women to themselves. The surveyor of woman in herself is male: the surveyed female. Thus she turns herself into an object—and most particularly an object of vision: a sight.[13]

---

[11]   For an analysis of this passage, see Richard Gustafson, *Leo Tolstoy, Resident and Stranger: A Study in Fiction and Theology* (Princeton, NJ: Princeton Univ. Press, 1986), 344–45.

[12]   Freud, of course, connects eyes with genitalia, both female (see, for example, *The Interpretation of Dreams*, chap. 6) and, especially, male (ibid., and also "The Uncanny").

[13]   John Berger, *Ways of Seeing* (London: British Broadcasting Corporation, 1972), 47; emphasis in the original. In her article "Learning How to Look: Nastasia Filippovna in *The Idiot*," Gina Kovarsky argues that in his novel, Dostoevsky challenges the prevailing contemporary ideas about the

Yet sometimes Masha ceases to be an object and attempts to act. Thus, she doesn't merely "watch herself being looked at" but, as the narrator of the novella, reports on her onlooker's visual activity. Even more importantly, at times she also assumes the role of the viewer. As Beth Newman puts it, "When a woman looks back she asserts her 'existence' as a subject, her place outside the position of object to which the male gaze relegates her and by which it defines her as 'woman.'"[14] It is noteworthy that Masha's visual activities markedly intensify when she takes an active role in the unfolding events. They also increase when she experiences sexual attraction. Let us examine the visual activity in the novella more closely.

Sergey Mikhailovich is by far the most active viewer in the novella. His gaze follows the heroine, watching, encouraging, exciting, and censuring her. Sergey Mikhailovich's eyes ("bright, intelligent") and his gaze ("kind, attentive") are the most prominent attributes of his face and are frequently described by the narrator (see 5:69; 71 and 5:71; 74, for example). In fact, his gaze is special, even unique: "He had his own particular look [vzgliad]: direct to begin with, and then more and more attentive and somewhat sad" (5:71–72; 74).

The main characters' interactions in the novella are primarily visual. Their first meeting is described in visual terms: "When he saw me he stopped, and looked at me for some time without greeting me" (5:69; 71). Looking is established as the main mode of interaction between the two: "I thought he would kiss my hand and I bent towards him, but he only squeezed my hand again and looked me straight in the eyes, steadily and cheerfully" (5:69; 71).

It is made clear from the beginning that Sergey Mikhailovich's gaze differs from those of other males: he refuses "to look with

---

authority of the male gaze and rejects the notion of the moral inferiority of the female gaze; see *Mapping the Feminine*, ed. Hoogenboom et al., 51–69.

[14]   Beth Newman, "'The Situation of the Looker-On': Gender, Narration, and Gaze in *Wuthering Heights*," in *Feminisms: An Anthology of Literary Theory and Criticism*, ed. Robin R. Warhol and Diane Price Herndl, 2nd ed. (New Brunswick, NJ: Rutgers Univ. Press, 1997), 453.

admiration" (*liubovat'sia*) at Masha. Furthermore, he disapproves of young ladies "who [are] alive only as long as [they are being] admired" and hopes that Masha is different (5:71; 74).[15] He seems not to care at all about Masha's appearance and even teases her about her "exterior deficiencies" (*naruzhnye nedostatki*; 5:77–78; 81). His gaze thus attempts to be asexual and not to express the erotic interest in the object of his observations that the etymology of the word *liubovat'sia* clearly suggests. Furthermore, by pointing out Masha's "exterior deficiencies," Sergey Mikhailovich also attempts to suppress her erotic view of herself.

Deliberately devoid of sexual interest, Sergey Mikhailovich's gaze is invested with moral authority. It can approve: "His kind, attentive gaze once more flattered and pleasantly disconcerted me" (5:71; 74; cf. 5:74, 5:78, and 5:83 of the original). It can also censure and teach:

> Many of my former tastes did not please him, and it was enough for him to show me, by a twitch of his eyebrow or a glance, that what I wanted to say displeased him; he had only to make his own particular, woeful and very slightly contemptuous expression, for me to think that I no longer liked what I had liked. (5:79; 82; cf. 5:83 and 5:87 of the original)

Sergey Mikhailovich's gaze shapes and changes Masha for the better, enabling her to see things differently, "to look at everything with different eyes" (5:79; 82).

Sergey Mikhailovich can also use his gaze to punish—at least this is what Masha thinks he is doing when he deliberately avoids looking at her. When it happens for the first time, she assumes that he is punishing her for being depressed:

> I already hoped to see him every day: I suddenly felt miserable, and afraid that my depression would return. I must have revealed this by my look and tone of voice.
> "You must study more—and don't mope," he said in a way which seemed to me too cold and forthright. "And in the

---

15   Note that, unlike admiration, *liubovanie* is necessarily a visual activity.

spring I will set you an examination," he added, letting go
my hand and not looking at me.
In the hall, where we were standing to see him off, he
hurriedly put on his fur coat, and again avoided looking at
me. (5:72; 74–75)

However, Masha also discerns a sexual aspect in his behavior:
"'There's no point in him trying like that!' I thought. 'Does he really
think I like it so much when he looks at me? He is a good man,
a very good man . . . but that's all'" (5:72; 74–75).

Masha is right: looking can be an erotic activity, and despite
Sergey Mikhailovich's initial reluctance, it soon becomes this for
him. When he cannot suppress his love for Masha anymore, it is
manifested in the special, penetrating gaze he directs at her. The
first time he looks at her in this manner he watches from far behind
her as she sits playing the piano. Masha, however, feels his gaze,
and whenever she turns around, it is indeed directed at her:

> He was sitting behind me, so that I could not see him; but
> everywhere—in the semi-darkness of the room, in the
> sounds, in my own self—I felt his presence. His every look
> and movement, although I could not see them, were echoed
> in my heart . . . I felt the delight that he was experiencing
> and without looking at him, I felt his gaze fixed on me from
> behind. Without stopping the unconscious movement of my
> fingers, I quite involuntarily looked around at him. His head
> was silhouetted against the light background of the night. He
> was sitting, leaning his head on his hand, and was looking at
> me intently, his eyes smiling. (5:87; 91)

Sergey Mikhailovich's intense gaze communicates love far more
efficiently than words do. In fact, visual communication in the
novella is clearly privileged over oral. In his oft-quoted denuncia-
tion of formal love declarations, Sergey Mikhailovich insists that
words should not be used to declare love:

> "A man can say that he is in love, but a woman can't," [Katya]
> said.
> "But I don't think a man should or can say he loves someone,
> either," [Sergey Mikhailovich] said.

"Why not?" I asked.
"Because it will always be a lie." (5:85; 89)[16]

In time, Masha realizes that Sergey Mikhailovich is right: "'There is no need for him to tell me that he loves me,' I thought now, vividly remembering this conversation. 'He loves me, I know'" (5:86; 90). The superiority of visual communication over verbal is confirmed later in the novella:

> I looked at him. One lime tree was missing from the row at the spot where we were—I could see his face clearly. It was so fine and happy...
> He said: "You are not afraid, are you?" but I heard him say: "I love you, my darling girl." "I love you, I love you!" his look and his hand repeated. (5:89; 93)

Because of the eloquence of his loving gaze, when Sergey Mikhailovich wants to conceal his love from Masha, he has to avert his eyes. Having realized that Masha was secretly observing him in the cherry-cage, he glances at her briefly and then "suddenly looked down and blushed, went crimson, as a child" (5:84; 88). While attempting to part with Masha and, later, resisting the temptation to admit his love to her, Sergey Mikhailovich again stubbornly refuses to look at her, only occasionally giving her a quick glance. To avoid looking at Masha, Sergey Mikhailovich looks down, averts his gaze, and covers his eyes with his hand (5:94–97; 99–101).

After Sergey Mikhailovich confesses his love for Masha, their looking activity becomes more symmetrical and its frequency markedly increases. It also acquires a clearly sexual feel. Now Sergey Mikhailovich looks Masha straight in the face, and his gaze is not just intense (*pristal'nyi*) but is invested with an irresistible mesmerizing force. Twice it is called "magnetic" (*pritiagivaiushchii*; 5:101; 107; and 5:103; 109). It also affects Masha in a way that is entirely new to her and clearly erotic:

> As he looked at me his gaze was steady and magnetic.

---

16   Cf. the Marquis D.'s declaration of love: "Je vous aime" (5:148; 140). Of course, one also recalls Pierre Bezukhov's ill-fated "Je vous aime" to Helen.

I did not answer, and looked involuntarily into his eyes. Suddenly something strange happened to me: first I ceased to see all my surroundings, then his face disappeared and only his eyes seemed to shine immediately in front of mine; then I felt that those eyes were inside me and everything became blurred, I could not see anything and had to close my eyes tightly in order to tear myself away from the feeling of delight and fear which this gaze produced in me. (5:101; 107)

A similar moment of erotic abandon occurs shortly after their wedding ceremony, on the way from the church to Sergey Mikhailovich's house. At this point, Masha is ready to give herself to her husband:

But at that very moment my heart suddenly began to beat faster, my hand trembled and pressed his hand, I began to feel hot, my eyes sought his in the dusk, and I suddenly felt that I was not afraid of him — that this fear was love, a new kind of love, a love more tender and strong than before. I felt that I was entirely his, and that I rejoiced in his power over me. (5:105; 111)

Masha's erotic awareness manifests itself in that she becomes an active viewer: "my eyes sought his in the dusk."

The newlyweds' first marital bliss is also described in visual terms. As they get to know each other, they do so by exchanging looks. The prayer scene is typical:

Once he came into my room as I was saying my prayers. I looked around at him and went on praying. He sat down at the table so as not to disturb me, and opened a book. But I felt that he was looking at me and looked around.

As Masha teaches him how to say his prayers, he too looks around at her, seeking approval (5:106; 112). Masha also continues to experience moments of erotic abandon when she looks at her husband: "I would look at his eyes, his moving lips, and not understand a word, but would simply rejoice to see him and hear his voice" (5:107; 113).

Their first quarrel likewise involves various kinds of visual activity. Irked by what she perceives as Sergey Mikhailovich's condescending attitude, Masha comes to her husband:

> He was sitting writing in his study. Hearing my footsteps, he looked around indifferently and calmly, and went on writing. I did not like the look he gave me; instead of coming up to him I stood at the table at which he was writing, opened a book and began looking at it. Once again he interrupted his work and looked at me.
> "Masha, you're in a bad mood?" he said. I replied with a cold glance.

The quarrel continues to unfold as a battle of glances ("He looked at me in surprise as if he were seeing something for the first time"; "I said, not looking at him"; "I said this and looked at him"). Finally, Sergey Mikhailovich calms Masha down with his loving gaze:

> I did not look at him. I felt that he must be looking at me at that moment either sternly or perplexed. I looked around: a mild, tender gaze was fixed on me, as if asking forgiveness. I took his hand and said: "Forgive me! I don't know myself what I was saying."

Peace between husband and wife also restores the harmony of visual activity:

> "Yes?" he asked, smiling and looking at me.
> "Yes," I said in a whisper; and suddenly we were both overcome with a fit of gaiety. Our eyes were smiling, and we made bigger and bigger steps and stood more and more on tiptoe . . . We reached the dining-room, where we stopped, looked at each other, and burst out laughing. (5:112–15; 119–23)

When their relations begin to fall apart in St. Petersburg, Sergey Mikhailovich first tries to bring Masha back to her senses with "his inquiring gaze, at once grave and searching," but she, so sensitive to his gaze in the past, fails "to grasp its significance" (5:118; 125). As she becomes more and more carried away by her

social success, her husband's gaze becomes less and less loving. It
is described as cold, malicious, and mocking (5:121; 128; and 5:123;
131). Most importantly, it becomes opaque, impenetrable to Masha's
gaze. At first, Masha is hurt:

> I wanted to tell him that I would not go and did not want to go
> to the party, when suddenly he looked around and frowned
> as he saw me, and the gentle and thoughtful expression of
> his face changed. Once more his look expressed perspicacity,
> wisdom, and patronizing calm. He did not want me to see
> him as an ordinary person: he always had to stand before
> me like a demi-god on a pedestal . . . I was annoyed that he
> should conceal his true self from me, and not want to remain
> the person I loved. (5:120–21; 128)

Masha tries to return to the visual intimacy of the past but in vain:

> "I hope it [the postponement of their return to the countryside]
> is not for my sake," I said, looking him straight in the eyes;
> but his eyes only looked back at me, and said nothing, as
> if they were somehow shrouded [zavolocheny] from me.
> (5:124; 132)

After an uneasy period of adjustment, Masha accepts it:

> He no longer had that penetrating [glubokii] look which used
> to embarrass and gladden me, there were no more prayers,
> no more transports of joy together, we did not even see each
> other very often—he was constantly away, and was neither
> afraid nor sorry to leave me alone; I was constantly in society,
> where I did not need him. (5:126; 134)

To describe the unease of her changing relations with her
husband, Masha extensively uses visual imagery, both idiomatic
(such as expressions s glazu na glaz [by ourselves], and nelovko bylo
smotret' drug na druga [it was embarrassing to look at each other])
and newly-coined (such as the simile kak budto mal'chiki begali
v glazakh [as if little boys were running around in our eyes]; 5:125).
She repeats the latter expression to mark their eventual adjustment
to the estrangement between them: "After a year's time, the little

boys ceased to run around in our eyes when we looked at each other"
(5:126). The FitzLyons translate the expression as "our eyes betrayed
an uneasy conscience" (133 and 134), and while their translation is
correct, it does not convey the full meaning of the original. Tolstoy
coins his simile by putting together three expressions: two idiomatic
phrases, *begaiushchie glaza* (wandering, evasive, guilty eyes),
mal'chiki v glazakh (said about someone who is dazzled, blinded),
and an expression from the monologue in Pushkin's *Boris Godunov*,
in which Boris describes his guilty conscience:

> И всё тошнит, и голова кружится,
> И мальчики кровавые в глазах.[17]

(And I feel nauseous and lightheaded, / and see bloodied
boys before my eyes.)

While "wandering eyes" indeed signify an uneasy conscience, the
reference to Pushkin's tragedy suggests the violent character of the
damage that Masha and Sergey Mikhailovich have done to their
relationship. Like Boris, they have killed—can we suppose that they
have killed Eros (who is a boy, of course)? The description of their
new sexual relations as "moments of quiet, restrained tenderness
which we sometimes had" (5:126; 135) seems to support such
a supposition. Fittingly, they feel uneasy in these moments: "I felt
something was wrong; something made my heart ache, and in his
eyes I seemed to read the same thing" (5:126; 135).

By the time the couple finally returns to the countryside,
Masha is, if not comfortable with the loss of both eros and visual
intimacy, then resigned to it. She ascribes this loss to the passage
of time:

> And he was just the same too, only with deeper furrows
> between his eyebrows, with more gray hair on his temples;
> only his profound and thoughtful gaze [*glubokii vnimatel'nyi*

---

17   Aleksandr Pushkin, *Boris Godunov*, in *Polnoe sobranie sochinenii v 16-ti tomakh*
       (Moscow: Izdatel'stvo Akademii Nauk SSSR, 1937–59), 7:27. Pushkin too
       modifies the idiomatic phrase in order to describe both Boris's physical
       illness and his alleged guilt as Dimitry's murderer.

vzgliad] was always shrouded [*zavolochen*] from me as if by a cloud. And I, too, was just the same, only I no longer had any love within me, or any desire for love. (5:135; 144–45)

However, Masha's old memories, revived by her playing the piano that witnessed their first love, prompt her to miss her husband's deep, penetrating, erotically charged gaze: "I finished playing the first movement and, quite unconsciously, from old habit glanced at the comer in which he once used to sit listening to me. But he was not there" (5:136; 145). She then attempts to revive his erotic love, but cannot. Sergey Mikhailovich's gaze has become permanently shallow: "But his eyes were clear and calm, and did not look deeply into mine [*i ne gluboko smotreli v moi*]" (5:142; 152). There is nothing Masha can do but accept the loss of eros in their marriage, and as soon as she accepts it, a measure of content and even happiness returns:

> And suddenly, as I looked at him, I felt easier in my heart, as if the painful moral nerve that had made me suffer had been removed. I suddenly understood clearly and calmly that the feeling of that time had passed irrevocably away like that time itself, and that it was not only impossible to retrieve it, but that it would be painful and embarrassing to do so. And indeed, had it really been so perfect, that time which had seemed to me so happy? And it was all so long ago already! (5:143; 152)

Eros thus turns out to be something painful, and its loss allegedly makes the couple happier.

While throughout their romance Masha predominately serves as an object of her lover's gaze, she also does some looking of her own, and the dynamics of her visual activities repays examination. Notably, her ability to look and see is influenced by Sergey Mikhailovich. Figurative usages of verbs of vision abound in Masha's description of her moral transformation at the beginning of their romance. Her view of things and people changes dramatically: she learns to appreciate books, the lessons she gives her younger sister, music, and her old governess Katya. Most importantly, Sergey Mikhailovich teaches Masha to love the common people:

> He taught me, too, to look at the people who worked for us—at the peasants, at the servants and girls—in quite a different way. Ridiculous as it may seem, I had lived amongst these people for seventeen years, and yet had remained more alien to them than I was to people whom I had never seen; I never once realized that they had loves and desires and regrets, as I had. (5:79–80; 83)

This new outlook translates for Masha into a new appreciation of her whole world: "Our garden, our woods, our fields became new and beautiful to me" (5:80; 83). Thanks to Sergey Mikhailovich and his love, she now sees things she has never seen before: "All that night I did not sleep, and for the first time in my life I saw the sunrise and the early morning; and never again have I seen such a night or such a morning" (5:89–90; 94). These new visual powers indicate Masha's moral growth and maturity.

In the sexual sphere, however, Masha's excessively active looking is often presented as inappropriate. Her looking closely at the Marquis D. is the most glaring example of this unseemly voyeurism:

> I looked at him. Without strength to speak or move, terrified, I waited and wanted something. All this lasted for an instant, but that instant was terrible! In the course of this instant I saw the whole of him so clearly. I so well understood his face, the abrupt, low forehead—so similar to my husband's—visible under a straw hat; the beautiful, straight nose with distended nostrils; the long, finely pomaded mustache and the little beard; the smoothly shaved cheeks and sunburnt neck. (5:131; 140)

But even in her relations with Sergey Mikhailovich, too much active looking on Masha's part gets her in trouble. One visual transgression is her attempt to see what she is not supposed to see. Masha secretly looks into the cherry-cage and observes Sergey Mikhailovich:

I wanted to see what he was doing there, how he looked, how he moved, when he supposed no one was looking at him. And then, at that moment, I simply did not want to lose sight of him for a minute . . . I looked round the interior of the cage . . . [and] saw Sergei Mikhailovich from under the crooked branch of an old tree. He probably thought I had gone away, and that no one could see him. Hatless, and with his eyes closed, he was sitting in the fork of an old cherry tree and was carefully rolling a lump of resin into a little pellet. Suddenly he shrugged his shoulders, opened his eyes and smiled, muttering something. The word he said and his smile were so unlike him that I began to feel ashamed of spying on him [*chto ia podsmatrivaiu ego*]. (5:84; 88)

When Masha realizes that Sergey Mikhailovich is pronouncing her name, she is so embarrassed that she stirs, and Sergey Mikhailovich notices her. First he blushes and lowers his eyes. Then he looks Masha straight in the face, silently admitting his love for her:

He smiled as he looked at me. I smiled, too. His whole face beamed with joy. This was no longer a fond old uncle and mentor, this man was my equal, loving and fearing me as I feared and loved him. We did not say anything and just looked at each other. (5:84; 88)[18]

Then, however, he shows a clear disapproval of her boldness:

But suddenly he frowned, his smile and the sparkle in his eyes vanished, and he turned to me coldly, once again more like a father, as if we had been doing something wrong, and as if he had come to his senses and advised me to do the same. (5:84; 88)

Masha then transgresses further, by climbing over the wall of the cherry-cage. Sergey Mikhailovich's disapproval increases, Masha feels guilty, and her guilt is expressed in visual terms:

I blushed and, trying to avoid his gaze, not knowing what to say, I started to pick the cherries, although I had nowhere to

---

18   The last sentence is missing in the FitzLyons' translation.

put them. I reproached myself, regretted what I had done, was frightened, and felt that by this act I had ruined myself forever in his eyes. (5:85; 89)

Benson rightly likens Masha's intrusion into the cherry-cage, "the locked garden of delights," to Eve's transgression—particularly as it is popularly portrayed.[19] The comparison is the more valid in that both Eve and Masha are guilty not simply of curiosity ("I wanted to see what he was doing there, how he looked, how he moved") but also of turning looking into a sexual activity: "Then the eyes of both were opened, and they knew that they were naked" (Genesis 3:7).[20] Furthermore, as in the Eden scene, in Tolstoy's episode it is the woman who is the active one. Like Eve, Masha destroys—or at least threatens—the Edenic asexual bliss of Sergey Mikhailovich's nascent love—in Benson's words, "disturbs his 'paradise.'"[21]

The sexual undertones of the cherry-cage scene are further augmented by the erotic symbolism that red berries have in Russian folk poetry. Pushkin uses it in "The Girls' Song," inserted into the erotically charged third chapter of his *Eugene Onegin*:

> When we lure the fellow on,
> When we see him from afar,
> Darlings, then, let's scamper off,
> Pelting him with cherries then,
> Cherries, yes, and raspberries,
> Ripe red currants let us throw!

---

[19]   The quote is from Benson, *Women in Tolstoy*, 30. In the popular interpretation of the Edenic episode, Eve is the one to blame for mankind's loss of innocence and thus its banishment from Eden. Most importantly, according to this view, she is improperly curious: as the Russian saying puts it, "Liubopytstvo Evu sgubilo" (Curiosity ruined Eve).

[20]   Gregg comments on the "shades of Genesis" in this episode ("Psyche Betrayed," 274) but misses the fact that Masha transgresses twice—first visually, by spying on Sergey Mikhailovich whispering her name; then by disobeying Sergey Mikhailovich and climbing over the fence. It is noteworthy that Psyche's transgression is also visual: she violates her lover's prohibition to see him. Gregg points this out in his retelling of Apuleius's story: "Not once is she allowed to *see* her lover" (ibid., 272; italics in the original), but misses the prominence of this motif in Tolstoy's novella.

[21]   Benson, *Women in Tolstoy*, 31.

In Pushkin's imitation of folk poetry, it is, appropriately, the male who is a transgressive onlooker and is punished for his misbehavior:

> Never come to listen in
> When we sing our secret songs,
> Never come to spy on us
> When we play our maiden games!

Like Masha, however, the girls are not passive objects of male aggression; on the contrary, they "lure the fellow on" in order to pelt him with red berries.[22]

Masha's transgression changes the nature of the relations between the two: it forces Sergey Mikhailovich to show, however briefly, his love for her. Masha continues to be visually active, and this finally makes Sergey Mikhailovich confess his love. Throughout their explanation, in particular, she does not once lower her gaze, whereas he consistently avoids looking at her. She begins the conversation: "'Why are you going away?' I asked in a measured tone and looking straight at him" (5:95; 100). Toward the climax, she looks at him again:

> I looked at him: he was pale, and his lower lip was trembling.
> I felt sorry for him. I made an effort and, breaking the power
> of silence that was fettering me, I began to speak in a quiet,
> even voice which I feared would break at any moment.
> (5:97; 102)

What she says finally breaks down Sergey Mikhailovich's resistance. Masha, the narrator, describes the happiness she felt at this moment of control as singular and irretrievable: "In my heart there was happiness—a happiness that has disappeared forever, a hap-

---

22   Alexander Pushkin, *Eugene Onegin*, trans. James E. Falen (Carbondale: Southern Illinois Univ. Press, 1990), 90. Yury Lotman, in his commentary to the novel, quotes a folk wedding song, in which the woman is called "berry" (*iagoda*) and the man, "cherry" (*vishen'e*). The woman picks berries to present to her bridegroom's father. See Iurii Lotman, *Roman A. S. Pushkina "Evgenii Onegin": Kommentarii* (Leningrad: Prosveshchenie, 1980), 232–33.

piness that has never returned [*schast'e, naveki ushedshee, nevozvra-tivsheesia schast'e*]" (5:97).[23]

Masha also displays visual assertiveness in the final scene with her husband, when she tries to revive his erotic love for her. In doing so, she not only looks at her husband but also forces him to look at her:

> I looked at him. He was sitting leaning his head on his hand, and he wanted to say something in answer to my look, but only sighed heavily and put his head on his hand again. I came up to him and took his hand away. He turned to look at me thoughtfully. (5:141; 151)

By looking straight into her husband's eyes, Masha tries in vain to bring back his penetrating, erotically charged gaze: "'Let everything be once more as it was before. It is possible, isn't it?' I asked, looking into his eyes" (5:142; 152). Sergey Mikhailovich's gaze, however, remains shallow. Masha no longer has the control over him that she used to have.

Not only is Masha an inappropriately active (and ultimately ineffective) viewer, she is also an exhibitionist of sorts. To mark this trait, Tolstoy mentions mirrors at two important points in the novella. As Berger argues, the function of the mirror in painting is "to make the woman connive in treating herself as, first and foremost, a sight" — that is, an object of erotic desire.[24] In his novella, Tolstoy uses this image to similar ends.

The mirror first appears at the very beginning of Masha's and Sergey Mikhailovich's romance, when he urges her not to change her simple country dress for his sake, claiming that he should be

---

[23]   This comment, of course, hints at the future trouble in her marriage. It is, however, so incongruous and unexpected at this point that both the FitzLyons and Aylmer Maude completely misread it. The FitzLyons translate it as "The happiness that had almost escaped me, but that had now returned again" (Tolstoy, "Family Happiness," trans. FitzLyons, 102); and Maude translates it as "Happiness which had now come back, after so nearly departing forever"; Leo Tolstoy, "Family Happiness," in *The Short Novels of Tolstoy*, trans. Aylmer Maude (New York: Dial Press, 1946), 108.

[24]   Berger, *Ways of Seeing*, 51.

no different to her than the old house servant Grigory. She does not believe him:

> But it seemed to me that, even as he was speaking, he was looking at me in a way that Grigory would never have looked at me, and I felt uncomfortable . . . "How strangely he looked at me," I thought as I hurriedly changed upstairs. "But anyway, thank goodness he's come: it will be more cheerful now!" I glanced at a mirror, ran downstairs gaily, and without concealing my haste I went out panting on the terrace. (5:74; 77)

The mirror clearly marks the first indication of Sergey Mikhailovich's erotic desire and Masha's awareness of it.

The second mention, in particular, betrays the mirror's erotic symbolism:

> In my room [kabinet], which [my mother-in-law] Tatyana Semyonovna furnished herself, stood the very best furniture of different centuries and styles and, amongst other things, an old cheval-glass which at first I simply could not look at without embarrassment, but which subsequently became as dear as an old friend to me. (5:106; 113)

The embarrassment (zastenchivost') suggests the erotic nature of the sights that used to be reflected in it. The appellation "an old friend," on the other hand, echoes what Masha says about her husband in the conclusion of the novella ("Not a lover, but an old friend was kissing me"; 5:142; 152), clearly denoting the eventual departure of eros from their relations.

By placing the mirror in Masha's intimate quarters, Tatyana Semyonovna may have unconsciously betrayed her own curiosity about the young couple's erotic life—the same curiosity that she manifests when she tries to peek discreetly at their evening activities:

> Mother often wanted to have a look at us in the sitting room, but she was probably afraid to embarrass us, and she would sometimes walk through the sitting room pretending not to look at us, with a pseudo-serious and indifferent expression on her face; but I knew that she had no reason for going to her room and coming back so quickly. (5:108; 115)

Tatyana Semyonovna's shy curiosity, however, does not satisfy Masha's exhibitionist streak. She wants her happiness to be exposed to the whole world: "I loved him and saw that I meant everything to him; but I wanted everyone to see our love" (5:111; 117). In St. Petersburg, she thinks that she has finally achieved this exposure and feels happy:

> I experienced for the first time the feeling of pride and self-satisfaction [*samodovol'stva*] when all eyes turned toward me as I entered a ballroom, but he would hasten to leave me and lose himself in a black crowd of tail-coats, as if ashamed to acknowledge his possession of me in front of the crowd. "You just wait!" I often thought, picking out his inconspicuous and sometimes bored figure at the other end of the ballroom. "Wait," I thought, "till we get home, and then you'll understand, and see for whom it was that I tried to be pretty and brilliant, and what it is I love best of all I see around tonight." (5:118; 126)

Masha enjoys being an object of general admiration and believes that it increases her sexual attractiveness in the eyes of her husband. At first, Sergey Mikhailovich is indeed affected along with other men: "Besides, I felt that, apart from his love for me, he now also admired me [*liubuetsia mnoi*]" (5:116; 124). Sergey Mikhailovich admits as much in a letter to his mother: "Everyone is delighted with her; even I can't admire her enough [*ne naliubuius' na nee*] and—if it were possible—I would love her even more!" (5:117; 124). Eventually, however, Sergey Mikhailovich grows ashamed of Masha's exhibitionism. The sexual favors that she apparently bestows on him afterward do not make up to him for the shame of her exposure.

Masha's encounter with the Marquis D. reveals to her the dangers of exhibitionism and teaches her the value of privacy. She is ready to withdraw to the countryside. The ability to see correctly, however, comes to her only at the very end of the novella, when she finds the right object for her gaze and the right mode of observation. When her final conversation with her husband is over, the nurse appears with her infant son. Formerly indifferent to her children,

Masha takes the child in her arms. The child looks at her and smiles: "Suddenly those eyes came to rest on me, the spark of thought shone in them, the fat, parted lips started to pucker and broke into a smile" (5:143; 153). Feeling a powerful surge of motherly love, Masha covers the infant with kisses. Remarkably, when her husband comes up to them and tries to play with the child, Masha does not want to share:

> My husband came towards me, and I quickly covered up the baby's face and then uncovered it again. "Ivan Sergeich!" said my husband, touching him under the chin with his finger. But I quickly covered Ivan Sergeich up again. No one but I should look at him for long. (5:143; 153)

Masha expresses a desire to look at her older child earlier in the novella, right after the incident with the Marquis D., when she rejoins her husband in Heidelberg. At that time, however, her wish to look at her child serves as a pretext to escape her husband's reproaching gaze:

> I imagined all he might think of me, and felt outraged by the dreadful thoughts that I attributed to him as I met his uncertain and seemingly shameful [*pristyzhennyi*] gaze directed at me. "No, he doesn't want to and can't understand me!" I said I was going to look at the child, and left him. I wanted to be alone, and to cry and cry and cry. (5:134; 142)

It is even doubtful whether she goes to see her child at all. In Pokrovskoe, however, Masha finally accepts and even welcomes the departure of eros from her marital relations. Now she is ready to change, and her younger child's innocent gaze teaches her that it is her children who are the rightful object for a woman's gaze. It also teaches her that a woman should be discreet in exhibiting her love, whether sexual or maternal, as well as in exposing the object of her love to an outside gaze—even to that of her husband. Having found her new identity as a mother, Masha can freely look her husband in the eye: "I glanced at my husband; his eyes were laughing as they met mine, and for the first time in many months I looked at him lightheartedly and joyfully" (5:143; 153).

* * *

Family Happiness is the first of many works in which Tolstoy wrestles with the problem of sexuality and its place in marriage. In the novella, he portrays the dynamics of sexual relations between the spouses in visual terms invested with powerful erotic symbolism. When expressing erotic desire, Sergey Mikhailovich's gaze is both penetrating and open for the heroine's reciprocal gaze. It plunges the heroine into an erotic trance. In contrast, when eros is gone from the characters' relations, Sergey Mikhailovich's eyes become shallow and impenetrable to Masha's.

The spouses' visual interactions are not symmetrical. Not only does Sergey Mikhailovich, by virtue of being male, do most of the looking, but Tolstoy also never suggests that his way of looking is improper. His deep, penetrating gaze signifies true erotic love and is favorably contrasted with the kind of superficial looking that expresses lust. The verb *liubovat'sia*, or to look with admiration, is used to denote a lustful gaze directed only at a person's outer appearance. This is how Masha is seen at the balls and how the Marquis D. and Masha see each other in their love scene: he looks at her neck and her breast; she, at his forehead, nose, nostrils, mustache, beard, cheeks, neck, and mouth. Sergey Mikhailovich not only refuses to look admiringly at Masha himself but also believes that, by accepting admiring gazes, she commits a sexual transgression.

In contrast, Masha's visual behavior is often wrong. For a female, she is an inappropriately active viewer and, furthermore, she enjoys being looked at and admired. She also wants her love for her husband to be exposed to outside observers. Her exhibitionist streak causes the marital rift and prompts Sergey Mikhailovich to purge eros from their marriage altogether. Only after Masha learns the dangers of enjoying an admiring gaze and realizes that both exhibitionism and active looking are wrong does she find a measure of family happiness in the privacy of her countryside home.

Masha's visual behavior is not only improper but also contradictory: she wants to be an active viewer (a sexual subject) and a recipient of the male gaze (an object of sexual desire) at the same time. Ultimately, she fails to achieve either. The only active looking that is permitted to her is asexual (or quasi-sexual, given the sensual undertones of the scene between her, her male child, and her husband at the conclusion of the novella). The only gaze that is appropriate for her to enjoy is her child's.

Sergey Mikhailovich's visual behavior, proper as it is, is inconsistent as well. On the one hand, he is an active onlooker, relegating Masha to the role of an object. (This is indirectly confirmed by his refusal to allow her to participate in his activities on the estate.) On the other hand, he tolerates and even invites Masha's reciprocal looking: his gaze is not only penetrating (*pronitsatel'nyi*) but also magnetic or attracting (*pritiagivaiushchii*). It seems that Sergey Mikhailovich accepts Masha as an equal in their sexual relations. Or does he?

Newman suggests that in order for desire to be reciprocal and productive, the male has to give up his superior position—be, as she puts it, figuratively castrated.[25] Sergey Mikhailovich is, if not "castrated," then certainly sexually tame: he is an older man, a father figure, reluctant to enter into sexual relations with the much younger heroine. Furthermore, his gaze is not quite masculine: it is described as quiet, sad, and purged of lust; most strikingly, it is portrayed as penetrating and deep at the same time. He may be Masha's superior morally but certainly not sexually. Hence the apparent equality of the characters' early sexual relations, which is reflected in the reciprocity of Sergey Mikhailovich's and Masha's visual activity at the apex of their love. Characteristically, their early marital life is filled with gaiety and laughter—another sign that the usual hierarchy of male and female is suspended in their relations.[26]

However, Sergey Mikhailovich cannot sustain this reciprocal and equal sexual relationship with his wife. His shy and tame sexual feelings are threatened by Masha's exuberant and unbridled ones. He is obviously intimidated by the idea that she is attractive to other men. He also may be afraid that her inappropriately bold

---

[25]   Newman, "'Situation of the Looker-On,'" 458–60, 464n17.

[26]   On the "emancipatory" power of laughter, see ibid., 460; Newman also refers to Patricia Yaeger, *Honey-Mad Women: Emancipatory Strategies in Women's Writing* (New York: Columbia Univ. Press, 1988), chap. 6.

visual behavior will castrate him even further.[27] In order to protect himself, Sergey Mikhailovich closes his gaze to Masha, regains his visual superiority, withdraws from eros, and chooses a safer mode of marital happiness, *philia*.

Tolstoy's character, however, does not admit—and, probably, does not even realize—that the loss of eros occurs because he is not up to equality in sexual relations with his wife. He clearly believes that it was Masha's sexual transgression that caused the trouble. Furthermore, he sees her transgression as having been inevitable. Like his creator, he considers women to be irrational creatures. The misquoting of Lermontov's poem by Sergey Mikhailovich and Tolstoy himself betrays this belief. Furthermore, Sergey Mikhailovich makes it clear that women are more vulnerable than men to what he calls "the nonsense of life" (5:141; 151)—that is, to the temptation of sexual desire. He therefore feels that he is powerless to keep his young wife from what he perceives as dangerous and destructive sexual experimentation:

> "Why, then, did you live through that nonsense with me and
> let me live through it, if you love me?" I said. "Because, even
> if you had wanted to, you couldn't have believed me; you had
> to find out for yourself—and you did." (5:141; 151)

In his view, a woman, as an erotic and irrational creature, inevitably succumbs to the temptations of lust—even when offered reciprocal and equal sexual relations. The only way to deal with female sexuality is to do away with it altogether and to replace eros in marriage with *philia*. Sergey Mikhailovich destroys his own erotic desire and, eventually, Masha's as well. With erotic love gone, Masha turns her gaze to an appropriate object—her child.

Mandelker, in chapter 1 ("The Myth of Misogyny: De-Moralizing Tolstoy") of her book argues, often convincingly, that, compared with his contemporaries, Tolstoy's views on women were relatively benign and sometimes even oddly feminist. She rightly points out that it was not just female sexuality, but sexuality

---

[27]   On the castrating powers of a female who looks back, see Newman, "'Situation of the Looker-On,'" 451.

in general—both male and female—which disturbed him.[28] While this is true, it is impossible to ignore Tolstoy's particular uneasiness about specifically female sexuality. I would suggest that he came to the idea of radical chastity—and thus the primacy of *agape* over both eros and *philia*—because he did not quite know how to deal with the fact that woman is a sexual creature and remains such in a marriage. This obviously made woman for him the source of instability in sexual relations. I believe that the seeds of this view can be seen in *Family Happiness*. It is not incidental, after all, that Tolstoy chose Matthew 5:28, the intertext central for the novella's message, as an epigraph for two of his most troubling works on erotic desire and female sexuality, "The Kreutzer Sonata" and "The Devil."

In *Family Happiness*, Tolstoy shows more respect for womankind than Michelet ever does in his *L'Amour*, but also far greater fear of female sexuality. While Michelet also presents woman as an irrational creature, in his interpretation she does not constitute any danger to the man or his marriage since the man is firmly in control. She is always an object, never a subject, and therefore cannot cause harm. According to Michelet, a man not only must but also can create his wife, whereas according to Tolstoy, he cannot. Ironically, the male's powerlessness in *Family Happiness* comes as the result of his attempt at equality in sexual relations: the male is hurt because he accords his female partner a measure of independence and the status of a sexual subject. To deal with female sexuality thus is dangerous. Characteristically, Michelet's treatise presents the stages that love undergoes (from platonic, to erotic, to familial love) as inevitable but also as natural and benign. In Tolstoy's novella, in contrast, only the first transformation appears as natural and good (although still marked with fear on the woman's part; 5:104–5; 94), whereas the second one is portrayed as outright painful and violent. Giving up eros is necessary to make family happiness possible, but the process is torturous and the loss is great.

Tolstoy makes Masha tell the story of her marital failures and sexual transgressions—the ultimate act of both exhibitionism and

---

[28]   Mandelker, *Framing Anna Karenina*, 29.

independence. As a reporter, Masha most clearly demonstrates her propensity to be an object and a subject at the same time: she not only is looked at, not only watches herself being looked at, but also reports on it. She usurps the right to "kiss and tell" normally reserved for men. The very act of narrating thus confirms for the reader her potential for causing harm.

At the same time, Masha serves her creator's narrative strategies, enabling Tolstoy to be as convincing as possible in the representation of the novella's events as well as in putting forth his ideas on the dangers of female sexuality and the tragic dynamics of family relations. A female narrator is instrumental to Tolstoy's narrative goals first of all as the focus of visual activities in the novella. As someone who is watched and watches herself being watched, she is in an excellent position to report on both activities. Only Masha could feel and report the magnetism of Sergey Mikhailovich's eyes and, later, watch as those eyes turn opaque. Only Masha could report her own lustful close-up with the object of her erotic desire, the Marquis D. Finally, only she could plausibly tell the reader about the impact of her baby's gaze.

Masha, the narrator, also helps Tolstoy to be ideologically convincing. In the conclusion of her analysis of the novella, Benson discusses a particular effect that Tolstoy's narrative strategies have upon young female readers: thanks to the novella's female perspective, those readers tend to perceive the novella as being "true."[29] While Masha's female perspective indeed makes her the most plausible reporter of her experience, it should not be forgotten that at the center of her experience is her sexual misbehavior and partial recovery with the help of her husband. Tolstoy thus uses her to validate his view of woman as an irrational and lustful creature whom no man, even the wisest and the kindest, can truly guide and control. Gender-biased as they are, when told in Masha's voice, Tolstoy's theses begin to look convincing.

---

[29]   Benson, *Women in Tolstoy*, 42, esp. n9. I can confirm Benson's observations from personal experience: as a young female reader, I used to be totally convinced by Tolstoy's argument and his apportioning of blame.

11. Tolstoy and Gogol: "Notes of a Madman"

As is well known, Tolstoy's first attempt at a work of fiction after his so-called conversion was the unfinished "Notes of a Madman." While its title unmistakably refers to Gogol's identically titled 1834 diaristic account of a clerk gone mad, little else about it does, at least at first glance. To begin with, contrary to the expectations the title creates, the genre of Tolstoy's story is different. It begins with a date ("1883. October 20"), suggesting a diary entry (compare Gogol's "3rd of October"), and the first several sentences are also in the style of a diary.[1] As in a diary, these sentences describe the events of the day when the entry is being written: "Today they took me for an examination to the Provincial Chancellery, and [the examiners'] opinions were divided. They had an argument and decided that I was not insane" (26:466). By the end of the first paragraph, however, these diaristic conventions are abandoned and the narrative assumes the tone of a memoir: "I will tell, in an orderly fashion, how and why this examination came about, how I became insane, and how I revealed my insanity" (26:466). Tolstoy smoothly substitutes a memoir for a diary thanks to the ambivalent meaning of the word "notes," *zapiski*, which can denote both. As I will show, this substitution has implications for the status of the story's narrator.

---

[1] Lev Tolstoi, "Zapiski sumasshedshego," in his *Polnoe sobranie sochinenii v 90 tomakh* (Moscow: Gosudarstvennoe izdatel'stvo khudozhestvennoi literatury, 1928–64), 26:466 (all future references to this edition are given in the text: 26:466); Nikolai Gogol', "Zapiski sumasshedshego," in his *Peterburgskie povesti*, ed. O. G. Dilaktorskaia, Seriia Literaturnye pamiatniki (St. Petersburg: Nauka, 1995), 110 (all future references to this edition are also given in the text). For an excellent and detailed discussion of Gogol's and Tolstoy's "Notes," see Eric de Haard, "Gogol's and Tolstoy's Madmen: Dimensions of Intertextuality," *Essays in Poetics: The Journal of the British Neo-Formalist Circle Produced at Keele University* 28 (Autumn 2003): 51–71. De Haard suggests reading Tolstoy's "Notes" as a parody of Gogol's piece, but as a serious, non-aggressive, and thus not-destructive parody. See ibid., 63–66.

The protagonists of the two stories also seem to be different in every respect: one is a petty bureaucrat unsure of his status as a nobleman but contemptuous toward everyone who is, in his view, his social inferior; the other is a wealthy landowner who initially has little awareness of those outside his social circle but who eventually arrives at the idea of his brotherhood with the common folk (*narod*).

Even more important, the protagonists' narrative ability and their status as narrators differ vastly. Tolstoy's protagonist is able to look back at changes he has undergone and to tell about them "in an orderly fashion," a task which is beyond Poprishchin's introspective and narrative competence. Unlike Tolstoy's narrator, who claims to be able to discern quite clearly the exact moments when the changes in the state of his psyche took place, Poprishchin is so unaware of what is happening to him that it is difficult for the reader to pinpoint the exact moment he becomes insane. As is characteristic of both a diarist and a true madman, Poprishchin is entirely inside both the narrative flow and the stream of psychopathological changes he undergoes, and therefore is unable to report credibly on what is happening to him. Tolstoy's memoirist, in contrast, is outside both the flow of events and the narrative flow. He is self-aware and capable of describing the process of his supposedly going mad. As a result, the fact of his madness becomes suspect: despite the narrator's repeated claims of insanity, the reader remains unconvinced. This paradoxical feature of Tolstoy's story is crucial for the understanding of its message.

Finally, the content of the two stories has little in common. Poprishchin's story can be read as a story of love that failed due to social inequality: while the reader tends to fault Poprishchin's human shortcomings for Sophie's inattention, he himself blames his inferior service rank. He thus suffers from what he perceives as social injustice or the inequity of the rank system. His sufferings do not change him internally, except to plunge him further into insanity. Tolstoy's protagonist, on the contrary, undergoes an existential crisis and a complete personality change: acute fear of death leads him to an understanding of the falsity of his life and a discovery of true Christian faith.

Tolstoy thus rejects the type of narrator created by Gogol, the genre this narrator uses to report his story, and the gist of the story itself. What, then, could be his reason for naming his story after Gogol's? In what way, in Tolstoy's view, does Gogol's title fit his fictional account of his character's conversion? How does the allusion to Gogol's "Notes of a Madman" (all aspects of which seem to have been cast away by Tolstoy) help convey the intended message of Tolstoy's story?

Perhaps, despite all the differences I have enumerated, it is possible to discern a few similarities between the stories. Let us begin with a similar formal feature: the use of the first-person voice, a rarity for both Gogol and Tolstoy. The advantages and disadvantages of first-person narrative are well-known: the first-person narrator is more believable, because he or she is either the protagonist or an eyewitness of the narrated events and thus "should know," and, at the same time, the first-person narrator is more suspect, because his or her view is of necessity limited and subjective. The competence and tone of the first-person narrator is of utter importance: a well-spoken and confident narrator tends to come across as trustworthy, while an inept and self-doubting one often fails to convince the reader. This rule works for Poprishchin, but not for Tolstoy's narrator. As a narrator, Poprishchin is awkward and disoriented, which supports the title's claim that he is a madman. His account of events is therefore always in doubt. Tolstoy's narrator, who is self-assured and eloquent, is supposed to be believable.[2] Paradoxically, it is his very competence that undermines his central claim in the story: that he is insane. As I have already mentioned, this proves useful in deciphering the story's message.

Another similarity between Gogol's and Tolstoy's stories concerns the changes their protagonists undergo beyond ostensibly losing their minds. As the stories progress, both characters become dissatisfied with their social status and try to change it, to leave their old social selves behind, and to become someone else. Poprishchin

---

[2]   For a discussion of one moment when eloquence fails the narrator, see "Tolstoy the Wanderer and the Quest for Adequate Expression," chap. 12 in this collection.

promotes himself to royalty, becoming, in his imagination, Ferdinand VIII. In contrast, Tolstoy's narrator claims to have left his high social position, joining the common folk. However, in a way he also assumes the status of a "king"—the king of Judea, Jesus Christ—when he says about himself at the conclusion of the story that he "went home on foot, talking to the people" (26:474). In the mirror symmetry to this change, at the conclusion of Gogol's story, Poprishchin momentarily becomes a human being devoid of discernable social markings, except, perhaps, those of a Russian peasant, one of "the common folk": "Now one can see the Russian huts. Is this my home I see afar?" (125).

Yet another similarity between the stories is, of course, their characters' insanity, obvious in the case of Poprishchin, and declared but dubious in the case of Tolstoy's protagonist. Poprishchin's insanity is evident in multiple ways: in his apparent belief in talking and corresponding dogs, in his increasing neglect of his service duties, in his inability to keep his dates in order, and, finally, in his conviction that he is Ferdinand VIII. Tolstoy's protagonist exhibits acute anxiety on several occasions, but never in the story is he actually out of touch with reality. The scholarly literature offers several medical explications of his condition, never seeing it as true madness.[3] It is obvious that Tolstoy's protagonist uses the word "insane" idiosyncratically. To understand his usage, it is important to point out that, by his own account, he becomes truly insane only when he finds faith:

> But my full insanity began even later, a month after this [his realization of his brotherhood with the common people].

---

[3]　It is widely accepted that "Notes of a Madman" is an autobiographical (or, in Richard Gustafson's term, autopsychological) story, and analyses of the narrator's psychopathology go hand in hand with discussions of Tolstoy's mental condition at the time of his religious crisis. While many scholars agree that Tolstoy (and his character) suffered episodes of anxiety, depression, and manic-depressive mood swings, nobody considers him truly insane. See, for example, Richard F. Gustafson, *Leo Tolstoy: Resident and Stranger* (Princeton, NJ: Princeton Univ. Press, 1986), 192–96; Daniel Rancour-Laferrier, *Tolstoy on the Couch: Misogyny, Masochism, and the Absent Mother* (Hampshire: Macmillan Press, 1998), 16–32, and Rancour-Laferrier, "Does God Exist? A Clinical Study of the Religious Attitudes Expressed in Tolstoy's *Confession*," *SEEJ* 49, no. 3 (2005): 445–73.

It began with my going to the church, attending the mass, praying properly, and being emotionally affected. And suddenly they brought holy bread to me, then everyone went to kiss the cross, began to hustle, then there were beggars at the exit. And suddenly it became clear to me that nothing of this should exist. Not only should this not exist, but it does not exist, and if it does not exist, then there is neither death nor fear, and the past tearing apart [*razdiranie*] in me is gone, and I am afraid of nothing. Then the light fully enlightened me, and I became what I am now. (26:474)

"What he is now," presumably, is the madman of the title. Effectively, Tolstoy's narrator is asserting that true faith and insanity are the same. Such an understanding requires some explanation.

The theme of insanity is also prominent in *A Confession* (*Ispoved'*, 1882), an account of the quest for faith that led to Tolstoy's conversion. In this work, the initial understanding of insanity is reversed in relation to "Notes of a Madman": those living without faith are repeatedly called insane. First, in chapter 2, Tolstoy recalls his time in St. Petersburg as a successful young writer; he reports about himself and his friends:

Through association with these people I acquired a new vice: an unhealthy pride and an insane conviction that I was called to teach people, though I didn't know what.
Now, when I recall that time, my frame of mind [*nastroenie*] then, and the frame of mind of those people (there are even now thousands of such people), I feel pity, horror, amusement: the same feeling arises that one has when visiting a madhouse. (23:6)

In the next paragraph, Tolstoy again compares the atmosphere in St. Petersburg in the 1850s to that in a madhouse (23:7). He concludes the chapter with yet another reference to the insanity of his younger faithless self and his St. Petersburg associates: "Now it is clear to me that it was no different from a madhouse. At that time I only vaguely suspected this, and, like all madmen, even called everyone else mad, except myself" (23:7).

Tolstoy continues to evoke insanity throughout the piece, but his understanding of the term changes. First he begins to use the word to denote his dissatisfaction with his life devoid of faith ("I felt that I was not quite sane mentally," 23:9; "minutes of bewilderment began visiting me," 23:10). Then Tolstoy arrives at an understanding of faith as insanity. Yet this understanding is different from the one in "Notes of a Madman": he uses the notion of madness negatively, implying that only an insane person can believe in certain aspects of Christian teaching:

> And this irrational [*nerazumnoe*] knowledge is faith, the very same that I was unable not to reject [*ne mog ne otrinut'*]. This was God as one and three; this was creation in six days, devils and angels, and everything that I could not accept unless I went mad. (23:33)

Finally, in chapter 11, Tolstoy returns to his understanding of life without faith as insanity, and now he even more clearly depicts his own faithless, egotistical, and unloving self as insane:

> An executioner who spends his life torturing and beheading, or a drunkard [*mertvyi p'ianitsa*], or a madman, who has locked himself for life in a dark room and who has dirtied his room but imagines that he would perish if he exited this room—what if they asked themselves: what is life? Clearly, they would not be able to give the question "what is life" any other answer than that life is the greatest evil. And the madman's response would be absolutely correct, but only for him. What if I am such a madman? What if all of us, the rich and educated, are such madmen?
> And I have realized that we are such madmen. And I in particular am certainly such a madman. (23:41–42)

Tolstoy thus comprehends (as he puts it in the opening of chapter 12) the "mistake of rational knowledge" (23:43), which, in turn, led him to embrace God the way He is accepted by the common people, and, eventually, to find true faith.

In Tolstoy's diary of 1884, the year when he worked most intensively on "Notes of a Madman," insanity similarly denotes the lack of a clear vision of truth. On May 28, Tolstoy writes about his conflict with family members over his newly acquired views:

"I seem to be the only non-madman [*ne sumasshedshii*] living in an insane asylum run by madmen" (49:99). Furthermore, Tolstoy also mentions his work on "Notes of a Madman" but refers to it by a title antithetical to Gogol's and his own eventual title: "Notes of a Non-Madman" ("Zapiski nesumasshedshego"; 49:75–76, 81). It is evident that at this point the word "insanity" meant for Tolstoy lack of faith and clear understanding. Apparently, he arrived at his idiosyncratic usage of the word "insanity" late in the process of working on the story.

Madness (both *bezumie* and *sumasshestvie*) as lack of understanding can also be found in Tolstoy's 1909 unfinished article "On Insanity" ("O bezumii"). Among other things, Tolstoy writes:

> In this way, it became clear to me that the majority of human beings, especially in the Christian world, live in our times a life that is directly opposed to both reason and feeling, and also to the most obvious benefits and comforts of all people—that they are in a state of perhaps temporary but total madness, insanity [*sumasshestviia, bezumiia*].[4]

He claims that there is no difference between the inmates in an insane asylum and their keepers:

> That we live an insane, totally insane, crazy life is not mere words, not a comparison, not a hyperbole, but the simplest statement of fact. Recently I had a chance to visit two enormous institutions for the mentally ill, and the impression I got was that I was seeing institutions set up by people with one common rampant form of insanity for people with diverse forms of insanity that did not match the common rampant form.[5]

It is clear from these passages that, in Tolstoy's view, people who consider themselves sane but who do not possess true faith are as insane as the madmen confined to insane asylums—or even more so.

---

4   Lev Tolstoi, "O bezumii," *Tolstovskii listok: Zapreshchennyi Tolstoi* 5 (Moscow: Press-Solo, 1994), 167.

5   Ibid., 169.

Remarkably, the article "On Insanity" has an epigraph that does not quite fit the content of the article. Its second sentence in particular recalls the usage of the word "madness" in the final redaction of "Notes of a Madman": "Ce sont des imbéciles. Un imbécile est avant tout un homme qu'on ne comprend pas."[6] It appears that Tolstoy vacillates between the more obvious usage of the word "insane" that defines unbelievers and the idiosyncratic one that denotes those who do believe and are misunderstood by other people. This vacillation is most clear in his eventual appropriation of Gogol's title for his own story.

Both Tolstoy's idiosyncratic usage of the word "insanity" and his adoption of Gogol's title can perhaps be better understood if we recall that Tolstoy was not the first Russian writer who very publicly announced his finding of true faith and that it was none other than Gogol in whose steps he was following.[7] Tolstoy's title acquires new significance when we recall that Gogol's contemporaries regarded his newfound religiosity and, particularly, his urgent desire to make it public in *Selected Passages from Correspondence with Friends* (1847) to be a result of mental illness. This was first suggested by Vissarion Belinsky in his "Letter to Gogol" (1847), in which he wrote: "Either you are ill, and you need urgent medical care, or—I do not dare to finish my thought."[8] Belinsky's opinion was shared not only by like-minded radicals but also by broad circles of Gogol's contemporaries, including some high-ranking members of the clergy and even some of Gogol's conservative friends like Sergey Aksakov.[9]

---

[6]   The publication in *Tolstovskii listok* erroneously has it "Un imbéciles est . . ."

[7]   Rancour-Laferrier, with a reference to Thomas Newlin, also mentions Petr Chaadaev, the author of *Apology of a Madman* (1837), as yet another possible role model for Tolstoy in writing his "Notes of a Madman" (see *Tolstoy on the Couch*, 206). I would argue, however, that Chaadaev (whose legacy Tolstoy largely ignored and whose alleged madness was not connected with religious conversion) is far less relevant for the interpretation of Tolstoy's story.

[8]   Vissarion Belinskii, "Pis'mo k N. V. Gogoliu," in his *Polnoe sobranie sochinenii* (Moscow: Izdatel'stvo Akademii Nauk SSSR, 1956), 10:214.

[9]   In his letter to I. S. Aksakov of January 11, 1847, S. T. Aksakov writes about *Selected Passages*: "Finally, three days ago we received Gogol's new book. . . .

In the 1850s, Tolstoy subscribed to the general harsh opinion of Gogol's religious writings of the late 1840s in general, and of *Selected Passages*, in particular. In 1857, after reading Gogol's letters published in his *Collected Works* edited by P. A. Kulish, Tolstoy wrote in his diary: "[Gogol] was simply a rotten person. Terribly rotten [*drian' chelovek, uzhasnaia drian'*]" (47:156).[10] Several weeks later, Tolstoy apparently had an argument with the Aksakovs about these letters. He wrote in his diary on November 17: "Evening at the Aksakovs', terrible pride. Needlessly argued about Gogol" (47:163). We can suppose that the argument was likely to have been about Tolstoy's harsh judgment of Gogol.

After his conversion, however, Tolstoy's view of Gogol and *Selected Passages* changed, becoming highly positive. In an October 1887 letter to N. N. Strakhov, he writes that he has reread Gogol's book for the third time and this time has found it impressive in many respects. He tells Strakhov of his plan to publish Gogol's *Selected Passages*, together with his biography, in *Posrednik*, as a publication intended for the common people: "This would be a wonderful vita [*chudesnoe zhitie*] for the people. At least they will understand" (64:107).[11]

From the letter to Strakhov, it is evident that Tolstoy had come to perceive Gogol as a fellow Christian writer who, like Tolstoy himself, was looking for new ways to address and serve his reader. In this, Tolstoy views Gogol as his model:

> Indeed, in regard to true art, I have rediscovered the America discovered by Gogol thirty-five years ago. The role of a writer

---

The best thing you can say about it is to call Gogol insane"; see S. T. Aksakov, *Sobranie sochinenii v trekh tomakh* (Moscow: Khudozhestvennaia literatura, 1986), 3:179. Cf. his letter to I. S. Aksakov of February 8 of the same year, ibid., 186. In his "Letter to Gogol's Friends," written soon after Gogol's death, Aksakov expressed a much more positive opinion of the book (ibid., 379–80).

10   For an overview of Tolstoy's changing opinion about *Selected Passages*, see I. P. Zolotusskii, "Tolstoi chitaet 'Vybrannye mesta iz perepiski s druz'iami,'" in *Gogol' i obshchestvo liubitelei rossiiskoi slovesnosti*, comp. R. N. Kleimenova (Moscow: Izdatel'stvo Academia, 2005), 211–22.

11   Cf. Tolstoy's letters to P. I. Biriukov (October 5, 1887) and F. N. Berg (January ?, 1888), ibid., 98–99 and 139.

in general is defined there (in his letter to Yazykov, [number] 29) in such a way that it is impossible to say it better. And the entire correspondence (if one excludes some personal things) is full of the most essential, profound thoughts. (64:105–6)

For Tolstoy, just as for Gogol, imaginative literature is now subordinated to the religious message: in the two copies of *Selected Passages* that Tolstoy owned and read in 1887 and again in 1909, he marks favorably passages in Gogol's work that make such claims.[12] Gogol's religiosity remained of the utmost importance for Tolstoy in his later years. In a diary entry of March 8, 1902, he remarks: "Belinsky, without religion, is from the lower floor. Gogol, religious, is from the upper one" (54:125; cf. 57:35–36). Tolstoy sums up his new understanding of Gogol as a writer and religious thinker in his 1909 article, written to mark the centennial of Gogol's birth. Even though Tolstoy never accepted Gogol's views in *Selected Passages* in their totality (he vehemently disagreed with Gogol's treatment of serfdom, his acceptance of church rituals, and his positive view of the Russian monarchy), he praises some of his literary works and those of his religious writings that, in his view, came from the heart:

> Gogol is a great talent, a beautiful heart, but a small, timid mind.
> When he submits himself to his talent, he produces beautiful literary works, such as "Old-World Landowners," the first part of *Dead Souls*, *The Inspector General*, and especially — the acme of a perfection of sorts — "The Carriage." When he submits to his heart and religious feeling, he produces in his letters — such as the letters "On the Significance of Illnesses," "On the Nature of the Word," and in many, many others — touching, often profound and instructive thoughts. (38:50)[13]

The "rotten person" becomes a fellow Christian writer and a model to emulate. The title of Tolstoy's story may thus refer to

---

[12]   See Zolotusskii, "Tolstoi chitaet," 214–17.

[13]   Cf. a diary entry of March 5, 1909, 57:34; and his notebook of the same time, 57:202.

his own similarity to Gogol as the author of *Selected Passages*, which the post-conversion Tolstoy recognized and wanted to highlight.

Tolstoy's continuing vacillation between the two understandings of insanity (unbelief and belief) can also point to his continuing unease about the fact that faith in God cannot be achieved rationally. This concern and the ensuing inconsistencies are evident in *A Confession* and, especially, in the article "On Insanity," whose epigraph contradicts the main text, and whose ending demonstrates Tolstoy's failed attempt to subordinate his argument to formal logic.[14] The same uneasiness can also be seen in Tolstoy's low opinion of Gogol's mind and preference for his heart, expressed in his centennial article.

Furthermore, the fact that Tolstoy's conversion did not completely resolve the issue that initiated his quest for faith—namely, the fear of death—could also have contributed to his inconsistent usage of the word "insanity." It is instructive to see what exactly leads the protagonist of Tolstoy's "Notes of a Madman" to his true faith: he realizes that there is something that should not exist, and if this something does not exist, then there is no death and no fear of death. It is pretty clear that it is fear of death that stands in the way of his faith ("light"), and once it is gone, the protagonist both finds faith and goes insane: "Then the light fully enlightened me, and I became what I am now" (26:474). What follows is that in order not to fear death, one needs to be insane.

This idea was not entirely new for Tolstoy at the time he was working on "Notes of a Madman": it first surfaced in his 1858 story "Three Deaths."[15] Let us also recall that in *A Confession* the reasoning faculty temporarily stands in the way of Tolstoy's accepting faith (23:33). In "Notes of a Madman," Tolstoy's protagonist does just that: in order to accept death without fear, he actually goes mad (or claims to have done so). It seems that, at some level, Tolstoy believes that only madmen are able not to fear death. It is possible

---

14   For Tolstoy's faulty logic in the conclusion of "O bezumii," see 167–68.

15   For a discussion of this idea in "Three Deaths," see "Turgenev's 'Death' and Tolstoy's 'Three Deaths,'" chap. 9 in this collection.

that this conclusion interfered with Tolstoy's ability to finish the story.[16]

The first literary work that Tolstoy completed after his conversion was "The Death of Ivan Il'ich," another story concerned with overcoming the fear of death. Tolstoy worked on the story simultaneously with his work on "Notes of a Madman," and much has been said about the common concerns of the two works.[17] In my view, it is also important to point out that "The Death of Ivan Il'ich" bears at least one point of similarity to Gogol's story: it is one of very few Tolstoyan works with a bureaucrat as its protagonist. True, Ivan Il'ich is no Poprishchin, in that he is a high-ranking bureaucrat successful in his career. Yet Tolstoy points out that he began his service in a very low rank (tenth class, 26:70—even lower than that of Poprishchin) and, like Poprishchin, he is mainly interested in his career (*poprishche*)—that is, until he faces death. It is likely therefore that Gogol's "Notes of a Madman" served as a point of departure for Tolstoy in this story. I would suggest that "The Death of Ivan Il'ich" is a rewrite, in a certain sense, of both Gogol's and Tolstoy's "Notes of a Madman," and that to picture the acceptance of death convincingly Tolstoy had to dispense with the idea of insanity altogether.

---

[16] For more on Tolstoy's inability to articulate a method of accepting death, see "Tolstoy the Wanderer and the Quest for Adequate Expression," chap. 12 in this volume.

[17] See, for example, the commentary to "The Death of Ivan Il'ich," in Lev Tolstoi, *Sobranie sochinenii v 20-ti tomakh* (Moscow: Khudozhestvennaia literatura, 1964), 12:474–78; Kathleen Parthé, in "Tolstoy and the Geometry of Fear," *Modern Language Studies* 15, no. 4 (1985): 84, while acknowledging the connection between the stories, emphasizes the difference in their presentation of death.

12. Tolstoy the Wanderer
and the Quest for Adequate Expression

The uncanny resemblance between Pushkin's 1835 poem "The Wanderer" ("Strannik," first published in 1841) and the events of the later years of Tolstoy's life has been pointed out by several scholars, but its implications have not yet been fully examined. The so-called "Arzamas terror," experienced by Tolstoy during an 1869 trip and described, at the time, in a letter to his wife and in "Notes of a Madman" in 1884; the persistent fear of death and the ensuing urge to change his life that caused the bitter conflict with his family; the suspicion among some family members that he had lost his mind; and, finally, the irresistible desire to leave his home (which, after several aborted attempts, ended in his departure from Yasnaya Polyana on October 28, 1910, and his death several days later at the railroad station Astapovo)—all closely resemble the description of the Wanderer's distress in Pushkin's poem.[1] More significantly, variations on "The Wanderer's" plot can be found in an astonishing number of Tolstoy's later works. There is therefore little doubt that, even though Tolstoy's knowledge of the poem is not documented, he knew it, and it affected him strongly.

As is well known, Pushkin's "Wanderer" is a transposition of the opening passages of John Bunyan's allegory *The Pilgrim's Progress* (published in 1668). Tolstoy knew Bunyan's work and, remarkably, disliked it: Dushan Makovitsky wrote in his diary on December 22, 1904, that it was its allegorical style that repulsed the writer. Tolstoy mentions *The Pilgrim's Progress* while criticizing Ján Komenský's *Labyrinth of the World and Paradise of the Heart* (1631). Makovitsky quotes his critical remark: "Yes, these are allegories—

---

[1]   For an analysis of the circumstances of Tolstoy's departure and his death, and, especially, of the "national narrative" that emerged about these events, see William Nickell, *The Death of Tolstoy: Russia on the Eve, Astapovo Station, 1910* (Ithaca, NY: Cornell Univ. Press, 2010).

I do not like them. For the same reason I also dislike the description of Bunyan's journey [*puteshestviia*]."[2] Dmitry Blagoy's arguments in favor of the biographical nature of the poem notwithstanding, Pushkin's poem is also allegorical.[3] Alexander Dolinin points out Pushkin's indebtedness to yet another allegorical journey, Dante's *Divine Comedy*.[4]

It is remarkable that the allegorical nature of both the original text and Pushkin's transposition did not preclude Tolstoy from trying to rewrite the Wanderer story time and again. If anything, it probably inspired him to do so, in order to put ideas that were of extreme personal importance to him in a proper form. One might say that in his later years the writer was obsessed with the Wanderer story, retelling it numerous times and in different genres: in letters and diaries, in "Notes of a Madman," in "Posthumous Notes of the Elder Fyodor Kuzmich," and in "Buddha." Other works about leaving one's normal life behind and trying to live a different one can also be added to this list: "Father Sergius," *The Living Corpse*, *The Resurrection*, several unfinished biographies of Buddha, and a 1904 story "Korney Vasil'ev." Taken together, these works illustrate Tolstoy's persistent interest in the motif of departure from one's home in quest of spiritual transformation.[5]

---

[2]   D. P. Makovitskii, *U Tolstogo, 1904–1910: "Iasnopolianskie zapiski,"* vol. 1, *1904–1905* (Moscow: Nauka, 1979), 106.

[3]   See D. D. Blagoi, "Dzhon Ben'ian, Pushkin i Lev Tolstoi," *Pushkin: Issledovaniia i materialy–1956*, Institut russkoi literatury (Pushkinskii dom) (Moscow: Akademiia nauk, 1962), 4: passim, but especially 60–63.

[4]   A. A. Dolinin, "K voprosu o 'Strannike' i ego istochnikakh," in *Pushkinskie chteniia v Tartu: Tezisy dokladov nauchnoi konferentsii 13–14 noiabria 1987 g.* (Tallin: [Tartuskii gos. universitet], 1987), 34–37. For a discussion of the poem's place in Pushkin's oeuvre, see Andrew Kahn, "Pushkin's Wanderer Fantasies," in *Rereading Russian Poetry*, ed. Stephanie Sandler (New Haven, CT: Yale Univ. Press, 1999), 225–47. Kahn interprets the poem as Pushkin's ironic rereading of Bunyan's allegory and of his own earlier poetry about wanderers.

[5]   For the most exhaustive overview of Tolstoy's treatment of the Wanderer *topos*, see A. Syrkin, "The 'Indian' in Tolstoy (part two)," in *Leo Tolstoy*, ed. Dragan Milivojevic, East European Monographs 518 (Boulder, CO: East European Monographs, 1998), 85–114; see also a discussion of what

I would like to examine three of Tolstoy's attempts to rewrite the Wanderer story: "Notes of a Madman," "Posthumous Notes of the Elder Fyodor Kuzmich," and "Buddha." I have chosen these works because, first, all three, different as they are, contain an autobiographical element, rooted in actual events in Tolstoy's life—in his conversion and (more importantly for my inquiry) in the "Arzamas terror" episode; second, all three contain the core elements of the Pilgrim/Wanderer plot (some of which could also have originated in the Arzamas episode): sudden and intense panic or distress, the ensuing urge to leave home, and, most crucially, the transformation of this unexplained spiritual turmoil into a quest to understand and accept death. In this paper, I would like to examine Tolstoy's different approaches to retelling the Wanderer story and try to determine what could have twice (in "Notes of a Madman" and "Posthumous Notes of the Elder Fyodor Kuzmich") prevented him from presenting it to his satisfaction and thus finishing these two pieces. I would also like to address the question of whether his characters in all three pieces in fact learn to accept death and, if so, whether they successfully formulate an explanation of how to do it.

The first text connected with the (future) Wanderer story is Tolstoy's letter to his wife, written in Saransk on September 4, 1869, on his way to visit an estate he was planning to buy. Tolstoy writes:

> The day before yesterday I spent the night in Arzamas, and something out of the ordinary happened to me. It was two o'clock in the morning, I was awfully tired, was sleepy, and not in any pain. But all of a sudden I was seized with anxiety [*toska*], fear, terror of a kind that I had never experienced. I will later tell you in detail what I felt, but I had never experienced such a tormenting sensation, and God forbid anyone should experience it. I got up at once [*vskochil*] and ordered the horses to be harnessed. While they were being harnessed, I fell asleep and woke up feeling well. Yesterday this feeling—

the author calls *arkhetip ukhoda* (the archetype of departure), in K. Kedrov, "'Ukhod' i 'voskresenie' geroev Tolstogo," in *V mire Tolstogo: Sbornik statei* (Moscow: Sovetskii pisatel', 1978), 248–73.

quite significantly weaker—returned during the ride, but I was ready and did not succumb to it, particularly since it was weaker. Today I feel well and happy [*zdorovym i veselym*], as much as I can be away from my family [*vne sem'i*].[6]

It is noteworthy that in this description Tolstoy does not mention the fear of death—the problem that would become central in later literary renditions of the event. Instead, he implies that his separation from the family is the likely cause of his emotional distress. He begins the description of the episode with anxious questions about the family's well-being: "How are you and the children? Has anything bad happened? I am tormented by worry for the second day in a row."[7] After having described the anxiety attack, Tolstoy returns to the subject of his family:

During this trip I felt for the first time to what degree I have grown together [*srossia*] with you and the children. I can be alone if I am constantly busy, as I am when I go to Moscow; but as I am now, without any occupation—I positively feel that I cannot be alone.[8]

It seems that at this point Tolstoy believes the way to deal with his anxiety is to reunite with his family, not to abandon it in search of a cure.

Tolstoy returns to the "Arzamas terror" in "Notes of a Madman" (1884), his first attempt at a literary work after his conversion. Tolstoy didn't finish the story in 1884 but kept coming back to it in 1887, 1888, 1896, and 1903; the only coherent extant text, however, is from 1884.[9] In this unfinished story, Tolstoy's description of the main character's experience is closer to Pushkin's "Wanderer" and

---

[6]   Lev Tolstoi, *Polnoe sobranie sochinenii v 90 tomakh* (Moscow: Gosudarstvennoe izdatel'stvo khudozhestvennoi literatury, 1928–64), 83:167–68.

[7]   Ibid., 167. The Russian form of the inquiry (*Chto s toboi i s det'mi?*) almost implies that something bad has indeed happened.

[8]   Ibid., 168.

[9]   For several additional fragments, most of them variants of the extant text, see Tolstoi, *Polnoe sobranie sochinenii v 90 tomakh*, 26:475–76.

the corresponding passage in Bunyan than to what he described in his 1869 letter. "Notes" contains all the crucial elements of Pushkin's and Bunyan's texts: the protagonist's sudden fear of death, his desire to leave his old, immoral life behind as a means of overcoming this fear, and his family's interpretation of his behavior as madness. Notably, Tolstoy abandons Bunyan's third-person narrative in favor of the first person, used by Pushkin, which highlights the autobiographical roots of the story. One puzzling detail is that the direction of the protagonist's progress seems still to be toward home, not away from it. Not only does the fear of death seize him when he is away from home (in Arzamas, in Moscow, in the woods), but the story ends as follows: "Right there, at the church porch, I gave away to beggars everything I had with me, thirty-six rubles, and went home on foot, talking to people [*poshel domoi peshkom, razgovarivaia s narodom*]."[10] Since the story is unfinished, we cannot be sure that this is his final destination. However, at the beginning of the story (a retrospective introduction that describes a medical evaluation of the protagonist's mental state and which chronologically follows the ending), the protagonist still seems to be with his family, who are presumably the ones labeling him as mad.

In "Notes of a Madman," the protagonist seems to have achieved what he has been looking for—acceptance of death—but how he has done so is not revealed in the extant draft. It seems to come as a revelation, but the exact nature of this revelation remains unstated. There are several possible explanations of this omission, and one is likely to be Tolstoy's (or his narrator's) inability to put his experience into words: the draft of the story available to us tries but fails to describe exactly how the protagonist comes to accepting death. It happens to him when he leaves the church after attending a service:

> И мне вдруг ясно стало, что этого всего не должно быть. Мало того, что этого не должно быть, что этого нет, а нет этого, то нет и смерти и страха, и нет во мне больше прежнего раздирания, и я не боюсь уже ничего. Тут уже

---

10   Tolstoi, "Zapiski sumasshedshego," in his *Polnoe sobranie sochinenii v 90 tomakh*, 26:474.

совсем свет осветил меня, и я стал <u>тем, что</u> есть. Если нет <u>этого ничего</u>, то нет прежде всего во мне.[11]

(And suddenly it became clear to me that <u>all this</u> should not exist. Not only should <u>this</u> not exist, but <u>this</u> does not exist, and if <u>this</u> does not exist, then there is neither death nor fear, and the old laceration within me is gone, and I am afraid of <u>nothing</u>. Then the light fully enlightened me, and I became <u>that which</u> I am now. If <u>all this</u> does not exist, it does not exist first of all in me.)

The large number of pronouns in this passage makes it impossible to grasp its exact meaning: "all this," "this should not exist," "this does not exist," "and if this does not exist," "if all this does not exist": what does "this" (*eto*) signify here? One may think that it signifies death or the fear of death, but they are mentioned separately, and it is the absence of the unidentified "this" that abolishes death and the fear of death. Furthermore, in "I became that which I am now," what is the meaning of "that" and "which"? Simply put, the language collapses here—which is not an unusual occurrence in Tolstoy's writings and tends to happen when he attempts to express ideas that are either too personal or resist rational expression.[12] Death—or rather the process by which one can accept death—appears to be one such idea for Tolstoy.

The next rendition of the Wanderer story I would like to discuss is "Posthumous Notes of the Elder Fyodor Kuzmich." Tolstoy had been thinking about this work and reading historical materials to prepare for it since 1890. He began writing it in late 1905 but never finished it.[13] The extant text consists of three parts: the author's introduction promoting the idea that Fyodor Kuzmich is Alexander I, and two parts told in the voice of Alexander/Fyodor

---

[11]   Ibid. Emphasis is mine.

[12]   For a discussion of one such example, see "Turgenev's 'Death' and Tolstoy's 'Three Deaths,'" in this volume, chap. 9. Another example can be found in the first three paragraphs of chap. 5 of "Kholstomer" ("Strider," 1885), packed with awkward repetitions of phrases filled with pronouns lacking antecedents.

[13]   For a description of Tolstoy's work on this piece, see Nickell, *Death of Tolstoy,* 159–62.

Kuzmich, in the form of a memoir, diary, or confession. The first of these two parts tells about Alexander's conversion:

> But God turned his eyes [*oglianulsia*] to me. And all the filth of my life, which I tried to justify for myself and for which I tried to shift the responsibility onto others [*svalit' na drugikh*], was finally opened to me in all its horror, and God helped me to get rid of — not evil: I am still full of it, even though I struggle with it — but participation in it. What kind of spiritual torments I have come through and what occurred in my soul when I recognized all my sinfulness and the necessity of atonement (not the belief that I have atoned, but the real atonement of sins through suffering) I will tell in its proper place.[14]

The narrative stops before Alexander/Fyodor Kuzmich fulfills his promise to describe the inner processes of his conversion. We may assume, however, that Tolstoy planned to draw on his own experience: even in the part that was written, the autobiographical element is quite obvious.[15]

Luckily for my project, Alexander/Fyodor Kuzmich fully describes exactly how he left his life as the emperor and became a Wanderer. It is essential, in my view, that the decisive impulse behind the tsar's departure is the death of his double, a soldier by the name of Strumensky, who has been "punished for running away" (*nakazan za pobeg*) and whose identity Alexander steals, thus becoming a fugitive or Wanderer himself. The realization that he is a murderer leads to the urge to abandon his wrongful life and disappear without anyone knowing about his departure. He easily achieves his goal:

> And what is surprising, the effecting of my intention turned out to be much easier than I expected. And my intention was as follows: to feign that I was ill, [that I was] dying, and, having persuaded and bribed the doctor, put in my place the

---

14   Tolstoi, "Posmertnye zapiski startsa Fedora Kuzmicha," in his *Polnoe sobranie sochinenii v 90 tomakh*, 36:60.

15   See Nickell, *Death of Tolstoy*, 160, for a textual comparison of Tolstoy's *Confession* and "Notes."

dying Strumensky and leave, flee, concealing my name from everyone.

Alexander specifically points out that his new life begins thanks to the man whose death he causes ("the soldier whom I tortured to death," *zamuchennogo mnoiu do smerti soldata*). [16]

The second part of the memoir tells about the memoirist's childhood. It is remarkable that the future emperor's first encounter with death produces a reaction very similar to that of the protagonist in "Notes of a Madman": both are about five years old when they become aware that death exists, and both respond with a fit of unstoppable weeping. Both later lose this sensitivity— until they undergo their conversions. Nickell suggests that this and some other details of Alexander/Fyodor Kuzmich's childhood are autobiographical. [17]

In this part of the memoir, the protagonist also grapples with the question of how to accept death. In contrast to "Notes of a Madman," where this acceptance comes to the protagonist unawares, Fyodor Kuzmich consciously attempts to formulate a rational approach to this task:

> And it occurred to me that if all life consists of the arising of desires and the joy of life [consists] in their fulfillment, then is there not a kind of desire that would be inherent in man, every man, always, and that would always be fulfilled or, rather, would [constantly] come closer to fulfillment? And it became clear to me that this would be so for a man who desired death. All his life would lie in approaching this desire's fulfillment, and this desire would certainly be fulfilled.
>
> At first this seemed strange to me. But, having thought it over, I suddenly realized [*uvidal*] that this is indeed so, that only this, approaching death, is a reasonable desire for man. A desire not for death, not for death itself, but for that movement of life that leads to death. . . . I came to this unconsciously. But if I were to define what is the highest good for me (and this is not only possible, but this has to be so), if

---

16   Tolstoi, "Posmertnye zapiski," 36:60, 44.

17   Nickell, *Death of Tolstoy*, 161.

> I were to consider that the highest good for me lies in liberation from the passions, in getting closer to God, then everything that would put me closer to death—old age, diseases—would be the fulfillment of my only and most essential [*glavnoe*] desire.[18]

It is noteworthy that the passage repeats the pronoun "this" (*eto*) almost as frequently as the last paragraph of the extant draft of "Notes of a Madman," but unlike the earlier story, in this passage it is clear what "this" signifies: the logic that leads to the acceptance of death. Yet logical as Alexander/Fyodor Kuzmich's reasoning may seem, accepting it is still difficult:

> This is so, and I feel this when I am healthy. But when, as it was yesterday and the day before yesterday, I have an upset stomach [*boleiu zheludkom*], I cannot summon this feeling and, even though I don't resist death, I cannot desire to get closer to it. Yes, this condition is the condition of spiritual slumber. I need to wait calmly [*nado spokoino zhdat'*].[19]

"Notes" breaks off before the protagonist reaches acceptance. Once again, we are dealing with a work that occupied Tolstoy for a very long time (at least fifteen years) and which, nonetheless, he left unfinished. It is, of course, impossible to know for certain why Tolstoy abandoned the piece. However, it seems significant to me that Tolstoy stops a couple of paragraphs after the just-quoted passage about the difficulty of accepting death rationally. It is noteworthy that in his letter (September 2, 1907) to Grand Duke Nikolay Mikhailovich (who had sent him his book debunking the idea that Fyodor Kuzmich was Alexander), he explains his abandonment of the story by the necessity of preparing for his own impeding death:

> Let it be that connecting the personalities of Alexander and Koz'mich [sic! Tolstoy uses one of the variants of the name Kuz'ma to form the patronymic] has been proven to be

---

18   Tolstoi, "Posmertnye zapiski," 36:72–73.

19   Ibid., 73.

historically impossible—the legend remains in all its beauty and truth. I started and abandoned [*nachal bylo*] writing something on this topic, but not only will hardly finish it—it is unlikely that I will even get around to continuing it. I have no time [*nekodga*], I need to pack for the impeding passage [*nado ukladyvat'sia k predstoiashchemu perekhodu*]. But I regret it strongly [*A ochen' zhaleiu*]. A captivating image.[20]

The necessity of preparing for his own death—and perhaps the renewed awareness of how difficult it would be to do it using one's reason—seems to prevent Tolstoy from granting his character the true acceptance of death for which he longs.

The last text I will examine is Tolstoy's retelling of Buddha's life, included in *The Circle of Reading*, a compilation of religious, philosophical, and literary writings by different authors, organized as a year-long series of weekly readings. Written in 1904 and first published in 1906, "Buddha" was significantly revised by Tolstoy for the second edition of *The Circle of Reading*, which was supposed to appear in 1908 but did not come out in Tolstoy's lifetime.[21] The biography is part of the "Weekly Readings" for February.

I will refrain from discussing Tolstoy's views of Buddhism and refer interested readers to more authoritative surveys of this topic.[22] However, we should remember that the life of Buddha closely occupied the writer at least since the early 1880s, when he included his first biography of Buddha (Sakyamuni) in his *Confession* (1882). In this rendition, Buddha's encounters with old age, illness, and death lead him to reject life:

> And Sakya-Muni could not find consolation in life, and he decided that life is the greatest evil; and he used all the strength

---

20 Tolstoi, *Polnoe sobranie sochinenii v 90 tomakh*, 77:185.

21 For the first version, see Lev Tolstoi, *Krug chteniia: izbrannyia, sobrannyia i raspolozhennyia na kazhdyi den' L'vom Tolstym mysli mnogikh pisatelei ob istine, zhizni i povedenii* (Moscow: Posrednik, 1906), 1:110–15; for the revised version, see Tolstoi, *Polnoe sobranie sochinenii v 90 tomakh*, 41:96–101.

22 See, for example, A. I. Shifman, *Lev Tolstoi i Vostok*, 2nd rev. ed. (Moscow: Nauka, 1971), 115–25; Dragan Milivojevic, "Tolstoy's Views on Buddhism," in *Leo Tolstoy*, ed. Milivojevic, 1–18.

of his soul to get free of it and to free others. To free them in such a way that even after death life would not recommence somehow, so as to destroy [*unichtozhit'*] life entirely, root and branch [*v korne*]. This is what all Indian wisdom says.[23]

Following Schopenhauer (whom he quotes soon after this passage: "Life is that which should not be; [it is] evil, and passage into nothingness is life's only goodness"), Tolstoy is concerned not so much with the acceptance of death as with the rejection of life's suffering.[24] The motif of leaving his home in quest of enlightenment is not part of this version.

In 1885–86, Tolstoy worked on "Siddhartha Called Buddha, That Is, the Holy One," a biography of Buddha of which he wrote only the beginning pages. The core motifs that interest me are not present in this fragment. V. G. Chertkov and some other members of Tolstoy's circle continued to work on this piece, encouraged and assisted by Tolstoy. The piece, however, was never finished. After Tolstoy's death, in 1916, Chertkov published what had been written, including the fragment produced by Tolstoy.[25]

In September of 1889, Tolstoy sketched a tale about "a young, handsome, healthy, and rich" tsar who happens to see an old person and a corpse. Like Buddha, he becomes disturbed and goes to a wise elder (*starets umnyi*). On the way he sees a young laborer, singing happily while he works. When asked whether he is always

---

23   Tolstoi, *Ispoved'*, in his *Polnoe sobranie sochinenii v 90 tomakh*, 23:26.

24   On Tolstoy's acceptance of Schopenhauer's view of Buddhism as "a pes-
      simistic, life-denying religion," see Milivojevic, *Leo Tolstoy*, 2. I would like
      to point out, however, that at times Tolstoy doubted this life-denying view.
      Cf., for example, an entry in his diary of September 12, 1884 (*Polnoe sobranie
      sochinenii v 90 tomakh*, 49:121) and the unfinished 1889 tale that I discuss
      later in this article.

25   See Tolstoi, "Siddarta, prozvannyi Buddoi, t. e. sviatym: zhizn' i uchenie
      ego," in his *Polnoe sobranie sochinenii v 90 tomakh*, 25:540–43; for the English
      translation by Dragan Milivojevic, see Milivojevic, ed., *Leo Tolstoy*, 141–44.
      For the history of the manuscript and Chertkov's work on it, see Tolstoi,
      Polnoe sobranie sochinenii v 90 tomakh, 25:887–90. Chertkov's publication can
      be found in *Edinenie* 1–2 (1916); for its translation, see Milivojevic, ed., *Leo
      Tolstoy*, 141–56.

happy, the laborer responds that he is. The wise elder suggests that the tsar follow the laborer's example and work for a year helping a widow and her small children. It is remarkable that in order to work for the widow, the young tsar leaves his home, but instead of departing secretly, he leaves with his wife's permission. Helping the widow cures the young tsar of his preoccupations: he comes back to the elder and informs him that "he feels as well as never before and that he has now begun to sing."[26] As we see, Tolstoy's solution to the problem of suffering and death offered here is quite different from the one presented in all his other attempts to solve it: working for the good of other people makes suffering and impeding death irrelevant. However, Tolstoy never finished this tale.

Finally, in February of 1910, Tolstoy wrote a letter to V. A. Posse, the editor of the journal *Life for All* (*Zhizn' dlia vsekh*), urging him to publish an essay on Buddhism by P. A. Bulanzhe. In Tolstoy's opinion, Bulanzhe's work was particularly valuable because, instead of presenting historical facts about Buddha's life, it concentrated on the religious and moral essence of his teaching. Bulanzhe's work appeared in *Life for All* in March of the same year, with Tolstoy's letter as an introduction.[27] Tolstoy's letter does not focus on the motifs that interest me in this article.

The only finished, polished, and published biography of Buddha produced by Tolstoy is the one he wrote for *The Circle of Reading*, and it is also the only one that presents a version of the Wanderer story, containing its core themes: when Siddhartha becomes aware of the existence of suffering, aging, and especially death, he is deeply affected, declares them contrary to human happiness, and leaves home in search of deliverance from the fear of death. That, of the three Wanderer stories that I consider, "Buddha" is the only one that was ever finished is, perhaps, understandable, because it is a summary of what Tolstoy knew about Buddha's life.[28]

---

[26] Tolstoi, "Zapisnaia knizhka no. 5," in his *Polnoe sobranie sochinenii v 90 tomakh*, 58:210.

[27] For Tolstoy's letter, see *Zhizn' dlia vsekh* 3 (March 1910), columns 105–9; for its translation, see Milivojevic, ed., *Leo Tolstoy*, 137–40.

[28] One of his immediate sources was the entry on Buddhism in the

Tolstoy uses the word *izlozhil* (retold) to describe his contribution. In addition, by the time he had written and, especially, revised the story, Tolstoy may have come to the conclusion that he had figured out how to write about death: he said as much to Makovitsky in December 1904, in the context of their discussion of Bunyan's allegory: "When the subject is important, one has to express oneself more simply. Sometimes one can [express oneself] as Christ did, in parables."[29] Indeed, "Buddha" is narrated in the simplest manner imaginable. This abstract narrative betrays its personal significance for Tolstoy only with the phrase that also appears in "Notes of a Madman": "This should not exist" (*etogo ne dolzhno byt'*). As in the earlier story, the phrase is used to discuss the fear of death. After Siddhartha discovers that death exists, he declares:

> How is it possible to rejoice in anything, do anything, how is it possible to live, knowing this? "This should not exist," he said to himself. "It is necessary to find deliverance from this. And I will find it. And, having found it, I will pass it on to people."[30]

Note Tolstoy's repetition of the pronoun "this," which, as in "Notes of a Madman," also lacks a clear antecedent. In the 1908 version, Tolstoy somewhat clarifies his usage: "How is it possible to rejoice in anything, do anything, how is it possible to live, knowing for sure that you will die?"[31] "This" now clearly signifies the foreknowledge of death.

   Tolstoy's "Buddha" attempts to deal with the fear of death much more explicitly than "Notes of a Madman" and in more detail

---

Brockhaus and Efron encyclopedia; see commentary on the story, in Tolstoi, *Polnoe sobranie sochinenii v 90 tomakh*, 42:592–93. For other sources of Tolstoy's knowledge of Buddhism, see Milivojevic, "Tolstoy's Views on Buddhism."

[29]   Makovitskii, *U Tolstogo, 1904–1910*, 106. There is a grammatical disconnect in the way Tolstoy formulates the idea in Russian (or, at least, the way Makovitsky writes it down): "Kogda vazhnoe delo, nado tem proshche vyrazhat'sia. Inogda mozhno, kak Khristos, — pritchami."

[30]   Tolstoi, "Budda," *Krug chteniia*, 112.

[31]   Tolstoi, "Budda," in his *Polnoe sobranie sochinenii v 90 tomakh*, 41:98.

than "The Posthumous Notes of the Elder Fyodor Kuzmich." It provides what seem to be instructions for escaping the fear of death:

> The path to salvation appeared to him as follows:
> Everything bodily is transient and should break down. As long as man is bound by the body, he is subject to suffering, destruction, and death. How can one be delivered of this? As long as soul is connected to flesh, it wants to live, and life with unsatisfied desires and the fear of death creates suffering. And this is why one needs to eliminate bad fleshly desires.[32]

The formulation of Siddhartha's discovery is followed by the description of four "truths," four steps leading to salvation, and ten rules, or commandments, that help one follow these steps.[33] In the second redaction of "Buddha," Tolstoy enumerates the "truths" and commandments but eliminates the step-by-step instructions; however, the directions he offers are still quite detailed. And yet, detailed as they are, they do not actually explain how they lead a person to accepting death without fear. When the time comes for Siddhartha to die, he is not afraid, but his disciples may be:

> But by the river Kharaneavata he stopped again and, sitting down under the tree, told his disciples: "I feel death approaching; remember in my absence all that I have told you." His favorite disciple Ananda, listening to him, could not contain himself and, stepping aside, wept. Siddhartha sent for him at once and, consoling him, said: "Enough, Ananda! Do not cry, do not worry. Sooner or later we have to part with everything that is dear to us. Is there anything everlasting in this world?"[34]

He then addresses all his disciples, reminding them:

> "Remember always that destruction is intrinsic for everything bodily, but that truth [*istina*] is indestructible and everlasting. And therefore seek your salvation in it."

---

[32] Tolstoi, "Budda," *Krug chteniia*, 113.

[33] Ibid., 113–14. The commandments resemble the biblical ones.

[34] Ibid., 115.

These were his last words. After this he closed his lips and
quietly left this life.[35]

The 1908 version of this passage does not differ from the
original one except in the last paragraph, which is even shorter
and simpler: "These were his last words."[36] Siddhartha's death is,
no doubt, valiant: he obviously dies without fear. But are his last
words to his disciples helpful in alleviating their own fear of
death? Do the disciples understand how Siddhartha achieved his
equanimity? There is no answer, and Tolstoy's formulation "These
were his last words" emphasizes this forcefully. Siddhartha's
disciples are left to search for their own ways of accepting death.

It seems that, however hard he tries, Tolstoy cannot formulate
directives for accepting death. When, in "Notes of a Madman,"
his autobiographical first-person narrator tries to tell the readers
how he has freed himself of the fear of death, he stumbles, and his
language falls apart. The reader cannot learn from his experience.
When Tolstoy's other autobiographical character, Fyodor Kuzmich,
manages to put the idea into words, it turns out that he cannot
follow his own guidelines. He does not know how to accept his own
reasoning once and for all and therefore cannot teach the reader
to accept it. Both language and reason fail Tolstoy, and the stories
remained unfinished. In the only finished story, we watch how a true
philosopher dies, calmly and bravely. But how does he do it? How
can his disciples—and the reader—emulate his behavior? There is
no answer. It looks as if the rational argument in favor of accepting
death resists verbal expression—even when a writer of genius
attempts to do it. It is likely that this knowledge is beyond words
and can be obtained only via experience. This is how Siddhartha
seems to have obtained it and perhaps Tolstoy himself did so as
well, when, at the end of his life, he reenacted the Wanderer story
and, through this reenacting, came to accept death.

---

[35]   Ibid.

[36]   Tolstoi, "Budda," in his *Polnoe sobranie sochinenii v 90 tomakh*, 41:101.

Part Four

RUSSIANS
IN LIFE AND LITERATURE

Preface

This part opens with an article on a little-known eighteenth-century poet, Alexey Rzhevsky, who stands out in the Russian tradition thanks to his intense interest in form and his bold experimentation with all kinds of exotic poetic devices. I examine several of his poetic experiments and briefly consider his possible sources and his few followers.

The next article is about the representation of time in the poetry of two turn-of-the-eighteenth-century poets. One, Mikhail Murav'ev, depicts the subjective perception of time. Interested in individual psychology, he focuses on time's discreet unites and their impact on the individual. Semyon Bobrov, in contrast, creates a grandiose mythology of time, presenting it in anthropomorphic shape and, at the same time, depicting it as deafeningly loud and overwhelming.

The final article of this part and the collection as a whole compares Dostoevsky's and Leskov's views of the code of honor. I argue that, unlike Dostoevsky, Leskov didn't believe in it as a living and useful institution. In one of his stories, he deconstructs and gently mocks Dostoevsky's rigid and unforgiving position on this issue. He argues that nothing in this world is as clear-cut and unambiguous as the code of honor demands it to be, and the exponent of his view is a childish and muddle-headed woman with a nickname that invites numerous and vaguely improper associations.

13. Alexey Rzhevsky, Russian Mannerist

In his 1927 book, *Russian Poetry of the Eighteenth Century*, Grigory Gukovsky devoted a chapter to Alexey Andreevich Rzhevsky (1737–1804), who until then had been remembered as a statesman and a prominent freemason, but not as a poet. "Nonetheless," Gukovsky writes, "in the eyes of his contemporaries he was a significant poet."[1] Indeed, during a very brief but extraordinarily productive literary career that spanned about five years, from 1759 to 1764 (after which he wrote little and published even less), Rzhevsky was perhaps the most prolific contributor to two early literary journals, *Useful Diversion* (*Poleznoe uveselenie*, 1760–62) and *Free Hours* (*Svobodnye chasy*, 1763), which largely shaped Russian literary life in the 1760s and beyond. According to Gukovsky, in his most active years, 1761–63, Rzhevsky published 225 works. In 1761, as Alexander Levitsky points out in his biography of Rzhevsky, some issues of *Useful Diversion* "were entirely his work."[2] And yet, for all his visibility and amazing productivity during these formative years of Russian literature, Rzhevsky's place in the history of eighteenth-century Russian literature has not been clearly defined. This is not surprising because in many respects Rzhevsky's literary production was unique for his time. Numerous features of his poetics seem to be out of sync with the contemporary context, do not have an easily identifiable genealogy, and lack any substantial following. All this makes it worthwhile to examine his idiosyncratic poetics and to consider its possible sources as well as its impact on the subsequent poetic tradition.

---

[1]   G. A. Gukovskii, "Rzhevskii," in his *Rannie raboty po istorii russkoi poezii XVIII veka*, ed. V. M. Zhivov (Moscow: Iazyki russkoi kul'tury, 2001), 157n.

[2]   Alexander Levitsky, "Aleksei Andreevich Rzhevsky (1737–1804)," in *Early Modern Russian Writers: Late Seventeenth and Eighteenth Centuries*, ed. Marcus Levitt, vol. 150 of *Dictionary of Literary Biography* (Detroit, MI: Gale Research / Bruccoli Clark Layman, 1995), 346.

Reintroducing Rzhevsky, Gukovsky presents him as a follower of Sumarokov. Indeed, Rzhevsky published in Sumarokov's *Busy Bee* (*Trudoliubivaia pchela*, 1759), and *Useful Diversion* and *Free Hours* came out under the editorship of Mikhail Kheraskov, who in his early years aligned himself with Sumarokov. At the same time, Gukovsky singles Rzhevsky out among Sumarokov's disciples for his intense interest in form—his penchant for rare and idiosyncratic tropes, such as antithesis, oxymoron, and polyptoton. Gukovsky argues that in this Rzhevsky differed from Sumarokov, who supposedly cultivated a neutral, natural-sounding poetic discourse. In contrast to Sumarokov, Gukovsky asserts, Rzhevsky "was the first in modern Russian literature to cultivate poetic trickery as such."[3]

In his 1986 article "Die Vergegenständlichung der Form im russischen Klassizismus," Joachim Klein disagrees with this view and argues that in fact, in his use of idiosyncratic poetic tropes, Rzhevsky was following Sumarokov's example. Klein asserts that, contrary to Gukovsky's claim, an intense interest in formal experimentation was also characteristic of Sumarokov and, indeed, of Russian Classicism in general. In Klein's presentation, Rzhevsky was not an isolated phenomenon, a "meteor" that briefly dazzled his contemporaries with his idiosyncratic poetry and disappeared without a trace, but a mainstream figure.[4] Charles Drage, in his overview of Russian *carmina curiosa* from the Baroque to late Classicism, seems to support this point of view: in addition to Rzhevsky and Sumarokov, he also names Ippolit Bogdanovich and Yury Neledinsky-Meletsky as practitioners of this genre.[5]

---

[3] Gukovskii, "Rzhevskii," 171, 180. In her "A. A. Rzhevskii i pretsioznaia poeziia," *Trudy po russkoi i slavianskoi filologii: Uchenye zapiski tartuskogo gos. universiteta* 748 (1987): 18–28, M. F. Grishakova calls Rzhevsky's interest in form "playful" (*igrovoi*).

[4] Joachim Klein, "Die Vergegenständlichung der Form im russischen Klassizismus," in *Festschrift für Herbert Bräuer zum 65. Geburtstag am 14 April 1986* (Vienna: Böhlau Verlag, 1986), 245–46.

[5] Charles L. Drage, *Russian Word-Play Poetry from Simeon Polotskii to Derzhavin: Its Classical and Baroque Context* (London: School of Slavonic and East European Studies, 1993), 92.

Klein bases his conclusion on the examination of Sumarokov's elegies and idylls, and many of his examples are convincing. However, they do not account for the fact that, as Irvin Titunik puts it in his entry on Rzhevsky in *Handbook of Russian Literature*, "a large number of his lyrics . . . were startlingly out of kilter with the Sumarokov style in displaying blatant features of the highly mannered tradition of *poesis curiosa*, such as shaped poems, poems consisting of exclusively one-syllable words, poems that could be read three different ways, and conceit and riddle poems."[6] Indeed, Sumarokov did not indulge in shaped poetry and other exotica, whereas Rzhevsky frequently used not just one but several sets of different rules to make his poems as difficult as possible. It seems that he was trying to test the limits of technical difficulty itself, to discover the point at which a poem ceases to be a work of art and becomes a curiosity.

In his foreword to the only substantial publication of Rzhevsky's works other than their original publications in the journals, Ilya Serman suggests that Rzhevsky's interest in experimenting with exotic poetic devices was stimulated by the poetry of Sumarokov's literary rival, Mikhailo Lomonosov. Alexander Levitsky seconds this opinion in his biography of Rzhevsky. Levitsky suggests that what set Rzhevsky apart from the rest of Sumarokov's group and marked his originality as a poet was his tendency to mix baroque and rococo features with classicist ones, which was also characteristic of Lomonosov's style.[7]

Levitsky agrees with Titunik that Rzhevsky's attraction to mannered poetry was a sign of the continuing coexistence of the Baroque and Classicism in eighteenth-century Russian literature.[8] Their argument is compelling but does not address the problem of Rzhevsky's models. Some features of his poetic style and certain

---

[6]   Irvin Titunik, "Rzhevsky," in *Handbook of Russian Literature*, ed. Victor Terras (New Haven, CT: Yale Univ. Press, 1985), 381.

[7]   Il'ia Serman, "A. A. Rzhevskii," in *Poety XVIII veka*, ed. Georgii Makogonenko and Il'ia Serman (Leningrad: Sovetskii pisatel', 1972), 1:190; Levitsky, "Aleksei Andreevich Rzhevsky," 345.

[8]   Titunik, "Rzhevsky," 381; Levitsky, "Aleksei Andreevich Rzhevsky," 345.

types of experimentation, including the "cultivation of such intricate forms as rondeau, riddle, bouts-rimés, sonnets, and so on," can be traced to French *précieux* poetry.[9] Rzhevsky's sources for other poetic tricks, especially shaped poetry, are more difficult to track down. We do not know, for example, if he was aware of Simeon Polotsky's shaped poetry, particularly since Polotsky's *Rifmologion*, which contains it, was never published and survived in just one manuscript copy. We can only speculate as to whether Rzhevsky knew Antiokh Kantemir's word-play poems, which Drage mentions. Before returning to these questions at the end of this chapter, I would like to offer an overview of some of Rzhevsky's experiments.

Rzhevsky's most frequently cited mannered poem is his "Fable 1: Husband and Wife" ("Pritcha 1: Muzh i zhena," 1761), which contains a rhombus-shaped section.[10] Whereas in shaped poetry the intended goal is generally the creation of a visual mimetic image, Rzhevsky's poem seems to focus on experimenting with metrics as much as on creating a rhombus as such. Writing in the context of discussions about the use of free rhymed iamb in the fable, which Sumarokov advocated in opposition to using lines of equal length, Rzhevsky apparently tries to demonstrate the flexibility of this meter. To do so, in the midst of the poem written in iambic hexameter, Rzhevsky inserts a portion that employs all possible variations of iamb, from one-syllable lines to hexameters. The shaped portion contains the husband's censure of his wife's alleged habit of leaving the house without good reason and the wife's witty response:

---

9   See Grishakova, "A. A. Rzhevskii i pretsioznaia poeziia," 24 and passim; K. Iu. Lappo-Danilevskii, "Rzhevskii Aleksei Andreevich," in *Slovar' russkikh pisatelei XVIII veka*, ed. N. D. Kochetkova et al. (Leningrad: Nauka, 1988–2010), 3:43–44.

10   It is mentioned in the best book on pattern poetry: Dick Higgins, *Pattern Poetry: Guide to an Unknown Literature* (Albany: State Univ. of New York Press, 1987), 146.

(1) «Нет,

(2) Мой свет,

(3) Неложно

(4) То, что с тобой

(5) И жить не можно,

(6) Как с доброю женой.

(7) С двора всегда ты ходишь;

(8) Тебя во вся дни дома нет.

(9) Не знаю, с кем приязнь ты водишь;

(10) Нельзя ужиться нам с тобой, мой свет.

(11) Гуляй, да только меру знать в том должно;

(12) Похвально ль приходить на утренней заре?

(13) По всякий день гулять тебе, жена, не можно,

(14) Лишь то льзя похвалять, что есть в своей поре.

(15) Ты худо делаешь, жена, неложно,

(16) А ходишь только, чтоб тебе гулять,

(17) И дом пустой ты оставляешь

(18) Хожу и я, да торговать;

(19) А ты всегда лытаешь».

(20) «Как мне бы не ходить,

(21) Где ж хлеб достати?

(22) Тебе так жить

(23) Некстати:

(24) Не всяк

(25) Так

Живет, как мы с тобою;

Иной не ссорится по смерть с своей женою».[11]

("No, my dear, it is true that it is impossible to live with you as with a good wife. You leave the house all the time, every day you are absent from home. I don't know who it is that you like; we cannot live together, my dear. You can go out, but within limits; is it good to return at dawn? You cannot go out every day. One can approve only what is appropriate. Truly, you behave badly, wife, and go out only to have a good time and you leave the house deserted. I also go out but on business, and you always idle." "If I don't go out, where would we get bread? You wouldn't like to live this way: not everyone lives like you and me. Some never quarrel with their wives.")

---

[11] Aleksei Rzhevskii, "Pritcha 1: Muzh i zhena," in *Poety XVIII veka*, 1:214. Line numbering is added.   Subsequent references to this edition will be given in the text of the article.

The poem ends with wife's teaching her husband a lesson: instead of going out to buy provisions, she obediently stays home and leaves her husband without a dinner.

Sumarokov also experimented with iambic lines of different length in his fables, including one-syllable verses. However, he never did so by creating an intricate pattern governed by strict rules. On the contrary, he randomly mixed iambic verses of different length to create an imitation of colloquial speech seemingly unimpeded by any rules but those of the language. In his 1761 fable "Snake and Saw," for example, the lines with different numbers of iambic feet are arranged as follows: 6623666645636262223542. No pattern can be detected, and the cadence approximates that of natural speech. All other of Rzhevsky's fables written in free iamb follow this model.[12]

Rzhevsky's experiment, which ostensibly is set to demonstrate the flexibility of free iamb, does so under overly restrictive conditions. Not only does his poem have a shape, but to make his task even more difficult, Rzhevsky creates an intricate rhyming scheme throughout the 25 lines that form the rhombus: aaBcBcDaDaBeBeBfGfGhIhIjj. To offset this complicated pattern, he uses a simple xYxY scheme in the opening quatrain and monotone couplets (XXyy, etc.) in the concluding portion of the fable. And what is he doing in the shaped portion? It is possible to interpret the 25-line rhombus as two overlapping sonnets. The rhyming scheme of the first one is reversed (it begins with line 14 and goes up to line 1 as follows: eBeB aDaD cBcB aa), and the rhyming scheme of the second mirrors that of the first (it begins with line 12 and goes down to line 25 as follows: eBeB fGfG hIhI jj).[13]

The two sonnets that comprise the rhombus are of the so-called Shakespearian variety (i.e., consist of three quatrains and a couplet), and the question arises whether Rzhevsky was familiar with

---

[12]   A number of Rzhevsky's fables are written in iambic trimeter.

[13]   I thank Margo Rosen for helping me figure out this complicated pattern. I also thank Michael Wachtel for his helpful critique of this part of the chapter.

Shakespearian sonnets: eighteenth-century Russians, including Rzhevsky himself, exclusively practiced the French and Italian sonnets (two quatrains and two tercets that form a sextet). We can thus only speculate as to whether Rzhevsky knew and imitated the Shakespearian sonnet or whether it is pure coincidence that his rhombus rhymes like two mirrored Shakespearian sonnets. Yet Rzhevsky's apparent experimentation with the sonnet form in "Husband and Wife" dovetails with his general love of sonnets and, especially, with his love of sonnets with added restrictions. Thus, he authored two sonnets written on pre-selected rhymes and two sonnets that can be read in three ways ("Read the whole thing sequentially, then only the first hemistiches and the other hemistiches," Rzhevsky instructs his reader in a subtitle to the first of these sonnets, 217; for the second sonnet, see 263; I will return to these poems later in this chapter).

Rzhevsky's play in this fable is not over. Lines 11 to 15, three of which (12, 13, and 14) are shared by both sonnets, seem to make an epigram:

> Гуляй, да только меру знать в том должно;
> Похвально ль приходить на утренней заре?
> По всякий день гулять тебе, жена, не можно,
> Лишь то льзя похвалять, что есть в своей поре.
> Ты худо делаешь, жена, неложно.

(You can go out, but within limits; is it good to return at dawn? You cannot go out every day. One can approve only what is appropriate. Truly, you behave badly, wife.)

It should be noted that the epigram was one of Rzhevsky's favorite genres, and he experimented with its form as well, creating several epigrams with an odd number of lines (five to nine).

Finally, the poem contains a verbal play: when the wife first says that if she doesn't go out they would have nothing to eat, one can easily assume that she means prostitution. However, in the concluding part of the poem it turns out that what she meant was simply going—or not going—to the market (or she pretends that this was the meaning of her retort to her husband):

"С двора я не ходила."
"Да для чего?" — "Ты сам мне не велел ходить;
Сидела дома я, кому же есть купить?" (214–15)

("I haven't left the house." "But why?" — "You yourself told
me not to; I stayed home, who else could buy food?")

Considering the complexity of Rzhevsky's play in "Fable 1," we
must conclude that supporting Sumarokov's proposed metric norm
for the fable is the least of Rzhevsky's concerns in this poem. He was
obviously interested in creating technical difficulties for himself
and then overcoming them.

Another poem that is cited as Rzhevsky's attempt to uphold
Sumarokov's view (in this case, his view of one-syllable words in
iambs and trochees) is his "Ode 2, Put Together from One-Syllable
Words" ("Oda 2, sobrannaia iz odnoslozhnykh slov," 1761). Unlike
Vasily Trediakovsky, who considered all one-syllable words equal
in respect to stress; and Lomonosov, who proposed a fixed three-
group system with some words always stressed, others never
stressed, and others stressed according to a poem's meaning;
Sumarokov advocated a flexible system entirely dependent on
meaning.[14] Rzhevsky's poem, written in trimeters, establishes an
iambic cadence in the first stanza:

Как я стал знать взор твой,
С тех пор мой дух рвет страсть:
С тех пор весь сгиб сон мой;
Стал знать с тех пор я власть. (213)

(Since I have begun to know your gaze/face, since then my
spirit is torn by passion: since then my sleep has vanished,
since then I have come to know domination.)

Even though it is possible to read the stanza as a trochaic
trimeter, to do so one must force the trochaic rhythm on the
poem. The repeated phrases ("stal znát'" and "s tekh pór"), which

---

14   M. L. Gasparov, *Ocherk istorii russkogo stikha: Metrika, ritmika, rifma, strofika*
      (Moscow: Nauka, 1984), 80–81.

maintain their stress pattern, strongly suggest and support the iambic reading. The iambic inertia then carries over to the next two stanzas:

> Хоть сплю, твой взор зрю в сне,
> И в сне он дух мой рвет:
> О коль, ах, мил он мне!
> Но что мне в том, мой свет?
>
> Он мил, но я лишь рвусь;
> Как рвусь я, ты то знай.
> Всяк час я мил быть тщусь;
> Ты ж мне хоть вздох в мзду дай.

(Even when I sleep, I see your gaze/face in my dream, and in my dream it tears up my spirit: it is so dear to me! But so what, my darling? It is dear, but I only long/am torn/grieve; you should know, how I long/am torn/grieve. Every hour I try in vain to endear myself to you. You should at least reward me with a sigh.)

The iambic cadence places into strong positions both fully meaningful as well as auxiliary words. Thus, if anything, Rzhevsky's poem supports Trediakovsky's position.

At the same time, the poem is full of verbal play unrelated to the problem of the status of one-syllable words. The poem plays on the two meanings of the word *vzor* (gaze and face) and the images of vision, sleep, and dreaming. The play is particularly evident in the first line of the second stanza: "Even when I sleep, I see your gaze/face in my dream." In the original, the play is augmented by the intricate phonetic arrangement and the fact that the words *vzor* and *zret'* have the same root: *vzor zriu v sne*. Rzhevsky also plays on two meanings of the word *son*, sleep and a dream: if in the first stanza it is clearly sleep, in the second one it is both sleep and a dream. In addition, Rzhevsky creates a tension between two words with the same root: *rvat'* (to tear, rip) and *rvat'sia* (to long, to be torn, and to grieve violently). The first is an active verb, and the lyrical hero is the object of the violent action: his spirit is torn by passion and by the vision of his beloved. The second is passive, and the violence is self-directed.

Finally, the poem's phonetics is also intricately organized. To begin with, the word *strast'* (passion) is inscribed in its first stanza: st t r t / s t r r str st' / s t r s s s / st s t t st'. The second stanza, as I have already noted, begins with the phonetically structured clause *tvoi vzor zriu v sne*. Furthermore, the first and the second halves of the poem are phonetically contrasted: the first is dominated by consonants *s, t, r, v, z*, which mimetically refer to the words *strast'*, *rvat'*, and *vzor*, whereas the second half adds consonants *m, l*, and *n*, which mimetically represent the words *mil* and *mne*, and are contrasted to *r* and *v* (the first line of the third stanza is a good example: *On mil, no ia lish' rvus'*).

It should be especially noted that this little intricate trinket is called an ode—the term mostly reserved in Russian eighteenth-century poetry for grandiose poems of forty to fifty ten-line stanzas written in iambic tetrameter, that is, solemn odes. For other poems called odes, a qualifier usually was needed: spiritual, anacreontic, or moralizing ode. It is obvious that, in addition to all the experimental devices described above, Rzhevsky is also testing the limits of the genre itself.

When Rzhevsky turns to fixed forms, he also is interested in testing the generic limits: more often than not, he imposes additional rules onto already challenging formulas. As I have already mentioned, he wrote sonnets that could be read three ways and thus constituted three sonnets, not one, with three different meanings (two of them are contrasting and the third one is a version of one of the contrasting two) and two sets of rhyming schemes. One such sonnet, published in *Useful Diversion* in 1761, is a love poem and a pledge of faithfulness, if read in its entirety. Its left half is a refutation of love, and its right half seems to proclaim eternal love for some other woman:

Вовеки не пленюсь	красавицей иной;
Ты ведай, я тобой	всегда прельщаться стану,
По смерть не пременюсь;	вовек жар будет мой,
Век буду с мыслью той,	доколе не увяну.
Не лестна для меня	иная красота;
Лишь в свете ты одна	мой дух воспламенила.

Скажу я не маня: свобода отнята –
Та часть тебе дана   о ты, что дух пленила!

Быть ввек противной мне   измены не брегись,
В сей ты одна стране   со мною век любись.
Мне горесть и беда,   я мучуся тоскою,

Противен мне тот час,   коль нет тебя со мной;
Как зрю твоих взор глаз,   минутой счастлив той;
Смущаюся всегда   и весел, коль с тобою. (217)

(1. I will never be captivated by a different beauty. You should know that I will be always charmed by you. I will not change until I die. My ardor will last all my life, I will always think so, until I wither. Different beauty does not attract me. You are the only one who has inflamed my spirit. I will tell you without deceit: my freedom is taken away, and this is your fate, O you, who has captivated my spirit! Do not be afraid that you can ever become repulsive to me. In this land, be the only one in love with me. I grieve and I am unhappy, I am in anguish, I detest the time when you are not with me. When I see your gaze, I am happy at this moment. I am always embarrassed and merry when I am with you.

2. I will never be captivated with you, you should know; I will not change until I die. I will always think so. In the whole world you are the only one who does not attract me. I will tell you without deceit: your fate is to be always repulsive to me. In this land, you alone are my grief and misfortune. I hate the time when I see your gaze. I am always embarrassed.

3. I will always be captivated by a different beauty. My ardor will last all my life, until I wither. Different beauty has inflamed by spirit. My freedom is taken away. O you, who has captivated my spirit! Do not be afraid that I will be unfaithful. Love me forever. I am in anguish when you are not with me. I am happy and merry when I am with you.)

In the left sonnet, Rzhevsky employs a rhyming pattern of abab cdcd eef ggf, and in the main and the right one he uses a pattern of aHaH iJiJ kkL mmL. It is worth pointing out that he complicates the French rhyming scheme in the first stanza by using the same ending (*oi*) for lines 1 and 3 of the main sonnet and lines 2 and 4 of the left sonnet. In his other "triple" sonnet, published in 1762 in *Useful Diversion* and constructed as a philosophical discussion on the question of whether life brings misery (both the left and the right sonnets) or happiness (the main sonnet), Rzhevsky also uses the French rhyming pattern: abab abab ccd ede for the left sonnet and fGfG fGfG HHi HiH for the main and the right sonnet. In this sonnet he strictly adheres to the prescribed rhyming scheme, keeping the same rhymes in the quatrains.

In his rondeaus Rzhevsky does not follow the prescribed pattern, which, in Mikhail Gasparov's view, suggests that the form had deteriorated, paving the way to "non-strophic free rhyming."[15] In the poems that Rzhevsky calls rondeaus, however, he does not simply dispose of the rules of the classic rondeau but creates his own, quite intricate, patterns. One of his rondeaus (published in *Useful Diversion* in 1761) is a poem structured as follows (R is the opening phrase, repeated in the conclusion of each quatrain, sometimes in a slightly different form, which I indicate as R'):

(R)aab(bR)aab(bR)aab(bR)aab(bR)aab(bR')aab(bR')

Rzhevsky differs from the prescribed pattern not only in the number of lines (twenty-four instead of fifteen) but also in that he integrates his repeated segment into the rhyming scheme:

> Не лучше ль умереть, ты часто рассуждаешь,
> Успехов в чем-нибудь когда не обретаешь;
> И часто говоришь: возможно ли терпеть?
> Не лучше ль умереть? (211)

("Isn't it better to die?" you think frequently, when you do not succeed in something. You say frequently: "Is it possible to endure. Isn't it better to die?")

Furthermore, he varies the repeated segment in the last two quatrains, changing it to "Isn't it better to endure?" (*Ne luchshe l' poterpet'?*, 212). While keeping the idea of repetition so crucial for the rondeau, Rzhevsky increases the complexity of the task and does it without making his poem sound stilted.

---

15   Gasparov, *Ocherk istorii russkogo stikha*, 101.

His other rondeau (*Useful Diversion*, 1761) is a variation of the above one, with the difference that the repeated segment is fully integrated into the last line of the quatrain:

> И всякий так живет, ты думаешь всечасно;
> Но худо извинять порок в себе пристрастно.
> Хотя бы утонул в пороках злых весь свет,
> Неправ и ты, хотя и всякий так живет. (218)

(Everyone lives like this, you think all the time; but it is wrong to excuse your own vice out of predilection. Even if the entire world drowned in evil vices, you are also in the wrong, even though everyone lives like this.)

The pattern continues for another two stanzas.

In his 1763 rondeau, published in *Free Hours*, Rzhevsky is even more inventive and daring. As the genre requires, it uses only two rhymes, but the rhyming scheme is as follows: aaaaaaab(br) aaaaaaaaaaab(br). The poem does not have an opening phrase, but has a refrain (r) that rhymes with the previous line (see 296). The poem is also a joke, playfully contrasting intellectual pursuits (the first sequence) with fashionable behavior (the second one). The first is presented as easy: "Everyone can do it" (*To mozhet vsiak*); and the second as difficult: "Not everyone can do it" (*Togo ne mozhet sdelat' vsiak*). Rzhevsky also plays with two meanings of the word used as a refrain: *Nikak* in the first case means "it seems," and in the second case, "no way": "To mozhet vsiak, / Nikak" and "Togo ne mozhet sdelat' vsiak / Nikak."

The list of Rzhevsky's mannered poems can be continued. To give but two more examples, in 1762, he published in *Useful Diversion* a poem that he calls "Idyll." Its most noticeable device is the use of homonymous rhymes:

> На брегах текущих рек
> Пастушок мне тако рек:
> "Не видал прелестнее твоего я стану,
> Глаз твоих, лица и век,
> Знай, доколь продлится век,
> Верно я, мой свет, тебя, верь, любити стану." (262)

(At the banks of flowing *rivers* a shepherd *told* me this:
"I haven't seen more charming *figure*, eyes, face, and *eyelids*
than yours. You should know that to the end of *time*, believe
me, I *will love* you faithfully, my dear.")[16]

As always, the poet complicates his task, imposing additional rules
(a more demanding rhyming scheme aaBaaB in the first stanza and
an intricate sound play in the other two). Rzhevsky also changes
the prescribed plot from idyllic to dramatic (or even tragic): the
shepherd of the poem abandons his shepherdess for another
lover, leaving her in mourning. Finally, Rzhevsky also introduces
dialogue into his poem, which usually is not part of the idyllic convention.

In yet another poem, the 1763 "Portrait," published in *Free
Hours*, Rzhevsky exclusively uses independent infinitives to create
a portrait of a man in love:

Желать, чтоб день прошел, собраний убегать,
Скучать наедине, с тоской ложиться спать,
Лечь спать, не засыпать, сжимать насильно очи,

and so on, to the concluding line:

Се зрак любовника, несчастного в любви! (288–89)

(To wish that a day would end, to avoid assemblies, to be
bored when alone, to go to bed in grief, to go to bed but not
to sleep, to close forcefully one's eyes . . . This is a portrait of
a lover who is unfortunate in love!)

The poem also abounds in antitheses, oxymora, and polymptota,
which very effectively convey the character's unsettled psychological state.[17]

---

16   In my translation, I italicized rhymes, to make it easier to follow Rzhevsky's
      rhyming game.

17   For a discussion of this poem, see Iu. I. Mineralov, *Lektsii po russkoi
      slovesnosti XVIII veka*, accessed February 1, 2011,
      http://mineralov.narod.ru/XVIII_vek.txt.

Gukovsky suggests that Rzhevsky's experimentations were necessary to foreground the importance of form, "to affirm the rights of manifest poetic construction as such," which, the scholar maintains, helped Russian poets realize anew, and fully, the conventional nature of verbal art.[18] This explanation sounds convincing but for two questions: why did Rzhevsky himself abandon his poetic experiments, and why did so few poets follow his example in formal experimentation? Besides Bogdanovich and Neledinsky-Meletsky, Derzhavin was the only one who tried his hand at some of the devices proposed by Rzhevsky. In his poem "Fashionable Wit" ("Modnoe ostroumie," two redactions: around 1776 and 1780), Derzhavin follows Rzhevsky in creating a poem based on independent infinitives.[19] In addition, in 1809, Derzhavin wrote a poem in the shape of a pyramid.[20] These experiments, however, were clearly not at the center of Derzhavin's poetic innovations, and after him, there is a hiatus. Not until the Modernists did Russian poets return to the regular use of "trickery as such" in their works.

Higgins points out that eighteenth-century European literatures generally were not interested in mannered poetry—with the exception of German and Polish literatures, where this interest was marginal; and French *précieux* poetry, whose place was also at the fringes of literature.[21] In Russia, too, opposition to mannerism was voiced, and its practice non-existent, except in the works of Rzhevsky and a very few others.[22] Could mannered poetry's unpopularity have compelled Rzhevsky to abandon it? Could it also

---

[18] Gukovskii, "Rzhevskii," 183.

[19] For a discussion of this poem and its two redactions, see Mineralov, *Lektsii*.

[20] The poem is mentioned in Higgins, *Pattern Poetry*, 146; it is reproduced and briefly discussed in Dmitrij Tschiževskij, *Formalistische Dichtung bei den Slaven*, Heidelberger slavische Texte 3 (Wiesbaden: Otto Harrassowitz, 1958): 42–43; and in Drage, *Russian Word-Play Poetry*, 12.

[21] See Higgins, *Pattern Poetry*, 84 and 135–36; Grishakova, "A. A. Rzhevskii i pretsioznaia poeziia," 19.

[22] For a discussion of one episode of polemics against mannerism, see V. P. Stepanov, "Kritika man'erizma v 'Primechaniiakh k vedomostiam,'" in *XVIII vek* (Leningrad: Nauka, 1975), 10:39–48.

have discouraged others from following his example? This certainly would explain why Rzhevsky's experiments were so thoroughly forgotten until Gukovsky rediscovered them. It is likely, however, that, as Grishakova suggests, Rzhevsky did influence contemporary poetry, but his influence was subtle, working not to introduce mannered poetry as a commonly accepted practice, but, by using playful technical tricks, to undermine Classicism's predominantly lofty propensities.[23] In my view, this was a significant contribution, for which Rzhevsky deserves to be remembered.

---

[23] Grishakova, "A. A. Rzhevskii i pretsioznaia poeziia," 25–26.

14. Imagery of Time and Eternity in Eighteenth-Century Russian Poetry: Mikhail Murav'ev and Semyon Bobrov

Eighteenth-century Russian poets exhibited considerable anxiety about the passage of time. This anxiety matched the greater awareness of time in eighteenth-century Europe in general and, in particular, reflected the Russians' assimilation of baroque ideas about the instability and changeability of human life.[1] At the same time, this anxiety anticipated the Romantic preoccupation with the concept of time as fleeting, changeable, and imperfect, and of eternity as infinite, unchanging, and perfect.[2]

---

[1] For an historical overview of human perception of time, see G. J. Whitrow, *Time in History: The Evolution of Our General Awareness of Time and Temporal Perspective* (New York: Oxford Univ. Press, 1988). For a discussion of the ideas of instability and changeability in seventeenth-century Russian literature, see A. S. Demin, *Russkaia literatura vtoroi poloviny XVII-nachala XVIII veka: Novye khudozhestvennye predstavleniia o mire, prirode, cheloveke* (Moscow: Nauka, 1977), esp. chap. 9 and 10. Hans Meyerhoff's *Time in Literature* (Berkeley: Univ. of California Press, 1968) offers a discussion of some theoretical aspects of the problem.

[2] Demin stresses a relatively optimistic interpretation of the ideas of changeability by seventeenth-century Russians, whereas Romantics

Many eighteenth-century poems addressed temporal themes such as the brevity of life, the futility of existence, and the inevitability of death. They combined traditional Greco-Roman and Christian mythology with contemporary scientific notions about time. They especially evoked Newton's model of time as an entity independent of space and matter, which evenly and steadily flows by. However, eighteenth-century poems about time were by no means philosophical treatises. In representing time, their authors as a rule were guided more by linguistic usage than by philosophy. The prevailing eighteenth-century imagery of time drew on temporal clichés, such as "time flies," "time flows," and "time passes"; it also drew on traditional auditory images such as a striking clock or a tolling bell.[3] Few poems that attempted a philosophical investigation of time stood out among the contemporary production.

Although they represent antithetical poetic styles, Mikhail Murav'ev (1757–1807) and Semyon Bobrov (1767–1810) explore time in a somewhat similar fashion. Both poets begin by using the prevailing poetic discourse and both end up deconstructing it—in different ways, however. Murav'ev creates ambiguity in meaning that encourages his readers to question time's power over man. Bobrov, on the other hand, boldly uncovers literal meanings in conventional poetic idioms, which allows him to resurrect ancient mythological notions of time as cyclical and thus to overcome the anxiety that linear concepts of time cause in modern man. Their approaches also differ philosophically: Murav'ev probes the individual's perception of time, whereas Bobrov explores time as a cosmic category. Murav'ev's analysis yields psychological insights and private moral lessons, while Bobrov constructs a grandiose mythology of time that encompasses nature, history, and man.

---

lamented the tragic imperfection of the temporal world vis-à-vis the harmoniousness of eternity. For a discussion of Romantic concepts of time, see F. P. Fedorov, *Romanticheskii khudozhestvennyi mir: Prostranstvo i vremia* (Riga: Zinatne, 1988).

[3]   For a prototypical and frequently quoted poem about time and its powers over man, see Alexander Sumarokov's poem "On Human Vanity" ("Na suetu cheloveka," 1763).

Murav'ev's 1775 poem "Time" investigates the idea of time's subjective character. The seventeen-year-old poet presents time both as duration and as a succession of separate instants. The poem fluctuates between portraying time's passage as an objective process and describing the lyrical hero's experience of it. Linguistically, it plays on literal and figurative meanings and polysemy; it also creates tension between syntactic structures and meaning.

The poem opens with a conventional reference to swiftly "running" time. Time's movement, however, manifests itself in recurrent natural processes, which strongly undermines the idea of time's irreversibility and diminishes the inherent sense of loss that accompanies time's passage:

> Постойте, вобразим, друзья, бегуще время:
> Недавно упадал без силы солнца свет —
> Се, в нивах брошено, проникло в класы семя
> И жателя зовет.
>
> Я солнце проводил вчера в вечерни воды.
> "Покойся; и тебе приятно в воды лечь," —
> Вещал я; но оно, обшедши антиподы,
> Умело день зажечь. [4]

(Wait, friends, let's imagine swiftly passing time: / just recently the sun's light fell [upon earth] powerlessly— / yet now, the seed that was cast into furrows has risen into ears of grain / and invites a reaper.

Yesterday, I saw the sun off into the evening waters. / "Repose; lying down in the waves is enjoyable for you too," / I said. But it circled the antipodes / and managed to light a [new] day.)

Murav'ev's representation of time's movement conveys a sense that even natural processes, such as plant growth and sunrise, require a certain effort in order to occur. In the first stanza, sunlight is initially portrayed as powerless, and only through some unspecified effort does it eventually cause the seed to grow and mature. Similarly, in the second stanza, the sun needs a special effort in order to rise:

---

[4]   Mikhail Murav'ev, *Stikhotvoreniia* (Leningrad: Sovetskii pisatel', 1967), 137. All subsequent quotations are from the same page.

it only "managed," *umelo*, to light a new day. Murav'ev's images put limits on time's powers, making it less threatening to human existence.

Furthermore, the observer remains still in these two stanzas (he even invites his readers to join him: "Wait/stop, friends"), whereas time is constantly on the move. The image of time flowing past and taking with it all life's delights usually emphasizes man's passivity in his encounter with time. In Murav'ev's poem, however, the lyrical hero's status as an observer, detached from temporal processes, increases his immunity to time's impact: while time passes by, he seems to remain unchanged. Murav'ev's poem deviates strikingly from the traditional poetic picture of time's power over man, which causes him to suffer irreversible changes.

The third stanza presents a different model of time—one in which man moves with it. Traditionally, this model presupposes that man totally submits to time's command over him. Again, Murav'ev breaks with tradition: in his interpretation, man is not a passive traveler through the river of time; rather, he himself acquires time's attribute, the ability to flow, while time remains still. The life that man lives loses the quality of something that time takes away but instead becomes active, almost personified:

> Однако, думал я, покоится мгновенье.
> Уже за третий люстр два года я претек.
> Счастлива жизнь! увы! ты бросилась в забвенье.
> Не сон ли целый век?

(However, I thought, an instant remains still. / I have already passed [lit.: flowed] two years beyond the third lustrum. / My happy life! Alas! You have rushed into oblivion, / Is not our whole life but a dream?)

The language of the stanza is ambiguous, allowing several interpretations. First of all, the syntax of the first line permits an alternate translation: "However, I have [or "had"] been thinking that an instant remains still." In this case, natural processes, including the lyrical hero's maturation, persuade him that time passes. However, the position of the word *odnako* undermines this reading, making the whole stanza an antithesis to the previous two.

Another ambiguity rests on the two possible readings of the verb *pretek*. While the Old Church Slavonic meaning of *tech'*, "to move, go," still persisted in the eighteenth century, the modern Russian meaning, "to flow," already predominated. The context makes this modern meaning especially relevant, as it reinforces the image of a "flowing" person.

Finally, the third line's structure contradicts its vocabulary: the words *uvy* and *zabven'e* are supposed to evoke a sense of loss and the idea of inexorable time. However, the vigorous exclamation point after the expression *schastliva zhizn'!*, the fact that the word *uvy* is tucked away in the middle of the sentence, and the predicate that pictures the happy life actively reinforce the reader's sense that life is happy and that it is not taken away but chosen to be forgotten. As a result, the process that the contemporary tradition usually portrayed as sad does not evoke sadness, and a sense of control emerges amidst a stanza designed to illustrate the futility of resisting time's passage.

For Murav'ev, man is not only independent of time's flow but also active. Indeed, man can influence time, either prolonging it or hastening it along its way:

> Во времени одну занять мы можем точку.
> Минута, кою жил, длинняе году сна,
> И бабочка, чья жизнь привязана к листочку
> Не тесно включена.

(In time we can occupy one point. / A minute lived is longer than a year of sleep. / Even a butterfly whose life is tied to a leaf / is not tightly confined.)

Murav'ev does not simply imply that duration of time is perceived differently by different persons. In fact, he deviates from Newton's idea of objective and independently flowing time. In the next stanza, he even ventures a claim that time acquires a moral dimension from a subject's behavior and mood:

> Мгновенье каждое имеет цвет особый,
> От состояния сердечна занятой.
> Он мрачен для того, чье сердце тяжко злобой,
> Для доброго — златой.

(Each instant has its own distinct color, / which is borrowed from [a person's] state of heart. / It is dark for him whose heart is heavy with malice, / but for a kind person—it is golden.)

The poem concludes optimistically: man has power over time and thus over his own fate. Although time passes, man can find enjoyment at every stage of life:

> Все года времена имеют наслажденья:
> Во всяком возрасте есть счастие свое.

(All seasons of the year have their joys: / every age has its own happiness.)

The passage of time is even beneficial, since it removes "the rust" of repentance from the "heart's tablet" and therefore allows man to recover happiness after his inevitable mistakes. In this poem, Murav'ev deconstructs the traditional imagery of time and thereby transforms existential anxiety about death into a practical philosophy for happy living.

By the end of the eighteenth century, Russians' anxiety about time intensified and acquired a more pessimistic character. They also shifted their focus from the realm of natural philosophy to the realm of historiosophy and, accordingly, from the personal level to the historical, concentrating on the fate of human civilization. Most works written at the turn of the century that are concerned with the passage of time—Nikolay Karamzin's 1794 prose piece "Milodor to Filaret. Filaret to Milodor," his poem of the same year "Epistle to Dmitriev," Alexander Radishchev's *Historical Song* (written in the late 1790s) and his poem "The Eighteenth Century" (1799–1801), Gavrila Derzhavin's poems on the beginning of the years 1797 and 1798, Bobrov's 1789 poem "The First Hour of the Year" and his four poems marking the beginning of the nineteenth century ("To the New Nineteenth Century," "The Hundred-Year Song, or The Triumph of Russia's Eighteenth Century," "Query to the New Century," and "The Century's Foreseen Response")—assumed a historical perspective and questioned (with various degrees of anxiety) the feasibility of social progress. It is noteworthy that works with nascent nationalistic sensibilities, such as Nikolay

L'vov's 1801 poems "The New Nineteenth Century in Russia" and "Popular Exclamation on the Entrance of the New Century," were considerably less troubled about mankind's future and the passage of time.

The general perception of social instability at the end of the century further intensified Russians' pessimistic outlook and turned their gaze away from personal concerns. In addition to the French Revolution and the execution of Louis XVI, which affected all Europeans and produced a sense of doom in many contemporaries, Russians had to deal with two important historical changes of their own: the death of Catherine the Great and Paul's succession in 1796, and Paul's assassination and Alexander I's accession to the throne in 1801. Russians perceived both events as the end of one epoch and the beginning of a completely new one. Significantly, for Russians these changes of reign, especially the events of March 11, 1801, almost completely overshadowed the great calendar milestone— the turn of the century. Even those few poems formally dedicated to the advent of the new century were mostly written after Paul's death and tended to treat the two beginnings—of the new century and of the new reign—as concurrent events. Similarly, odes greeting Alexander usually referred both to the change of reign and to the calendar change of centuries.[5]

Despite the shifts in perspective, the imagery of time in Russian literary production at the turn of the century remained mostly unchanged: as in earlier poetry, time was depicted as passing, flying, flowing, and generating sound. The turn of the century, however, drew attention to time's destination. As a result, an image of eternity

---

[5] See Mark Altshuller, "Poeticheskaia traditsiia Radishcheva v literaturnoi zhizni nachala XIX veka," section "Radishchev i Bobrov," in *XVIII vek* (Leningrad: Nauka, 1977), 12:118–19. Natan Eidel'man, in his *Gran' vekov: Politicheskaia bor'ba v Rossii. Konets XVIII—nachalo XIX stoletiia* (Moscow: Mysl', 1982), 5–6, points out that New Year's eve celebrations in late eighteenth-century Russia were relatively unimportant due to poor methods of keeping time, slow communications, and the novelty of having January 1 begin the new year. This indifference apparently contributed to the mute reaction to the beginning of the new century. The double meaning of the Russian word *vek* (both "century" and "age") facilitated the discussion of the change of reign in terms of calendar change and vice versa.

as a depository of passed time emerged: time was presented not just as passing/flowing/flying away, but as flowing into the ocean, pool, or whirlpool of eternity.[6]

Semyon Bobrov's poetry betrays the author's continuous intense interest in the topics of time, eternity, and death. His approach to the portrayal of time was highly original: his poetry transformed the prevalent poetic idioms of passing time and offered a striking image of eternity as a vast grave containing past and future years and centuries. Combining common idioms, mythological images, Masonic symbols, and contemporary scientific concepts, the poet created images of years and centuries as living creatures, able to fly, converse, menace men, and die. The result was a grandiose and idiosyncratic picture of a living universe, which Bobrov's contemporaries, unreceptive to the cosmic scale of his poetry, found difficult to appreciate.

Bobrov favors the image of time flying. However, unlike his predecessors, Bobrov consistently uses the expression "time flies" literally: in his poetry, time is a winged creature. For example, in "The First Hour of the Year," the old year flies into eternity on "decrepit wings," whereas the new year flies out to replace it "on the wings of youth." Similarly, in two of his poems greeting the beginning of the nineteenth century, Bobrov calls the new century "the winged son of eternity" and "the winged herald of the Almighty."[7] The

---

[6]   Alexander Radishchev's "The Eighteenth Century" opens with such a description:

> Урна времян часы изливает каплям подобно:
> Капли в ручьи собрались; в реки ручьи возросли
> И на дальнейшем брегу изливают пенистые волны
> Вечности в море; а там нет ни предел, ни брегов.

(The urn of times pours out hours like drops: / drops gather into streams, streams grow into rivers / and at the farthest shore pour their foaming waves / into the sea of eternity. And there are no bounds, no shores.)

Later in the poem, Radishchev speaks of the vortex and "furious whirlpool" (*omut iaryi*), which has swallowed eighteenth-century hopes for happiness. For a discussion of the Romantic concept of time as flowing between two eternities (the past and the future), see Fedorov, *Romanticheskii khudozhestvennyi mir*, 118–41.

[7]   Semen Bobrov, "Pervyi chas goda," "K novostoletiiu XIX," and "Stoletniaia pesn', ili torzhestvo os'mogonadesiat' veka Rossii," in *Poety 1790–1810*

image of winged time apparently emerged, on the one hand, as a way of realizing the prevalent poetic idiom and, on the other hand, as a result of the image of Chronos as a winged creature. Thus, in "The First Hour of the Year," years come to Earth with Chronos's traditional attribute, the scythe, in hand (77, 78).[8]

Another distinctive feature of Bobrov's time imagery is the noise that accompanies time's passage. Some of this noise arises from the flutter of time's wings: in "Query to the New Century," the nineteenth century flies in "noisily" (*shumlivo*, 102). Similarly, in "The Century's Foreseen Response," it is called "a loud-feathered herald" (*gromkopernatyi vestnik*, 104). The beginning of the new year or century is also signaled by a clock striking or a bell tolling:

> Чу!—Первый час столетья *звукнул*! (101; Bobrov's emphasis; cf. 77, 92)
>
> (Listen! The first hour of the century *has sounded!*)

Notably, Bobrov presents this sound as time's voice, once again personifying time:

> Звукнул времени суровый
> Металический язык;
> Звукнул—отозвался новый,
> И помчал далече зык. (119)
>
> (The stern metallic tongue / of time has sounded. / It has sounded: a new [sound] responded / and the roar rushed far away.)

While the metallic sound suggests a tolling bell, the word *iazyk*, with its double meaning of "tongue" and "clapper," suggests some fantastic creature, made of metal, but alive and conversing with other similar creatures.[9] Notably, two of Bobrov's poems dedicated

---

godov (Leningrad: Sovetskii pisatel', 1971), 77, 91, 102. Cf. also 92, 94, 101, and 108. Further references to this edition are given in the text.

[8]   For a discussion of Orphic depictions of Chronos as a multi-headed winged serpent, see Whitrow, *Time in History*, 39. For a contemporary image of winged time, see F. Guenther's sculpture "Chronos" (around 1765–70).

[9]   L. O. Zaionts, in "Iung v poeticheskom mire S. Bobrova," *Uchenye zapiski Tartuskogo gosudarstvennogo universiteta* (Tartu: Tartu Riiklik Ülikool, 1985), 73n10, traces this image to the following lines in Edward Young's

to the beginning of the nineteenth century, "Query to the New Century" and "The Century's Foreseen Response," are two statements in a dialogue between the new century and men. In the former, Bobrov directly comments on the century's ability to speak:

То скажет *век*, — мы внять готовы. (103; Bobrov's emphasis)

(The *century* will say that, and we are prepared to heed.)

The sound of a tolling bell or a striking clock betokens mysterious and awesome events that, for Bobrov, accompany time's passage. When a new year replaces the old one, the vast vault opens, revealing an eternity that contains both past and future centuries:

> Час бил; отверзся гроб пространный,
> Где спящих ряд веков лежит;
> Туда протекший год воззванный
> На дряхлых крылиях летит. (77)

(The hour has struck. The vast grave, / where a row of sleeping centuries lie, has opened. / Summoned thither, the past year flies / on decrepit wings.)

The changing of centuries occurs in similar fashion:

> [Полночный час п]робил — завеса ниспадает;
> Я вижу длинный зал сквозь тень;
> Вдали — там свет лампад мелькает;
> Висит над ними бледный день,
> Подобно как в туманну осень.

"Complaint, or Night Thoughts on Life, Death, and Immortality" (1742–43). See *The Poetical Works of Edward Young* (Westport, CO: Greenwood Press, 1970), 1:3:

> The bell strikes one. We take no note of time
> But from its loss. To give it then a tongue
> Is wise in Man.

However, despite his vivid metaphor, Young remains in the realm of the abstract, whereas Bobrov, by realizing the trope, creates a mythological picture. In general, despite their undeniable importance for Bobrov, Young's images and ideas of time and cosmos remained but one element in Bobrov's complex and idiosyncratic mythology of time. Young's poem became a major influence in Russia in the 1770s. His image of "time's tongue" also influenced Derzhavin, especially his 1779 poem "On Prince Meshchersky's Death"; see L. V. Pumpianskii, "Sentimentalizm," in *Istoriia russkoi literatury* (Moscow: Akademiia nauk, 1947), 432.

Там ряд веков лежит особый;
На них планет влиянья нет;
Стоят в помосте тусклы гробы. (92)

([The midnight hour] has struck, and the veil is dropping. /
I see a long hall through the haze. / There, far away, the light
of lamps gleams. / The pale day hovers over them / as if
during the foggy autumn.
There lies a separate row of centuries. / The planets do not
influence them. / Faded coffins stand on the scaffolding.)

The vault of eternity is separated from the temporal world by the
door, or gates, of time (101, 108). When this door opens to release
a new year or century, a terrifying noise can be heard:

Се там столетья страшна дверь.
Подобно грому заревела
На медных вереях теперь!
Ты слышишь звуки их ужасны. (93)

(This is the terrible door of the century over there. / It roared
just now / like thunder on its bronze ropes! / You hear their
terrible noise.)

The image of the door is crucial for Bobrov's concept of time: it
marks the boundary between timeless eternity and the mortal
world where time exists in the form of discrete units personified as
mortal creatures.

When the vault of eternity opens, the "wheels of time" (119)
turn—an image indicating a concept of the universe as a mechanical
clock or a machine.[10] In Bobrov's poetry, this popular seventeenth-
and eighteenth-century concept is associated with the Romantic
idea of the universe as sounding spheres.[11] Bobrov begins "The
Hundred-Year Song" with Urania supervising a clocklike universe:

Глубока ночь! — а там — над бездной
Урания, душа сих сфер,
Среди машины многозвездной

---

[10] On the idea of the clocklike universe, see Whitrow, *Time in History*, 120–32.

[11] On the Romantic concept of the resounding universe, see Fedorov,
Romanticheskii khudozhestvennyi mir, 52–56. Zaionts, in "Iung v poeticheskom
mire Bobrova," 79, suggests Kepler's influence.

Дает векам прямой размер;
Бегут веков колеса с шумом. (92; Bobrov's emphasis)[12]

(It's deep into the night! And there—over the abyss / *Urania*, the soul of these spheres, / inside the multi-star machine, / gives the direct measure to centuries. / The wheels of centuries run noisily.)

However, unlike the Romantic image of harmonious music accompanying the workings of the universe, in Bobrov's poems the sound of running time is a discordant mixture of noises; the sound of time's wings, the opening of time's gates, the striking of the clock, the sound of wheels rotating, groans, and sighs form a wild chorus. Instead of representing the universe's live soul, this cacophony evokes death:

Я слышу—стон там проницает;
Пробил, пробил полночный час!
Бой стонет—мраки расторгает,
Уже в последний стонет раз;
Не смерть ли мира—вздох времен? (92)

(I hear—a groan penetrates over there. / The midnight hour has struck, has struck! / The sound [striking of the clock] groans—it opens the darkness; / it already groans for the last time. / Is not this sigh of time—the world's death?)

Indeed, the end of a time unit constitutes its death, and the vault of eternity to which it returns resembles the underworld: it is a dark, dimly lit space where years and centuries lie in deep, death-like sleep.

This death-like slumber is not a final state, however, but an ambivalent one, pregnant with new possibilities. Appropriately,

---

12   Zaionts (in "Iung v poeticheskom mire Bobrova," 79–80) contrasts Bobrov's picture of the universe with the one offered by Young. In Young's poetry, the image of the universe as a clock is also present, but it works noiselessly. In her essay "K simvolicheskoi interpretatsii poemy S. Bobrova 'Tavrida,'" Zaionts also points out the paradoxical, vertical organization of Bobrov's world: the upper sphere is occupied by the immaterial universe, invisible and incomprehensible, whereas the physical universe, containing the stars and the moon, occupies the lower sphere; see *Trudy po znakovym sistemam* (Tartu: Tartu Ülikool, 1992), 24:97n16. Such an organization allows the volt of eternity and the arch of the sky to be identical.

the vault of eternity is the realm of the two-faced Janus, the god of beginnings and endings, of entrances and exits, who also symbolizes annual renewal. In "The Hundred-Year Song," Bobrov first presents Janus as an old man, "bowed by age" (93). However, as the old century is replaced by the new one, Janus becomes a youth:

> Сие рек старец—обратился;
> Что зрю?—Я зрю в нем юный лик!
> Куда же старец мой сокрылся?
> Иль, возродяся, вновь возник? (100)

(The old man has spoken—and turned around. / What do I espy? I espy his youthful face! / Whither hast my old man disappeared? / Or, having been reborn, appeared anew?)

In fact, Janus is simultaneously old and young. He always has two faces, one looking back toward the past and another forward toward the future. The change of a year or century thus not only brings humans closer to death but also brings them renewal. The new year's advent is marked by signs of revival and awakening:

> Сын вечности неизъясненной,
> Исторгнувшись из бездны вдруг,
> Крылами юности снабденный
> Слетает в тусклый смертных круг;
> *Фемиды* дщери воскресают
> И пред лицом его играют;
> Весна усопшие красы
> Рассыпать перед ним стремится
> И вместо вихрей вывесть тщится
> Спокойны в *январе* часы. (77; Bobrov's emphasis)

(The son of inexplicable eternity, / ejected suddenly from the abyss, / outfitted with the wings of youth, / flies down into the dim circle of mortals. / The daughters of *Themis* revive and play before his face. / Spring longs to scatter her dead [sleeping] / beauty in front of him / and attempts to usher in quiet hours / in *January* instead of whirlwinds.)

In "To the New Nineteenth Century," the poet addresses the new century, asking it to bring renewal to Russia:

> Обнови нам ныне ты
> Век *сивиллин* золотой! (92; Bobrov's emphasis)

(Renew for us now / the golden *Sibyl's* age!)

It is crucial for Bobrov's concept of time that this renewal happens in the form of a return to the past—to the golden age. On an historical scale, such a view implies periodic renewal:

> Преходит век—и всё с веками;
> Единый род племен падет
> И пресмыкается с червями,
> Как из червей другой встает;
> И всё приемлет новый образ. (92; cf. 102–3)

(A century ends, and everything ends with the centuries. / As soon as one genus of tribes falls / and begins crawling with worms, / another rises from amidst the worms, / and everything takes on a new image.)

Bobrov regards this cyclical concept of history as a source of optimism, even if an individual fate is less than happy. In "An Unfortunate's Song for His Benefactor on the New Year" (1795, 1804), he depicts the eternal renewal of life on Earth:

> Снова солнцы покатились
> По палящим небесам;
> Снова шумны обратились
> Времени колеса там.
>
> Будьте вновь благословенны,
> Земнородны племена!
> Будьте паки восхищенны,
> Как и в прежни времена! (119–20)

(Suns have rolled again / through fiery skies. / The noisy wheels of time / have rotated again there.

Be blessed again, / earthly tribes! / Be rapturous again, / as [you were] in past times!)

At the conclusion of the poem, the poet translates his belief in periodical renewal into anticipation of personal happiness:

> [В] новом годе
> Не пролью я новых слез;

После бурь в другой погоде
Осушу их средь очес. (121)

([In] the new year / I will not shed new tears. / After storms, in
different weather, / I will wipe them from my eyes.)

Even a person's death brought by time passing is not final
but resembles sleep. In "The First Hour of the Year," addressed to
the poet's friend P. P. Ikosov (1760–1811), Bobrov maintains that his
friend's possible death will not be final:

Но если я твой одр суровый
Слезой обмою в год сей новый
И ты—в свой темный гроб сойдешь,
Возможно ль, ах!—при смерти люты
Иметь тебе тогда минуты?
Любезный друг!—ты лишь уснешь. (78)

(But if in this new year / I will wash your somber death-bed
with my tears / and you will descend into your dark grave, /
is it possible that in fierce death / you will then have minutes?
/ My dear friend! You will but fall asleep.)

Years and men thus die in like manner, and the state of human death
resembles eternity: in both death and eternity, time is temporarily
inactive, and both death and eternity include the possibility of
rebirth. Characteristically, the state of death is free of discrete
time units ("minutes"), which, in Bobrov's view, represent time's
mortality.

Despite its cosmic scale and its apparent absence of interest
in the subjective experiencing of time that fascinated Murav'ev,
Bobrov's mythology of time also addresses the question of how to
deal with time's passage and its inevitable destructive influence on
man. Bobrov presents time's passage and human death as reversible
and promises periodic renewal both in nature and in human
life. Bobrov accomplishes his task by reviving the mythological
connotations dormant in the poetic clichés of his time, returning to
their original, literal meaning. His philosophy of time becomes for
him a source of historical optimism, as well as of personal solace.

By deconstructing the prevailing imagery of time in their
different ways, both Murav'ev and Bobrov created philosophies of

time that provided personal consolation and anticipated different trends in Russian literature. Murav'ev is an acknowledged initiator of the psychological tradition in Russia.[13] By regarding time as a succession of instants rather than as a duration, he prepared the ground for late eighteenth- and early nineteenth-century literary explorations of human psychology, memory, and individuality.[14] While Bobrov's mythic vision of time was not appreciated by his contemporaries, it portended the development of cosmic themes in the work of such poets as Lermontov, Tyutchev, and Mandelstam.

---

[13]   See G. A. Gukovskii, *Ocherki po istorii russkoi literatury i obshchestvennoi mysli XVIII veka* (Leningrad: Khudozhestvennaia literatura, 1938), 251–98.

[14]   Whitrow points out the connection between science's examination of time as a succession of instants and literature's interest in psychology (*Time in History*, 170–71).

15. Dishonor
by Flogging and Restoration by Dancing: Leskov's Response to Dostoevsky

Dostoevsky held strong grudges against several Russian literary characters, including Pushkin's Silvio and Lermontov's Pechorin, because he believed they had a harmful influence on Russian society. But by far the most hateful of all Russian literary characters for Dostoevsky was Lieutenant Pirogov, one of the two protagonists in Gogol's story "Nevsky Prospect." As we remember, Pirogov courted the pretty wife of the locksmith Schiller, a German residing in St. Petersburg, who happened to return home at the unfortunate moment when Pirogov was attempting to kiss her. In drunken indignation, Schiller gave Pirogov a thorough flogging, helped by his similarly drunken and indignant German friends Hoffman and Kunz. Initially the flogged Pirogov plans a terrible revenge: "He considered Siberia and the lash to be a small punishment for Schiller."[1] However, on the way to file a complaint, he drops by a pastry shop, where he becomes distracted by puff-pastries and a few newspaper articles in *The Northern Bee*, calms down, and forgets the whole affair.

Dostoevsky mentions the dishonored and dishonorable Pirogov time and again. The flogged lieutenant's name appears in *Notes from the Underground*, in *The Idiot*, in Dostoevsky's critical essay "A Number of Articles about Russian Literature," in the article "Something about Lying," published in 1873 in the *Diary of a Writer*, and in the notes for the *Diary*.[2] Often Pirogov's name appears in the plural, thus epitomizing ignominy.

In Dostoevsky's view, Pirogov's crime lay in doing nothing about the insult he had suffered at the hands of Schiller:

> [Gogol] was in the end forced to have [Pirogov] flogged to satisfy the outraged moral feelings of his reader, but, seeing that the great man merely shook himself and, to fortify himself after the severe punishment, ate a puff-pastry, he just threw up his hands in amazement and thus left his readers.[3]

Presumably, his readers would make up their own minds about Pirogov's conduct. In Dostoevsky's portrayal, Gogol is perplexed by his character's behavior; Dostoevsky, in contrast, is indignant. Dostoevsky firmly believes that a competent person who has been physically violated cannot go on living without doing something to remove the dishonor.[4]

---

1   Nikolai Gogol', "Nevskii prospekt," in his *Peterburgskie povesti*, ed. O. G. Di-laktorskaia (St. Petersburg: Nauka, 1995), 28.

2   See Fedor Dostoevskii, *Polnoe sobranie sochinenii v 30-ti tomakh* (Leningrad: Nauka, 1972–90), 5:128, 8:385, 18:59, 21:124-25, 24:79, 102; 25:241. All subsequent references to Dostoevsky's works are given to this edition.

3   Dostoevskii, *Idiot*, 8:385. I am using the translation of the novel by David Magarshak, with some modifications: Fyodor Dostoevsky, *The Idiot* (Harmondsworth, UK: Penguin, 1955), 443.

4   I do not discuss here Dostoevsky's treatment of physical violence toward subjects not *sui juris*, such as children or peasants. With respect to them, Dostoevsky's views were quite different.

How could one remove a disgrace such as Pirogov's, however? To have a physical confrontation with the aggressor, as Pushkin half-seriously suggested, pointing toward British tradition, was not socially accepted.[5] A complaint to the police or other authorities would bring punishment upon the offender, the severity of which would depend on how the offense was classified. For a "simple offense" (*obida prostaia*), the offender was supposed to pay a fine to the offended, the so-called dishonor money (or simply dishonor, *beschest'e*). For a "grave offense" (*obida tiazhkaia*), the punishments varied: the offender could have been obliged to ask the offended for forgiveness and to pay the dishonor money—or could have been arrested, dismissed from service, imprisoned, or subjected to corporal punishment, all depending on the gravity of the offense.[6] However, none of these punishments would remove the damage to Pirogov's honor. Furthermore, the law did not even acknowledge damage to one's honor in cases of physical offense: "No kind of offense can diminish the honor of the one offended."[7] In addition, accepting the dishonor money, which was customary among all social classes in pre-Petrine Russia, was decisively rejected by the post-Petrine nobility as incompatible with the very idea of honor. Dostoevsky, in particular, considered "the right to dishonor," that is, the right to receive monetary compensation for physical offense, profoundly immoral.[8]

Nor did Dostoevsky believe in legal recourse in cases of personal offense. In his notes for the *Diary of a Writer*, he writes:

---

[5] Aleksandr Pushkin, "Razgovor o kritike," in his *Polnoe sobranie sochinenii v 16-ti tomakh* (Moscow: Izdatel'stvo Akademii Nauk SSSR, 1937–59), 11:90.

[6] *Svod zakonov Rossiiskoi Imperii: Svod zakonov ugolovnykh*, 2nd ed. (St. Petersburg: Tipografiia Vtorogo Otdeleniia Sobstvennoi Ego Imperatorskogo Velichestva Kantseliarii, 1842), 15:87 and 88.

[7] Ibid., 87.

[8] On the Russian nobility's rejection of the idea of monetary compensation for physical offenses, see Irina Reyfman, *Ritualized Violence Russian Style: The Duel in Russian Culture and Literature* (Stanford: CA: Stanford Univ. Press, 1999), 121–23 and 247–48 (Dostoevsky's view). Dostoevsky criticizes "the right to dishonor" in 10:288; 13:454; 22:11, 22:101, 23:154; 24:178 and 229.

"There are cases that cannot be brought to open trial. True, man belongs to society. Belongs, but not entirely."[9] He describes an incident that proves the legal system's apparent uselessness and demonstrates a nobleman's lack of faith in it: "A coachman beat a gentleman [*barin*]. A scandal [*istoriia*]. The gentleman was a sort of professor. He didn't complain. But what if he had complained? 'Nothing would happen.'"[10] From Dostoevsky's other record of the same incident, it is clear that the last words are the remark of the offending coachman: *Nichego ne budet*, that is, "The authorities would do nothing to punish me."[11]

Dostoevsky looked for extra-legal means to deal with personal offenses and regarded dueling as one such means. Dueling, of course, was problematic for Dostoevsky, because of both its violent nature and its foreign origin, but in the absence of other recourse, he saw it as an acceptable and, moreover, a necessary evil. In 1876, he writes in his notes for the *Diary of a Writer*:

> By the way, what safeguards honor and what can replace the duel? . . . And the duel is not at all silly: those who repudiate it offer only an idea, and one that is not yet *complete*, whereas the duel has been a fact from the beginning of the century. Generals who claimed that the sword had been given to them to protect their fatherland did not know or kept forgetting that those who drew it for the protection of their honor were also the ones who could stand up against the enemy, while complacent people and Pirogovs turned out to be quartermasters and "skeptics."[12]

Dostoevsky seemed to believe that the very existence of the institution of dueling could serve as a deterrent not only against personal offenses but also against corporal punishment meted out by authorities. He implies this much in *The House of the Dead*, where his narrator explains the authorities' reluctance to flog noblemen by

---

9   Dostoevskii, "Zapisi k 'Dnevniku pisatelia' 1876 g.," 24:135; cf. 24:136.

10   Ibid., 24:103.

11   Ibid., 24:102.

12   Ibid.

the influence of the exiled Decembrists, notorious for their readiness to duel.[13]

Dueling, however, was a class institution, practiced by noblemen (and, later in the nineteenth century, sometimes also by the educated *raznochintsy*). It was suitable only for removing dishonor inflicted by a peer. If a commoner assaulted a nobleman, as was the case with Pirogov and the nameless professor beaten by a coachman, it was of little use. Perhaps the only recourse for Pirogov would be suicide. It could be argued that Gogol suggested as much by making Pirogov's foil in the story, the idealistic artist Piskarev, commit suicide upon discovering that a beauty he was trying to woo was a vulgar prostitute totally satisfied with her lot. In real life, Pushkin contemplated suicide after rumors spread in the early 1820s that he had been flogged in the Secret Chancellery.[14] It is noteworthy that Pushkin, not unlike Pirogov, also decided against turning to the authorities. In September of 1825, he wrote in a rough draft letter to Alexander I: "[My friend] advised me to seek justification from the authorities—I thought it to be useless." [15]

Christian ethics suggests another possible response to physical violation: forgiveness. The narrator in *The House of the Dead*, continually anxious about corporal punishment (like Dostoevsky himself, he had been stripped of his noble rank and thus become subject to corporal punishment), relates the story of a Polish political prisoner, a former professor of mathematics, Zh-ski, who is flogged by the prison superintendent for his alleged insubordination. The old man's response to the flogging is that of a Christian: after the punishment,

> Zh-ski, averting his eyes from everyone, his face pale and his bloodless lips quivering, passed between the convicts who had gathered in the prison yard, having learned that

13   See Dostoevskii, *Zapiski iz mertvogo doma*, 4:212.

14   For an analysis of Pushkin's reaction to the rumors, see I. V. Nemirovskii, "Smyvaia 'pechal'nye stroki,'" in his *Tvorchestvo Pushkina i problema publichnogo povedeniia poeta* (St. Petersburg: Giperion, 2003), 19–44.

15   Aleksandr Pushkin, rough draft of a letter to Alexander I, July–September, 1825, in his *Polnoe sobranie sochinenii v 16-ti tomakh*, 13:227; original in French.

a nobleman was being flogged; he walked into the barracks, went straight to the place assigned to him on the plank bed, and without saying a word got down on his knees and began to say his prayers.

One may assume that he was praying to be given strength to forgive or, at least, accept the violation. His Christian behavior as well as his fortitude earned him the respect of the commoners, but, significantly, not of his fellow noblemen.[16]

Dostoevsky never stopped having doubts about the Christian response to physical violation, fearing that it could be used to mask cowardice and ignominy. In the late 1870s, he wrote in his notes for the *Diary of a Writer*:

> *Man is man*: the highest ideal is to forgive and to subdue unintentionally by the greatness of one's equanimity, of one's composure when insulted. But when will people become like that? Meanwhile, the law forthrightly demands the ideal: forgive. And it does not consider the answer: "But I wear a sword, where is honor? Otherwise there's cynicism, and harm for you and society." Yet to forgive for the sake of an ideal is true holiness, but to forgive out of cynicism, infamy, cynical egotism, that is, out of cowardice, is base.[17]

The only character in Dostoevsky's works who is allowed to forgive physical assault is Prince Myshkin, an indisputable holy fool. In contrast, Stavrogin's forgiving the slap in the face he receives from Shatov is a clear sign of his profound depravity. For Dostoevsky, it follows, to be beaten and either to fail or to be unable to remove the dishonor by dueling means to be dishonored for good. Corporal punishment thus leaves a person of honor in an utterly tragic situation, with no way out.[18]

---

[16]   Dostoevskii, *Zapiski iz mertvogo doma*, 4:210–11. I am using the translation of *Zapiski* by David McDuff: Fyodor Dostoyevsky, *The House of the Dead* (Harmondsworth, UK: Penguin, 1985), 325–26.

[17]   Dostoevskii, "Zapisi k 'Dnevniku pisatelia' 1876 g.," 24:262.

[18]   No doubt the question had personal significance for Dostoevsky because

Pirogov, of course, is not that tragic person, tormented by his dishonor. He neither contemplates suicide nor prays: he eats his puff-pastries. Furthermore, it may be suspected that he keeps quiet about the flogging because he is afraid of being dishonorably discharged from his regiment.[19] In any case, by the end of the day Pirogov recovers so nicely that he appears at "a very delightful assembly of civil servants and officers. There he spent the evening with pleasure and was so good at the mazurka that not only the ladies but also the cavaliers were in raptures."[20] Gogol writes about Pirogov's dancing with light irony, but Dostoevsky's discussion of this episode oozes with venom:

> Recall that right after his adventure the lieutenant ate a puff-pastry and distinguished himself the very same evening in the mazurka at one eminent civil servant's name-day party. What do you think, when he danced [*otkalyval*] the mazurka and, performing the steps, wrenched his so recently offended limbs, did he think about the fact that just two hours ago he had been flogged? No doubt he thought. But was he ashamed? No doubt he was not![21]

---

of the persistent rumors that he was flogged during his time in the Siberian prison camp. On the rumors and their falsity, see M. M. Gromyko, *Sibirskie znakomye i druz'ia F. M. Dostoevskogo, 1850–1854 gg.* (Novosibirsk: Nauka, Sibirskoe otdelenie, 1985), 44–51.

[19]   O. G. Dilaktorskaia, "Primechaniia," in Gogol', *Peterburgskie povesti*, 267.

[20]   Gogol', "Nevskii prospekt," 28–29.

[21]   For Pushkin, too, the scene depicting Pirogov dancing after his flogging is negatively marked. In his October 1834 note to Gogol, in response to Gogol's worry that the censor would not allow the flogging scene to be printed, he wrote: "It would be a pity to omit the flogging [*sekutsiiu*]: it is, I think, needed for the full effect of the evening mazurka" (*Polnoe sobranie sochinenii v 16-ti tomakh*, 15:198). Pushkin's brief note, however, seems to refer to the artistic effect, rather than to pass moral judgment on Pirogov's behavior. Gogol's fear proved well-founded, and the story was first published without the flogging scene. Gogol could only hint at the unfortunate incident: "These three craftsmen . . . treated him so rudely and impolitely, that I must confess I cannot find the words to depict this unfortunate event" (cited in commentary to Gogol, "Nevskii prospekt," 266).

Dostoevsky presents Pirogov's shamelessness as a specific feature of post-Petrine Russian behavior:

> The two-hundred-year absence of any independence of character and the two-hundred-year spitting in our own Russian face expanded the Russian conscience to such a fatal boundlessness [*bezbrezhnost'*] from which... what can one expect from it, what do you think?[22]

The horrible act Dostoevsky suggests that the reader imagine is Pirogov's marriage proposal to his dancing partner:

> I am convinced that the lieutenant was capable ... —perhaps the very same evening during the mazurka—of declaring his love to his partner, the host's elder daughter, and proposing to her formally. The image of this young lady, flittering around with this young fellow in a charming dance and not knowing that her partner was flogged just an hour ago and that he didn't care in the least, is utterly *tragic*.

Furthermore, Dostoevsky even suspects that, to make things worse, the young lady would have accepted the proposal from her flogged suitor even if she had known of the flogging. He exclaims bitterly: "Alas, she would accept him without fail!" [23]

* * *

Nikolay Leskov was no less interested than Dostoevsky in violence, corporal punishment, and proper responses to physical violation. His approach to these problems was, however, very different and much more flexible. His view of physical force against an individual was broader and included the epic tradition that did not find it insulting at all. Furthermore, he did not see any value in dueling and did not believe in its power to remove dishonor or

---

[22] Dostoevskii, "Nechto o vran'e," 21:124. On Dostoevsky's view of the harmful influence of Peter the Great's reforms on the Russian national character, see Deborah Martinsen, *Surprised by Shame: Dostoevsky's Liars and Narrative Exposure* (Columbus: Ohio State Univ. Press, 2003), 34.

[23] Dostoevskii, "Nechto o vran'e," 21:125; emphasis is Dostoevsky's.

safeguard against personal offenses. He also did not believe that physical violation irreparably ruined a person's character. Most importantly, unlike Dostoevsky, he trusted Christians to be able to forgive their offenders sincerely.

I suggest that Leskov formulated his view of these issues partly in response to Dostoevsky's position. I have argued elsewhere that Leskov's 1889 story "Figura" is a response to the story of Elder Zosima's life in Dostoevsky's *Brothers Karamazov*.[24] Zosima, as we remember, undergoes conversion on the eve of a duel, and yet, instead of directly apologizing to his opponent, he first withstands his opponent's shot. And even this is not sufficient to safeguard his honor: he is restored in the eyes of his comrades only after they learn that he has resolved to take monastic vows. Dostoevsky makes sure his reader sees Zosima's behavior as truly "holy," not "base."

In Leskov's story, the "righteous man" (*pravednik*) nicknamed Figura, while still a commissioned officer, receives a slap in the face from a drunken subordinate, a commoner. His first impulse is violent: he wants to kill his offender on the spot. His next thought, however, is about Christ and the virtue of forgiveness. In contrast to Zosima, Figura insists on his right to forgive the offender without formally associating himself with Christian institutions. Like Pirogov, Figura decides against reporting his offender to the authorities, but the motivation behind his decision is consideration for the assailant: Figura doesn't want him to suffer the severe corporal punishment the authorities would inflict on him. His actions dishonor him in the eyes of his peers and even in the eyes of his extraordinarily religious commanding officer. To save Figura's honor, the commanding officer suggests that he take vows, but Figura refuses and simply resigns his commission. He is not ashamed of his ostensibly dishonorable status: "I'm a beaten officer, and besides, I haven't got any noble pride [*bez usiakoi blagorodnoi gordosti*]."[25]

---

[24] See Reyfman, *Ritualized Violence*, 265, 268–70.

[25] Nikolai Leskov, *Sobranie sochinenii v 12-ti tomakh* (Moscow: Pravda, 1989), 7:247. The story was first published with the subtitle "From Memoirs about Righteous Men."

As we see, Leskov easily resolves the problem that seemed irresolvable to Dostoevsky. In his and his character's view, no external justification for Christian behavior is needed. Man himself is his own judge. Upon deciding to resign his commission, Figura is sure that he has made the right decision:

> I was absolutely calm, because I knew that the most precious things for me are my own will; the possibility of living according to one testament [*zavet*], not according to several; [the possibility] of not arguing, not pretending; and [the possibility] of not having to prove anything to anyone, if this person doesn't have a higher understanding [*esli emu ne iavleno svyshe*] . . . I decidedly didn't want any kind of service—neither that which requires a noble pride, nor that which requires no pride at all.[26]

Dostoevsky distrusts human nature and is afraid that without firm principles to guide him—be they Christian ethics or the aristocratic honor code—man will transgress. In contrast, Leskov believes in man's ability to find the right path.

I propose that Leskov also responded polemically to Dostoevsky's description of the flogged Pirogov's dancing the mazurka with the unsuspecting young girl. Leskov's story "Unappreciated Services," written between 1888 and 1891 and first published by Olga Maiorova in 1992, focuses on the theme of dancing with men who have been flogged.[27] In contrast to Dostoevsky's indignant descriptions of the shameless Pirogov, Leskov comically describes the sudden appearance in St. Petersburg

---

26   Ibid., 7:246.

27   Nikolai Leskov, "Neotsenennye uslugi: Otryvki iz vospominanii," ed. Ol'ga Maiorova, *Znamia* (January 1992): 155–79. Leskov's title, "Unappreciated Services," is a play on the idiomatic expression *neotsenimye uslugi* (invaluable services). In the text of the story, his narrator uses the phrase *neotsenennye uslugi* in the sense of "invaluable services": *A vot, pozhaluista, slushaite, i razberite: kto v samom dele okazyvaet inogda samye neotsenennye uslugi* ("Here, please listen and decide who, in fact, sometimes renders the most unappreciated/invaluable services"; 171; cf. 160, where the narrator uses another corrupted idiom, *neotsenimye zaslugi*, "invaluable deserts/merits").

of scores of Bulgarians ostensibly flogged by K. A. Panitsa, the leader of the 1887 anti-Austrian uprising. The diplomat Baron Alexander Genrikhovich Zhomini (Jomini), Leskov's narrator in the story, reports: "All of a sudden, from there to here Bulgarians began to arrive, who complained that their own people had treated them without respect; simply put, they complained that they had been flogged!" The number of complainants seems to grow exponentially:

> They arrived in larger and larger numbers, and every one said: "They flogged me, brother," — "They flogged me too," "Oh, and I was flogged as well." . . . At the beginning we comforted the first arrivals somewhat using our means; but this was a mistake. After this a whole stream of sufferers poured from there, and every one wanted to be comforted... It began to seem strange: it meant that the vicious Panitsa was flogging his poor compatriots every day left and right.[28]

The comicality is created by the ever-increasing numbers of the supposed sufferers, by their eagerness to report their experience, and by the implied reason for this eagerness: monetary compensation.

As I have mentioned, Dostoevsky believed that accepting money in compensation for physical offense was beyond ignoble. Leskov's narrator, however, is concerned not about the impropriety of the Bulgarians' accepting money for their sufferings but about the expense. He complains:

> We tried to get this affair off our hands, letting another agency take care of the "flogged heroes" [*vysechennye muzhi*], but all of a sudden this other agency turned out to be very shrewd and devoid of noble ambition [*blagorodnoe chestoliubie*]. It refused to accept the "insulted heroes" [*oskorblennye muzhi*], and our situation was becoming very sensitive. (161)

The wording of Jomini's report deliberately, and humorously, combines two cultural codes of behavior: the heroic code, which does

---

28   Leskov, "Neotsenennye uslugi," 160. All subsequent references are given in the text.

not see physical violence against an individual as insulting, and the aristocratic honor code, which finds it utterly dishonoring. To do so, Jomini repeatedly calls the flogged Bulgarians *muzhi*, evoking their heroic—or epic—status, and, at the same time, uses expressions pertaining to the honor code discourse, such as "insulted" and "noble ambition."

Help for Jomini arrives in the persons of Olga Alekseevna Novikova (dubbed in the story Cybele) and Vissarion Vissarionovich Komarov (Corybant), conservative figures of the Pan-Slavic persuasion.[29] They take up the cause of the flogged Bulgarian brothers. Corybant works hard to dispel doubts about the veracity of the flogging stories by personally examining some of the flogged Bulgarians in the editorial office of his newspaper. He also displays their injuries to visitors:

> And I have [in my office] a pair of garden-fresh [*samye svezhie*] flogged Bulgarians. Do you want to see them? They are in my office and are telling their story . . . It is very interesting how they were flogged... . . . Please, go in and wait for me there—I'll just greet some ladies and join you, we will ask one of them to take his clothes off again... You will see what Mr. Panitsa does!.. I'll convince them... They are, you see, very simple, epic [*epicheskie*], as it were, people, and anyway, why have scruples [*da i chego stesniat'sia*]?! (162–63)

Corybant's flippant tone and his evident lack of concern for the Bulgarians' dignity—as well as his apparent lack of awareness that their submission to examination may be improper—comically clash with the alleged violence done to them. His evoking the heroic code when he calls Bulgarians "simple, epic" people, while at the same time using the modified vocabulary of the honor code ("scruples" instead of "shame") heightens the comical effect—the more so in that, unlike Jomini, Corybant seems to be totally unaware of the discrepancy between these two cultural codes.

---

[29]   See Maiorova, commentary to Leskov, "Neotsenennye uslugi," 178n10. Notably, Novikova was a sister of A. Kireev, the author of the pro-dueling *Pis'ma o poedinkakh* (St. Petersburg, 1899; first serialized in the newspaper *New Times*).

Like her Corybant, Cybele is not in the least disturbed by the Bulgarians' readiness to demonstrate evidence of their dishonor. Furthermore, she wants to get involved and organizes a "brilliant soirée," attended by scores of dignitaries and high society ladies. Among the guests is a lady nicknamed Pitulina and her young daughters. Corybant greets Pitulina with the stories of the flogged Bulgarians, pointing them out to her one by one. Pitulina first expresses incomprehension, then bewilderment, and, finally, after she sees one of the flogged Bulgarians dancing, indignation. She exclaims: "What! And this one too... the one who's dancing!" (164).[30] She then immediately collects her daughters and departs, repeating on her way out that it is improper to dance with men who have been flogged (*s vysechennymi ne tantsuiut;* 165).

It seems that Pitulina shares Dostoevsky's opinion that it is improper to dance with the flogged. She explains to Corybant: "When I heard that these, the ones who were there, had been brutally [*ochen'*] flogged, I remembered how it was proper to act in such cases [*kak v etikh sluchaiakh priniato*], and took my daughters home" (166). She recalls a lesson from her youth:

> I remember very well that when they brought me and my sister home to Orlovskaia *guberniya* from the institute, there... we had in our *uyezd* one landowner, Koziul'kin... . . . And *maman*, when she took us out for the first time to the ball at the assembly during the elections, instructed us very severely that we could dance with all cavaliers but not with Koziul'kin, because he had been flogged [*ego sekli*]. (167)

Having learned from Pitulina that Koziul'kin was flogged by some cuirassiers stationed in their *uyezd*, Corybant refuses to see the similarity, but Pitulina insists:

> Why cannot [these incidences] be compared? It's all the same. Koziul'kin... I also remember him well... I saw him... he even was a very handsome young man and dressed well, and besides he spoke French better than many others, but nobody

---

30   Pitulina stumbles as she speaks, and Leskov marks her frequent stumbling with ellipses.

danced with him, and everyone was even amazed at just how
he could appear for elections and the assembly after he had
been flogged but didn't kill them in a duel. (167)

At the same time, Pitulina defends Koziul'kin when Corybant
suggests that he was just "some kind of a provincial slicker, surely
a rogue . . . and even if he was flogged, he was flogged because he
deserved it" (167). She retorts:

> Let me tell the truth and defend him... Even though
> Koziul'kin died long ago . . . , he was flogged not for some
> fraud but simply for his courage, because one officer did
> a bad thing to one poor young girl who was a governess and
> left her, and this Ivan Dmitrich Koziul'kin, he was a bachelor
> then and had very strange ideas. When the landowners [in
> whose house the girl was the governess] threw her out, he
> picked her up from the inn and hid her in the priest's house,
> and went immediately to the officers and began to reason
> with them and to rebuke them, and they, naturally, ordered
> their orderlies to lay him down, rolled him up in a wet sheet,
> and flogged him, and after that they took him in a cart to his
> estate and left him there. (167)

After the incident, Koziul'kin behaves remarkably similarly
to Lieutenant Pirogov as imagined by Dostoevsky: he proposes to
the girl. Unlike Dostoevsky's imagined bride, the girl refuses him;
Koziul'kin takes her to Moscow to her family, marries a peasant
girl, and lives his life ostracized by his neighbors. Like the beaten
officer Figura in Leskov's earlier story, Koziul'kin does not consider
it necessary "to prove anything to anyone" and to submit to the
dictates of the honor code at the expense of his Christian beliefs. He
obviously does not want to kill anyone in a duel (Pitulina's naive
formulation "and he did not kill them in a duel" —a on ikh ne zastrelil
na dueli—underscores the violent aspect of dueling, as opposed to
the ritual aspect). He simply does what he deems right and lives
with the consequences.

Figura's and Koziul'kin's behavior forces us to rethink
Pirogov's conduct. Granted, unlike Leskov's righteous characters,
Pirogov is a thoughtless fop who is trying to seduce someone else's

wife out of boredom. It is very likely that his choice not to pursue his offender springs from the baseness of his own character and not from high moral principles, but would it be better if he followed through with his complaint and had Schiller lashed and exiled to Siberia, perhaps to his death, as he initially intended? In his numerous philippics against Pirogov, Dostoevsky does not consider this question. For Leskov, however, it is of paramount importance. His characters choose dishonor and social ostracism over taking another man's life.

Koziul'kin eventually regains his status in the community thanks to a local lady, Anna Nikolaevna Zinov'eva. She arrives from Europe to live on her estate, learns his story, and restores his reputation—by dancing with him. Pitulina reports:

> [She] immediately became our first lady . . . she somehow heard about all of Koziul'kin's antics... from the archbishop, I think . . . , and she asked him: why do all the noblemen despise Koziul'kin? And the archbishop told her, and she immediately sent her servant to ask for Koziul'kin's acquaintance, and, having invited him to her name-day ball, opened the dances by dancing the Polonaise with him. And all of a sudden she changed everyone's attitude toward him. (168)

The name-day ball (absent in Gogol's text—he speaks of an evening party) may be another reference to Dostoevsky's "Something about Lying." This is all the more probable in that the dance Zinov'eva and Koziul'kin are dancing is, like the mazurka, of Polish origin. Most importantly, Dostoevsky concludes his report of the imaginary dancing scene with praise for the high moral qualities of Russian women: right after suggesting that the young lady would have accepted the flogged Pirogov's proposal of marriage, he notes that in general Russian women are less affected by the post-Petrine moral degradation and typically behave more honorably than men. Dostoevsky returns to this idea several times in his *Diary of a Writer*. Characteristically, however, Dostoevsky is also concerned that women, like men, won't be able to find the right path without the help of formalized principles:

Women are our great hope; [they], perhaps, will serve all
Russia in her most fateful moment. But here is the problem:
even though we have many, very many honorable [women],
you see, they are kind rather than honorable, and none of
them know what honor is and they absolutely do not believe
in any kind of code of honor [*formula chesti*]—they even reject
the clearest old formulas, and this is everywhere and applies
to everyone—what a marvel![31]

In contrast, Leskov's Zinov'eva, like his other righteous characters,
disregards established rules and the honor code (which she, of
course, knows well, having arrived from Europe); instead, she
is governed by wisdom and higher understanding. And higher
understanding is precisely what she needs to guide her, as the rest
of Leskov's story demonstrates.

Pitulina's report gives Corybant an idea of how to help the
flogged Bulgarians:

Your Koziul'kin, even though he is a petty and insignificant
person, is in a way touching, but this Anna Nikolaevna
Zinov'eva is simply charming and even beautiful! In her you
present to everyone a living example and a lesson on how
a true lady of high rank should act. (168)

Without much delay, he convinces Cybele to save the Bulgarians:

The proposition was to perform a "restoration of honor"
[*restavratsiiu chesti*]: that is, as Zinov'eva restored the human
dignity of the flogged Koziul'kin, insulted by universal
ostracism, so all the "first ladies" of our time should restore
"the Bulgarians' dignity." For this it was necessary to
organize a very big ball, and at this ball the ladies would
have to take by the hand all the Bulgarians who had suffered
vexation from Panitsa and dance the Polonaise with them.
(170)

Preparations are well under way when Jomini discovers
that the stories of Panitsa's cruel treatment of his compatriots are

---

31   Dostoevskii, "Odna nesootvetstvennaia ideia," 23:24.

false, and that the Bulgarians actually received their injuries in St. Petersburg. His search for truth begins with the realization that their stories do not add up. As he later explains to Cybele, "People flogged in Bulgaria, in Sophia, could not have preserved [*ne mogli by dovesti*] their welts all the way to Petersburg" (176). The welts therefore had to have been created locally. Jomini's conclusion is confirmed by one of his friends, who discovers that to get flogged the Bulgarians visit an apartment in the building where he himself lives. The friend's story generates speculations among the listeners about the reason the Bulgarians get themselves flogged:

> Some thought that it was something sectarian—nowadays there are so many sects; others were inclined to see in this "a means of Spartan training" to help them prepare themselves for Panitsa [*v dukhe kotorogo nedurno ukrepit' sebia pri Panitse*], and yet others thought that it was simply "exaction" [*pravezh*], because this Bulgarian lent money at interest and probably flogged insolvent debtors. (174)

They all are wrong, however: according to Jomini's informant,

> This Bulgarian—or even not a Bulgarian but a Persian or an Armenian—came here to trade, but went bankrupt and started to heal—started to offer something like massage . . . He has discovered some kind of a healing action that he called "beneficial patting." And sick rheumatics and paralytics would come to him, and he "would beat them a little bit, and they would pay him a little bit, and everyone benefited from this." (174)

The friend's story and its interpretations, notably, leave unexplored the questions of the Bulgarians' blaming Panitsa for their welts and accepting the comfort money.

Significantly for my argument, the story of how the Bulgarians' machinations were discovered is framed as a polemic with Dostoevsky—or, rather, as a parody of his idea that everyone, including society girls, has much to learn from [male] kitchen servants (*kukhonnyi muzhik*). To assure that the reference to Dostoevsky is unmistakable, Leskov makes his narrator Jomini remark:

I have to admit that at that time I thoroughly enjoyed the stories about Dostoevsky who, in the house of the poet Tolstoy, urged a young lady and educated people [in general] to go to the kitchen, "to learn from the kitchen servant." Nobody listened to him: the young lady U<sha>kova suggested that he himself should go and learn from the kitchen servant how to be polite. (171)[32]

Jomini, however, doubts that the *kukhonnyi muzhik* can help against Cybele's "venture to lead the flogged Bulgarians in the Polonaise" (171). But he is wrong: it is precisely his friend's kitchen servant who helps discover the flogging clinic and thus destroys Cybele's plans for the "restoration of honor" ceremony. Accused by his employer of having an affair with a female cook employed in the same apartment building, the servant explains that he met with the cook on the service staircase not out of love but

> out of pity [*po zhalosti*], and she went there out of fear [*po strasti*], that is, because at home she felt <u>fear</u> [*doma ei stanovilos' strashno*], since she lived at a Bulgarian's, and when other Bulgarians of their faith visited him, they played a game in which they flogged each other, and she got fearful [*ei eto strashno*] and went to the staircase, and he sat there with her out of compassion [*po sostradaniiu*]. (174; Leskov's emphasis)

Leskov plays on the different meanings of the root *strast'*, which can mean both passion and fear, as well as on the meaning of the word *zhalost'*, which can also mean love, casting doubt on the servant's claim that he "kept himself pure," *sobliudal sebia v chistote*, and thus on Dostoevsky's advice to society girls to learn from kitchen servants. Leskov draws attention to his wordplay by graphically marking the word *strashno*.

---

[32] The episode took place in the early 1870s at the house of S. A. Tolstaya, the widow of A. K. Tolstoy. A similar scene unfolded several days earlier in the house of Yu. D. Zasetskaya. Leskov tells both stories in his 1886 essay "O kufel'nom muzhike i proch.: Zametki po povodu nekotorykh otzyvov o L. Tolstom," in Nikolai Leskov, *Sobranie sochinenii v 11-ti tomakh* (Moscow: Izdatel'stvo khudozhestvennoi literatury, 1958), 11:147–51.

Dostoevsky's faith in the wisdom of kitchen servants, however, turns out to be right, but in a comical way. Jomini reports:

> I liked this story not only because it was simple, intriguing, and funny but [also because] I heard in it something consoling and invigorating [*uteshitel'noe i bodriashchee*]. But what was it exactly? I couldn't determine, but [I felt] as if <u>something</u> strong and powerful supported my view [*stalo na moiu storonu*] and tripped up the political Polonaise with a huge foot wrapped in a felt puttee and clad in a bast shoe. The kitchen servant fished something out, and a really resourceful mind with a lively imagination would have done something with it, and would have done exactly what was needed to break up the Polonaise! (174; Leskov's emphasis)

Leskov plays with grammar here: while the word "mind" (*um*) is in the singular, the verb that goes with it is in the plural (*sdelali*). This grammatical play capitalizes on the fact that the third-person plural can convey the idea of someone or something impersonal but powerful. This idea is reconfirmed and clarified by the use of the passive voice in the next sentence: "And this, please note, all this has already been <u>done</u> [*bylo uzhe sdelano*]!" (174; Leskov's emphasis). The presence of a Higher Authority is clear here.

Whether Dostoevsky was also right in his aversion to dancing with people who had been flogged is more difficult to determine. True, the falsely flogged Bulgarians are improper dancing partners, but Koziul'kin is not. The problem obviously requires a more flexible approach. One character who is capable of such an approach is Pitulina. Despite her slightly jumbled speech and her somewhat confused ideas about proper behavior, she is correct in her assessment of the Bulgarians: they are tricksters and extortionists, and "educated girls" certainly should not dance with them. And she is also right in her positive assessment of Koziul'kin and of Zinov'eva's treatment of him. Pitulina thus seems to be the transmitter of higher understanding—even though she herself may not be aware of this.

What marks Pitulina as an exponent of higher truth is evidently her nickname, which she received as a little girl. Jomini reports: "Still in the institute, the girls nicknamed [*prozvali*] her

'Pitulina.' It was not her name, but a nickname [*klichka*], and with it she lived her entire life" (163). The very wording of this passage draws attention to the heroine's unusual nickname. Furthermore, the system of names and nicknames that Leskov creates in the story gives Pitulina's nickname a truly unique place. The naming system in "Unappreciated Services" is complex. Some characters have real names, such as Jomini and Panitsa, although there is no guarantee that these characters will behave like their historical counterparts. Then there are names that are plausible Russian names but are obviously fictitious, such as Anna Nikolaevna Zinov'eva and Koziul'kin. Leskov, however, tries to pass them off as the names of real people. Pitulina reports about Koziul'kin: "He... in truth [*vzapravdu*] had... such a last name" (167).[33] Finally, there are characters who are given nicknames by the story's ostensible narrator Jomini: Cybele and Corybant. The origin and meaning of these nicknames are clear, and the corresponding characters have identifiable prototypes.

Pitulina is entirely different. She does not have an identifiable prototype, her nickname comes from outside the story (her schoolmates gave it to her long before the narrated story began), and its origin and meaning are murky yet surprisingly rich in associations. It is likely that Pitulina is a childish version of the name Kapitolina. This connects the heroine to the martyr Capitolina of Cappadocia (beheaded in 304) and signals her potential for Christian higher understanding. At the same time, an association with Lupa Capitolina (or Ca*pitulina*), the she-wolf who nursed Romulus and Remus, introduces the idea of *pitanie* (nourishing), with which the nickname Pitulina is paronomastically connected. This association is supported by the existence of many phonetically similar words in Slavic languages that express the idea of nourishment. For example, Dahl lists a plant called *pitul'nik*, with a reference to *pikul'nik*, *Galeopsis versicolor*, also known in Russian as *sladkie-soski* (sweet nipples). In Czech, *pitulnik* is the name of a similar plant, *Lamium*

---

33   In the commentary to Leskov, "Neotsenennye uslugi," 178n13, Maiorova suggests that the probable prototype's last name was Kozelkin—a similar but less comical-sounding name.

galeobdolon. Jan Karłowicz's dictionary of the Polish language (1902) lists *pitul* and *pitula,* "fodder, feed," and also the verb *pitulić* and the noun *pitulenie,* both of which refer to hasty and careless cooking. In Czech, the recent coinage *pitulina* is a feminine version of the masculine *pitomec,* which means "idiot, half-wit," but etymologically is connected to **pitati,* "to feed, nourish."[34]

Similar phonetic patterns can be found in Romance languages, where they have both "childish" and obscene connotations. For example, in the dialect used in the Italian town of Massa, *pitulin* is a term of endearment for a child.[35] In contemporary Italian slang, however, *pitulina* connotes female genitalia, and *pitulino,* cunnilingus. Spanish-speaking children use the word *pitulina* for penis.[36]

Some of the listed names and words Leskov was bound to have known (the martyr Capitolina, Lupa Capitolina, *pitul'nik/pikul'nik*), some he was likely to have known (he spoke Polish and therefore could have been aware of the Polish cluster), and some he obviously could not have known (all the new coinages). What is important for my argument, however, is that, considered collectively, these names and words strongly suggest childishness, ambiguity, and suspect intellectual and moral status. When they imply food, this food is dubious: a child's treat (the sweet juice of *Galeopsis versicolor*), the she-wolf's milk that nourishes human children, cattle fodder, or carelessly cooked food. When they connote people, these people are either young, and thus not entirely competent, or feeble-minded. Some of these words directly refer to vulgar sex or urination. Even the martyr Capitolina implies not only sainthood but also eros, as signified by the name of the servant martyred together with her, Eroteis.

---

34   I thank Kateřina Harwood (born in Prague, Czech Republic) for the information on the contemporary usage of the word *pitulina* in Czech.

35   Enrico Novani, *Vocabolario del dialetto massese* (Massa: Stampato in proprio, Ceccotti, 1998).

36   I thank Maria Belen Reyfman (born in San Juan, Argentina) for this information. I would also like to express my gratitude to Anna Frajlich-Zajac, Christopher Harwood, and Paola Castagna for their help with Polish, Czech, and Italian usages of the words phonetically similar to the nickname Pitulina.

Childishness, ambiguity, and feeble-mindedness perfectly fit Leskov's heroine: Pitulina is "a matron of majestic size" (163) who goes by her childhood nickname; she has trouble explaining her position, even though she seems to know right from wrong quite well; she is a society lady who can easily forget "all good tone and manners" (165), and yet she behaves exactly as is proper; her reputation for being somewhat dim (*neumnaia*, 163) is directly mentioned by Jomini. Furthermore, Pitulina's nickname itself makes her intellect suspect: being a corrupted name, it illustrates her linguistic incompetence, the poor grasp of the Russian language that the narrator points out (163–64) and which is obvious in her hesitant, awkward speech throughout the story.

The ambiguity of Pitulina's status makes her similar to many of Leskov's other righteous characters, who are often morally suspect and frequently occupy a marginal place in society. They reject the accepted rules and principles (Dostoevsky's *formula chesti*, "code of honor"), but, like Pitulina, they know how to act in morally confusing situations and thus can serve as examples for other people.[37] Their higher understanding easily allows Leskov's righteous characters to distinguish between dishonorable and noble behavior, even when these two types of behavior seem to look alike.

---

[37]   For the most insightful discussions of Leskov's righteous characters as marginal and far from ideal, see Irmhild Christina Sperrle, *The Organic Worldview of Nikolai Leskov* (Evanston, IL: Northwestern Univ. Press, 2002), 36–37, 92, and 101; for their failure to rely on well-formulated rules in choosing how to behave, see 40–41 and 61.

Sources

Articles in this collection first appeared or were presented in the following venues:

Part One: Rank, State Service, and Literature

1. "Writing, Ranks and the Eighteenth-Century Russian Gentry Experience," in *Representing Private Lives of the Enlightenment*, ed. Andrew Kahn, SVEC 11 (Oxford: Voltaire Foundation, 2010): 149–66.

2. "Kak sdelat'sia dvorianinom? Poprishchin Gogolia kak nesostoiavshiisia *honnête homme*," *Trudy po russkoi i slavianskoi filologii: Literaturovedenie*, n.s., 6 (Tartu: Tartu Ülikooli Kirjastus, 2008), 97–107.

3. "Prose Fiction," in *The Cambridge Companion to Pushkin*, ed. Andrew Kahn (Cambridge: Cambridge University Press: 2006), 90–104.

4. "Pushkin the Chamberlain: Pushkin's Social Reputation in the 1830s" (paper presented at the VIII World Congress of ICCEESS, Stockholm, July 2010).

Part Two: Pushkin as the Other

5. "Poetic Justice and Injustice: Autobiographical Echoes in Pushkin's *The Captain's Daughter*," *Slavic and East European Journal* 38, no. 3 (1994): 463–78.

6. "Kamer-iunker v 'Zapiskakh sumasshedshego' (K voprosu ob otnoshenii Gogolia k Pushkinu)" (paper presented at the Iubileinaia mezhdunarodnaia nauchnaia konferentsiia, posviashchennaia 200-letiiu so dnia rozhdeniia N. V. Gogolia, Moscow, St. Petersburg, September 2009); abstract published in *Iubileinaia mezhdunarodnaia nauchnaia konferentsiia, posviashchennaia 200-letiiu so dnia rozhdeniia N. V. Gogolia: Tezisy* (Moscow: IMLI RAN, 2009), 74–76.

7. "Death and Mutilation at the Dueling Site: Pushkin's Death as a National Spectacle," *Russian Review* 60 (Winter 2001): 72–88.

8. "'Shestaia povest' Belkina': Mikhail Zoshchenko v roli Proteia," in *Cultural Mythologies of Russian Modernism: From the Golden Age to the Silver Age*, ed. Boris Gasparov, Robert P. Hughes, and Irina Paperno (Berkeley: University of California Press, 1992), 393–414.

Part Three: Tolstoy

9. "Turgenev's 'Death' and Tolstoy's 'Three Deaths,' in *Word, Music, History: A Festschrift for Caryl Emerson*, ed. Lazar Fleishman et al., Stanford Slavic Studies 29 (Stanford, CA: Stanford University, Dept. of Slavic Languages and Literatures, 2005), 1:312–26.

10. "Female Voice and Male Gaze in Leo Tolstoy's *Family Happiness*," in *Mapping the Feminine: Russian Women and Cultural Difference*, festschrift for Marina Ledkovsky, ed. Hilde Hoogenboom, Catharine Theimer Nepomnyashchy, and Irina Reyfman (Bloomington, IN: Slavica, 2008), 29–50.

11. "Tolstoy and Gogol: 'Notes of a Madman,'" in *The Petersburg Tradition: Essays in Honor of Nina Perlina*, ed. John Bartle, Michael C. Finke, and Vadim Liapunov, Indiana Slavic Studies 17 (Bloomington, IN: Slavica, 2012), 1–11.

12. "Tolstoy the Wanderer and the Quest for Adequate Expression" (paper presented at the conference of the Neo-Formalist Circle, "Tolstoy 100 Years On," Mansfield College, Oxford, UK, September 2010).

Part Four: Russians in Life and Literature

13. "Aleksey Rzhevsky, Russian Mannerist," *Ulbandus, the Slavic Review of Columbia University* 9 (2005/2006): 3–17.

14. "Imagery of Time and Eternity in Eighteenth-Century Russian Poetry: Mikhail Murav'ev and Semen Bobrov," *Indiana Slavic Studies* 8 (1996): 99–114.

15. "Telesnye nakazania, tantsy i restavratsiia chesti: Dialog Leskova s Dostoevskim," in *Fol'klor, postfol'klor, byt, literatura: Sbornik statei k 60-letiiu Aleksandra Fedorovicha Belousova*, ed. A. K. Baiburin et al. (St. Petersburg: Sankt-Peterburgskii gos. universitet kul'tury i iskusstv, 2006), 281–89; and "Dishonor by Flogging and Restoration by Dancing: Leskov's Response to Dostoevsky," *Ulbandus, the Slavic Review of Columbia University* 13 (2010): 109–25.

Index*

* Boldface indicates principal treatment of a topic.

CPSIA information can be obtained at www.ICGtesting.com
Printed in the USA
BVOW03*0121250214

345877BV00004B/18/P